AF194443

PLANNING, SCHEDULING AND CONSTRAINT SATISFACTION: FROM THEORY TO PRACTICE

Frontiers in Artificial Intelligence and Applications

FAIA covers all aspects of theoretical and applied artificial intelligence research in the form of monographs, doctoral dissertations, textbooks, handbooks and proceedings volumes. The FAIA series contains several sub-series, including "Information Modelling and Knowledge Bases" and "Knowledge-Based Intelligent Engineering Systems". It also includes the biannual ECAI, the European Conference on Artificial Intelligence, proceedings volumes, and other ECCAI – the European Coordinating Committee on Artificial Intelligence – sponsored publications. An editorial panel of internationally well-known scholars is appointed to provide a high quality selection.

Series Editors:
J. Breuker, R. Dieng, N. Guarino, R. López de Mántaras, R. Mizoguchi, M. Musen

Volume 117

Recently published in this series

ISSN 0922-6389

Planning, Scheduling and Constraint Satisfaction: From Theory to Practice

Edited by

Luis Castillo

Departamento de Ciencias de la Computación e Inteligencia Artificial,
Universidad de Granada, Spain

Daniel Borrajo

Departamento de Informática, Universidad Carlos III de Madrid, Spain

Miguel A. Salido

Departamento de Ciencias de la Computación e Inteligencia Artificial,
Universidad de Alicante, Spain

Angelo Oddi

ISTC-CNR Institute for Cognitive Science and Technology,
National Research Council, Italy

IOS
Press

Amsterdam • Berlin • Oxford • Tokyo • Washington, DC

© 2005, The authors mentioned in the table of contents

All rights reserved. No part of this book may be reproduced, stored in a retrieval system, or transmitted, in any form or by any means, without prior written permission from the publisher.

ISBN 1 58603 484 7
Library of Congress Control Number: 2004116331

Publisher
IOS Press
Nieuwe Hemweg 6B
1013 BG Amsterdam
The Netherlands
fax: +31 20 620 3419
e-mail: order@iospress.nl

Distributor in the UK and Ireland
IOS Press/Lavis Marketing
73 Lime Walk
Headington
Oxford OX3 7AD
England
fax: +44 1865 750079

Distributor in the USA and Canada
IOS Press, Inc.
4502 Rachael Manor Drive
Fairfax, VA 22032
USA
fax: +1 703 323 3668
e-mail: iosbooks@iospress.com

LEGAL NOTICE
The publisher is not responsible for the use which might be made of the following information.

Preface

This book compiles a series of papers selected from two peer-reviewed workshops of the European Conference on Artificial Intelligence 2004: the Workshop on Constraint Satisfaction Techniques for Planning and Scheduling Problems and the Workshop on Planning and Scheduling: Bridging Theory to Practice.

Bringing artificial intelligence planning and scheduling applications into the real world is a hard task that is receiving more attention every day by researchers and practitioners from many fields. In many cases, it requires the integration of several underlying techniques like planning, scheduling, constraint satisfaction, mixed-initiative planning and scheduling, temporal reasoning, knowledge representation, formal models and languages, and technological issues. Most papers included in this book are clear examples of how to integrate several of these techniques. Furthermore, the book also covers many interesting approaches in application areas ranging from industrial job shop to electronic tourism, environmental problems, virtual teaching or space missions.

The book comprises both theoretic and applied papers. The former focus on the use of constraint satisfaction techniques in planning and scheduling frameworks. This is an extremely rich interdisciplinary area that is arising as an integrating technology for planning and scheduling techniques. It provides powerful techniques that allow building fully deployable applications to solve real problems. On the other hand, papers more focused on the practice are updated reviews of many of the most interesting areas of application of these technologies, showing how powerful these technologies are in overcoming the expressiveness and efficiency problems of real world applications. Other topics covered are knowledge representation, and algorithms and execution techniques for the whole lifecycle of any real application.

Acknowledgements

We would like to thank the following contributors that made this book possible: the Research Group TIC-175 Intelligent Systems Group of the Andalusian Regional Government, the project funded by the Spanish Ministry of Education and Science number TIC2002-04146-C05-05, the Department of Computer Science of the University of Alicante in Spain, the Institute for Cognitive Science and Technology of the National Research Council of Italy and the ECAI 2004 Organization team for contributing to a successful holding of both workshops.

Contents

Planning, Scheduling and Constraint Satisfaction: From Theory to Practice
L. Castillo et al. (Eds.)
IOS Press, 2005

1

Some Issues in Chromosome Codification for Scheduling with Genetic Algorithms

Ramiro VARELA, Jorge PUENTE, Camino R. VELA
Centro de Inteligencia Artificial. Universidad de Oviedo,
Campus de Viesques, 33271 Gijón, Spain
e-mail: ramiro@uniovi.es , http://aic.uniovi.es/ramiro
puente@aic.uniovi.es , http://aic.uniovi.es/puente
camino@aic.uniovi.es , http://aic.uniovi.es/camino

Abstract. Chromosome codification is one the most important issues in designing genetic algorithms for CSP. In this work we consider two codification schemas for scheduling: conventional permutations and permutations with repetition. First we analyse their characteristics in terms of probabilities for a given gene appears before to another one. This leads us to the observation that permutations with repetition have a bias towards a kind of natural orders. Then we present results from an experimental study showing that this bias produce, in general, a better convergence for permutations with repetition than for conventional ones; and that the convergence relies much less on the characteristics of the initial population.

Introduction

In this work we face the problem of design codification schemas for Genetic Algorithms (GA). We focus on the Job Shop Scheduling (JSS) problem and on two common codification schemas: conventional permutations and permutations with repetition. The analysis of these schemas shows that permutations with repetition have a bias towards particular regions of the search space. The reported experimental results show that this bias improves the GA convergence and makes it much more independent of the particular characteristic of the initial population.

The remaining of the paper is organized as follows. In section 1 we formulate the JSS problem. Section 2 describes various search spaces of interest for JSS problems. Section 3 outlines the application of GA to JSS. Here we focus on the analysis of the two codification schemas of our interest. Section 4 reports results from an experimental study.

1. The Job Shop Scheduling Constraint Satisfaction Problem

The Job Shop Scheduling (JSS) requires scheduling a set of N jobs $\{J_0,...,J_{N-1}\}$ on a set of M physical resources or machines $\{R_0,...,R_{M-1}\}$. Each job Ji consists of a set of operations $\{\theta_{i0},...,\theta_{iM-1}\}$ to be sequentially scheduled. Each operation has a single resource requirement and a fixed processing time of du_{il} time units. Once a starting time st_{ij} is determined for the operation θ_{ij}, this operation must be processed during the time interval $[st_{ij}, st_{ij} + du_{il}[$ with no preemption.

Furthermore, there are two non-unary constraints of the problem: *precedence constraints* and *capacity constraints*. Precedence constraints defined by the sequential routings of the operations within a job translate into linear inequalities of the type: $st_{il} + du_{il} \leq st_{il+1}$. Capacity constraints that restrict the use of each resource to only one operation at a time translate into disjunctive constraints of the form: $st_{il} + du_{il} \leq st_{jk} \vee st_{jk} + du_{jk} \leq st_{il}$. The objective is to come up with a feasible schedule such that the completion time of the whole set of operations, i.e. the makespan, is minimized.

In the following a problem instance will be represented by a directed graph $G = (V, A \cup E)$. Each node of the set V represents an operation of the problem, with the exception of the dummy nodes *start* and *end* which represents operations with processing time 0. The set A represents the precedence constraints and the set E represents the capacity constraints. The set E is decomposed into subsets E_i with $E = \cup_{i=0..M-1} E_i$, such that there is one E_i for each resource R_i. Figure 1 shows an example with three jobs and three physical resources. The arcs are weighed with the processing time of the operation at the source node.

A feasible schedule is represented by an acyclic subgraph Gs of G, $Gs=(V, A \cup H)$, where $H = \cup_{i=1..m} H_i$, H_i being a hamiltonian selection or partial schedule of E_i. The makespan of the schedule is the cost of a longest path in Gs from node *start* to node *end*. Therefore, finding out a solution can be reduced to discover a partial schedule for each machine so that the resulting solution graph has no cycles.

2. Search space for the JSS problem

The whole space of feasible schedules is extremely high and furthermore many of the solutions of this space are actually of no interest. Therefore it is worth to look for alternative spaces with a much lower size while these spaces are complete. In this sense there are three spaces which are often of interest: the spaces of semi-active, active and non-delay schedules. A schedule is *semi-active* if to start earlier any operation on a given machine, at least the relative order of two operations must be modified. A schedule is *active* if to start earlier any operation, at least another one should be delayed. Finally a schedule is *non-delay* if it is never the case that a machine is idle at the same time that an operation can be processed on that machine. Non-delay schedules are a subset of active schedules, and active schedules are a subset of semi-active ones. The experience demonstrates that the mean value of makespan is much higher for semi-active schedules than for active schedules; and that it is much higher for active schedules than for non-delay schedules too. But at the same time the only spaces that are guaranteed to contain at least one optimal schedule are semi-active and active schedules.
Semi-active schedules has mainly interested to a number of researchers in the field of

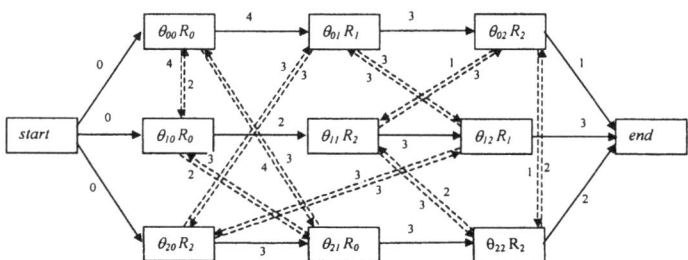

Figure 1. A directed graph representation of a *JSS* problem instance with three jobs. The release date is 0 and the due date is 15. The resource requirement of every operation is indicated within the boxes. Arcs are weighted with the processing time of the operation at the outcoming node.

genetic algorithms. The main reason for this interest is that it is easy to envisage encoding mechanisms, such as for example the permutations with repetition proposed by C. Bierwirth [1], that codifies all partial schedules as they appear within the actual schedule. Moreover, a variety of local search methods have been developed that can only be efficiently exploited when used in conjunction with semi-active schedules, for example those methods proposed by D. Mattfeld [2].

However active schedules are in fact the most interesting space. This is mainly due to the existence of the well-known G&T algorithm proposed by B. Giffler and G. L. Thomson [3]. This is a greedy algorithm that produces an active schedule in a number of $N*M$ steps. At each one of these steps the G&T algorithm makes a non-deterministic choice. Every active schedule can be reached by taking the appropriate choice at each step.

Figure 2 shows the G&T algorithm, although this is not the original G&T algorithm but a modified version termed as *hybrid G&T*. This hybrid version enhances the original one with a filtering mechanism that allows for constraining the search to a subset of the active schedules. This is achieved by means of a reduction parameter $\delta \in [0,1]$. When $\delta=1$, sentence 6 has a null effect and hence we have the original G&T algorithm. In this case, it is possible to envisage a non-deterministic sequence of operation selections that gives rise to an optimal schedule. Otherwise, i.e. if $\delta < 1$, the search is restricted to a subset of the active schedules; thus guaranteeing the existence of an optimal sequence is no longer possible. The algorithm produces a *non-delay* schedule at the extreme $\delta=0$. The *hybrid G&T* was first proposed by Storer, Wu and Vaccari [4] and adapted for state space searching; and was further used as chromosome-decoding schema by Bierwirth and Mattfeld [5] within the framework of a Genetic Algorithm. In this work, Bierwith and Mattfeld demonstrate that filtering becomes more and more effective as long as the instance size increases.

3. Scheduling with Genetic Algorithms

Genetic Algorithms (GAs) are among the most outstanding methods to confront scheduling problems. Due to their parallel and stochastic nature GAs are able to cope with the huge search spaces involved in this class of problems; in particular they are able to escape from

Algortithm G&T hybrid
1. A = *set containing the first operation of each job;*
   while $A \neq \varnothing$ **do**
2. *Determine the operation* $\theta' \in A$ *with the lowest completion time if scheduled in the current state, that is* $st\theta' + du\theta' \le st\theta + du\theta, \ \forall \theta \in A;$
3. *Let* M' *be the machine required by* θ', *and* B *the subset of* A *whose operations require* M';
4. *Delete from* B *every operation that cannot start at a time lower than* $st\theta' + du\theta'$;
5. *Determine operation* $\theta'' \in B$ *with the lowest possible start time, let* $st\theta''$ *be this time;*
   /* *the least start time of every operation in B, if it is selected next, is a value of the interval* $[st\theta'', st\theta' + du\theta']$ */
6. *Reduce the set B such that*
       $B = \{ \theta \in B \ / \ st\theta < st\theta'' + \delta((st\theta' + du\theta') - st\theta'') \}, \ \delta \in [0,1] \};$
   /* *now the interval is reduced to* $[st\theta'', st\theta'' + \delta((st\theta' + du\theta') - st\theta'']$ */
7. *Select* $\theta^* \in B$ *and schedule it at its lowest possible start time to build a partial schedule corresponding to the next state;*
8. *Remove* θ^* *from A and insert the succeeding operation of* θ^* *in set A if* θ^* *is not the last operation of its job;*
   endwhile;

Figure 2. The hybrid G&T algorithm; $st\theta$ stands for the start time of operation θ and $du\theta$ for its processing time.

local optima. Even though a basic GA usually produces moderate results, the experience demonstrates that its effectiveness actually improves when it is hybridized with other techniques such as gradient based methods. Moreover GAs are often so flexible that allows for incorporating any kind of heuristic knowledge from the problem domain in some of the genetic operators.

On the last decade various approaches were proposed to face the JSS and related problems by means of GAs. Maybe the first remarkable approaches are by Syswerda [5]; Fang, Ross, and Corne [6]; and Dorndorf, and Pesch [7]. Then Bierwirth [5] proposed the codification based on permutations with repetition. This is a single and effective codification that was afterward exploited by other researches. For example Mattfeld [2] exploits this schema together with a semi-active decoder. Furthermore he enhances a conventional GA with a variety of gradient based search methods and structured populations. Bierwirth and Mattfeld [8] exploit an active decoder based on the hybrid G&T algorithm. They studied the effect of restrict the search space by means of parameter δ. Their experimental study demonstrates that a value of δ around $0,5$ produces the best results. Yamada and Nakano [9] introduced local search methods with active scheduling.

A conventional GA starts from an initial population of potential solutions to the problem. Then this population is transformed by means of a simulated evolution process in such a way that good solutions tend to survive and recombine to generate new ones. While the worsen solutions tend to disappear. One of the key issues in designing a GA is to maintain an appropriate equilibrium between exploitation and exploration. Exploitation is achieved by means of crossover operators. A crossover mates two or more selected parent solutions and produce new ones. It is expected that these new solutions inherit some of the characteristics of their parents and therefore they are in the nearby within the search space. Exploration is mainly achieved by the mutation operators which make small random variations in a number of solutions. This way the GA performs a parallel search over the whole space of solutions, but the search is more intensive around regions containing good solutions. Figure 3 shows the structure of a conventional GA. In the following subsections we describe the elements we have chosen to adapt this algorithm to the JSS problem, that is: the chromosome codification, the evaluation function, and the genetic operators of selection, crossover, mutation and acceptance.

3.1 Chromosome codification

To codify chromosomes we have considered two schemas: the conventional permutation schema that codifies a chromosome by means a permutation of the set problem operations; and the permutation with repetition schema proposed by C. Bierwirth [5]. A permutation with repetition is in principle a permutation of the set of operations of the problem in which

Conventional Genetic Algorithm
1. *Generate the Initial Population;*
2. *Evaluate the Population;*
   while *No termination criterion is satisfied* **do**
   3.   *Select chromosomes from the current population;*
   4.   *Apply the Crossover and Mutation operators to the*
        chromosomes selected at step 1. to generate new ones;
   5.   *Evaluate the chromosomes generated at step 4.;*
   6.   *Apply de Acceptation criterion to the set of chromosomes*
        selected at step 3. together with the chromosomes generated
        at step 4.;
   endwhile;
5. *Return the best chromosome evaluated so far;*

Figure 3. Structure of a conventional genetic algorithm.

an operation is represented by only its job number. This way every job number appears so many times as the number of job operations. For example, the permutation with repetition

(0 1 1 2 2 0 0 2 1)

codifies a feasible chromosome to the problem of Figure 1. In this codification the first *1* represents to the first operation of job *1*, the second *1* the second operation of job *1*, and so on. If we identify the problem operations by numbers *0, 1, ..., N*M-1*, starting with the operations of the first job, the former chromosome will be represented in the permutations schema by

(0 3 4 6 7 1 2 8 5)

In either case a chromosome expresses a linear order, or partial schedule, for the operations demanding each resource. Even thought these partial schedules are only tentative, due to they might be finally not maintained in the actual schedule depending on the type of schedule the evaluation function builds up. Both of the schemas have a number of interesting characteristics that are desirable for a codification schema. Maybe the most important is that every permutation represents a feasible chromosome and consequently it is quite easy to design efficient crossover and mutation operators that guarantee feasible offspring. Moreover these schemas allow for a variety of decoding mechanisms to build a schedule from a given chromosome. In the sequel we refer to the permutation with repetition schema as RP and to the conventional permutations as CP for short.

In addition to the former properties the RP schema has another important characteristic which the CP does not hold: a RP tends to represents *natural orders*. We explain this by means of an example. Let us consider the operations θ_{12} and θ_{20} of the problem of Figure 1. As we can observe these operations require the resource R_1; and θ_{12} is the third operation of job 2 while θ_{20} is the first operation of job 3. Therefore the most natural or probable order among these two operations within an optimal (or at least a good) schedule can be considered in principle as $(\theta_{20} \ \theta_{12})$. The intuition behind this assumption is that the operation θ_{12} has to wait for at least the two operations θ_{10} and θ_{11} to be processed, while the operation θ_{20} could be processed with no waiting at all. Now if we consider the probability that the operation θ_{20} appears before the operation θ_{12}, in a random RP this value is *0,95* while in a conventional permutation is *0,5*. In general, the probability that operation θ_{li} falls in a former position that operation θ_{mj} in a random RP depends only on the operations position *i* and *j* respectively and is calculated by

$$P(\theta_{li} < \theta_{mj}) = (j+1) * \binom{M}{j+1} * \sum_{k=i+1}^{M} \binom{M}{k} \bigg/ \left(\binom{2M}{k+j+1} * (k+j+1) \right) \quad (1)$$

while this probability is always *0,5* for random CPs. Figure 4 shows these probability values for a problem with 15 machines.

Natural orders are neither preserved by other codifications such as the machine preference list codification proposed by F. Della Croce, R. Tadei and G. Volta [10]. The ability to preserve natural orders might be relevant when non-direct codifications are used, that is codifications that should be decoded in order to obtain a schedule, for two main reasons. Firstly due to random chromosomes, for example those of the initial population, hopefully are to be better. And furthermore the random effect (often referred to as mutation effect) of the genetic operators tends to be much less disruptive.

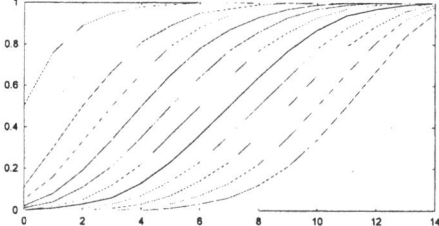

Figure 4. Probability profiles for a problem with $M=15$ calculated by expression (1) that correspond to random RPs. In any case each of the curves represents the values of $P(\theta_{li}, \theta_{kj})$ for a fixed i while j ranges from 0 to $M-1$. The curves from up to bottom correspond to values of i from 0 to $M-1$ respectively.

Direct codifications are also a good possibility to represent chromosomes. For example T. Yamada and R. Nakano [9] represent a chromosome by means of an actual schedule. This representation requires much more sophisticated genetic operators to generate feasible schedules. In order to do that Yamada and Nakano have exploited a local search method. Their proposed method is one of the most effective GA based approaches to the JSS problem.

3.2 Chromosome evaluation

As we have pointed, we have chosen to restrict the search over the set of active schedules. This way it is natural to exploit the G&T algorithm as a decoder mechanism. Hence to decode a chromosome we apply the G&T algorithm to build up a schedule with ties broken, at step 7. (see Figure 2), in favour of the leftmost operation.

3.3 Genetic operators

Both of the former codification schemas allow for simple and effective genetic crossover and mutation operators. Here we have considered the order based crossover (OX) for CP, which can be adapted to RP as well, being in this case named generalized order crossover (GOX). We clarify how operator GOX works by means of an example. Let us consider the following two chromosomes are selected as parents for mating

Parent1 (0 1 2 2 1 0 0 2 1)   *Parent2 (2 2 1 0 0 1 1 2 0).*

Firstly a substring is selected from Parent1 and it is inserted in the Offspring at the same position as in Par-ent1. Then the remaining positions of the Offspring are completed with the genes of Parent2 after removing the selected genes of Parent1. If the selected substring is the one remarked in Parent1, the resulting Off-spring is

Offspring (2 1 0 2 1 0 0 1 2).

This way, GOX preserves the order and position of the selected substring from Parent1 and the relative order of the remaining genes form the Parent2.

Regarding selection and acceptation operators, our choice was first select all the chromosomes of the cur-rent population and organize them into random pairs. Then the crossover is applied to each pair accordingly to the crossover probability to obtain two offsprings. These offsprings, or the original parents in case of no crossover, are mutated accordingly to the mutation rate. Finally the acceptation criterion consists in selecting the best two chromosomes among the parents and offsprings. Only if the two best chromosomes have the same makespan value, the second is discarded and the third one in the ranking is selected instead.

4. Experimental Study

In this section we report the results of an experimental study about the comparison of the two codification schemas summarized in the former section. As we have pointed, what we tried to analyze was the influence of the capability to represent natural partial schedules of the RP schema. This ability produces a bias towards particular regions of the search space so that the convergence is conditioned in anyway. In this study we have experimented with a set of selected problems taken from a well-known repository: the OR library. These selected problems are recognized as hard to solve for a number of researches such as Applegate and Cook [11] and Mattfeld [2].

In the first set of experiments we have compared the quality of random initial populations composed by sets of random RP and random CP respectively, as well as the GA convergence in any case. Figure 5 shows, for the problem instance ABZ7, the

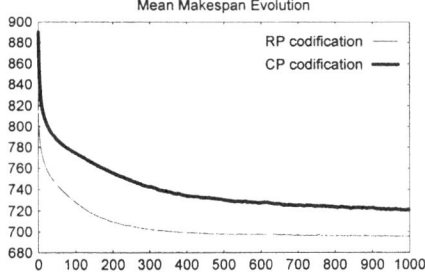

Figure 5. Mean makespan evolution with RP and CP codifications for the problem instance ABZ7. In either case the GA was run 30 times starting from random initial populations. That is random RPs and random CPs respectively.

convergence pattern of the mean makespan for both codification schemas. As we can observe, with RPs the mean value of the makespan for the initial population is much lower than it is with CPs. Moreover the convergence is much faster with RPs as well and so the GA reaches finally a lower value of mean makespan. Similar results were obtained for almost all the 12 instances of the set of selected problem instances. Table 1 shows results from the remaining problem instances, but in this case the GA final results refer to the best solution reached and the standard deviation in 30 trials.

In addition to the GAs starting from random RP or CP, we have considered the evolution of the GAs starting from equivalent populations. We have generated initial chromosomes by means of three different methods in order to do that. These chromosomes are firstly codified into RPs, and as a RP can be translated directly into a CP with the same meaning and structure, we can compare both versions of the GA starting from actually equivalent initial populations. The first method consists in generating random RPs and then trans-forms them directly into CPs. The other two methods consist in applying the G&T algorithm, with ties bro-ken at random in the second, while with ties broken in favor of the operation with the largest index within its job in the third. Clearly the first two methods are quite natural, while the third one is not. In fact this method generates quite bad chromosomes, this way we obtain initial populations with different characteristics which is

Table 1. Summary of results from different codifications. In either case the GA was ran with a population of 100 chromosomes generated initially at random, 1000 generations, crossover probability 0,7 and mutation probability 0,2. The value of parameter δ was 0,5.

Problem characteristics				RP codification			CP codification		
					GA Results			GA Results	
name	size	Best known	Init. Pop. Mean	Mean of Best solution	SD	Init. Pop. Mean	Mean of Best Solution	SD
abz7	20×15	665	816	688	5,9	890	708	6,5
abz8	20×15	670	850	709	6,5	919	727	11,0
abz9	20×15	686	892	723	6,9	923	741	9,9
ft10	10×10	930	1195	957	6,4	1253	958	10,4
ft20	20×05	1165	1531	1185	7,2	1541	1183	6,3
la21	15×10	1046	1332	1075	7,1	1394	1088	9,3
la24	15×10	935	1197	968	13,1	1294	974	12,7
la25	15×10	977	1240	996	7,5	1353	1002	9,2
la27	20×10	1235	1553	1271	6,5	1643	1292	11,1
la29	20×10	1153	1488	1213	14,8	1631	1236	11,4
la38	15×15	1196	1538	1253	11,1	1631	1248	14,9
la40	15×15	1222	1520	1266	10,3	1617	1270	14,5

useful for the purpose of comparison. Figure 6 shows the results obtained for the problem in-stance ABZ7 for the two versions of the GA, RP and CP respectively, when they start from initial populations with different characteristics. As we can observe, the RP version relies much less on the quality of the initial population, and in almost all the cases converges towards a better value than the CP version.

The former experimental study suggests that in the context of a simple GA the RP codification is better than the CP codification. But this conclusion should not be considered as quite general. Maybe if more sophisticated GAs are exploited or more specific initialization methods are considered, as the method proposed by Varela et al. [12] for bottleneck problems, the conclusion is rather different.

References

[1]   Bierwirth, C. (1995) "A Generalized Permutation Approach to Jobshop Scheduling with Genetic Algorithms." OR Spec-trum 17, 87-92.

[2]   Matfeld, D. C. (1995) "Evolutionary Search and the Job Shop. Investigations on Genetic Algorithms for Production Scheduling." Springer-Verlag.

[3]   Giffler, B., and G. L. Thomson. (1960) "Algorithms for Solving Production Scheduling Problems." Operations Research 8, 487-503.

[4]   Storer, R. H., S. D. Wu, and R. Vaccari (1992) "New search spaces for sequencing problems with application to job shop scheduling." Management Science 38, 1494-1509.

[5]   Syswerda, G. (1991) "Schedule Optimization Using Genetic Algorithms," Handbook of Genetic Algorithms, Ed. L. Davis, Van Nostrand Reinhold, New York, pp. 332-349.

[6]   Fang, H.L., P. Ross, and D. Corne. (1993) "A promising genetic algorithm approach to job-shop scheduling, reschedul-ing, and open-shop scheduling problems", Proceedings of the Fifth International Conference On Genetic Algo-rithms, 375-382.

[7]   Dorndorf, U., and E. Pesch. (1995) "Evolution based learning in a job shop scheduling environment," Computers & Operations Research 22, 25-40.

[8]   Bierwirth, C., and D. Mattfeld. (1999) "Production Scheduling and Rescheduling with Genetic Algorithms." Evolution-ary Computation 7(1), 1-17.

[9]   Yamada, T. and R. Nakano. (1996) "Scheduling by Genetic Local Search with multi-step crossover". Fourth Int. Conf. On Parallel Problem Solving from Nature (PPSN IV), Berlin, Germany, pp.960-969.

[10]   Della Croce, F. D., R. Tadei and G. Volta (1995) "A genetic algorithm for the job shop problem" Computers and Op-erational Research 22, 15-24.
[11]   Applegate, D., and W. Cook. (1991) "A Computational Study of the Job–Shop Scheduling Problem." ORSA Journal of Computing 3, 149-156.
[12]   Varela, R., C. R. Vela, J. Puente, and A. Gómez. (2003) "A knowledge-based evolutionary strategy for scheduling prob-lems with bottlenecks." European Journal of Operational Research 145, 57-71.

Planning, Scheduling and Constraint Satisfaction: From Theory to Practice
L. Castillo et al. (Eds.)
IOS Press, 2005

Topological Constraints in Periodic Train Scheduling

M.A. Salido[1], M. Abril[2], F. Barber[2], L. Ingolotti[2], P. Tormos[3], A. Lova[3]

DCCIA[1], Universidad de Alicante, Spain

DSIC[2], DEIOAC[3], Universidad Politécnica de Valencia, Spain

{mabril, msalido, lingolotti, fbarber, }@dsic.upv.es

{ptormos, allova}@eio.upv.es

Abstract.

It is well known that many scheduling problems can be modeled as constraint optimization problems. The scheduling of train services can be considered as a problem subject to a number of constraints describing railway infrastructure, required train services and reasonable time-intervals for waiting and transits. Railway optimization problems are known to be hard problems and a good solution or the best solution is a rather difficult task. In this work, we propose a topological constraint optimization technique for solving periodic train scheduling, developed in collaboration with the National Network of Spanish Railways (RENFE). This topological technique transforms the railway optimization problem in subproblems such that a traffic pattern is generated for each subproblem. These traffic patterns will be periodically repeated to compose the entire running map. The results show that this technique improve the results obtained by well known tools as LINGO and ILOG Concert Technology (CPLEX).

1 Introduction

Over the last few years, railway traffic has increased considerably, which has created the need to optimize the use of railway infrastructures. This is, however, a hard and difficult task. Thanks to developments in computer science and advances in the fields of optimization and intelligent resource management, railway managers can optimize the use of available infrastructures and obtain useful conclusions about their topology.

The overall goal of a long-term collaboration between our group at the Polytechnic University of Valencia (UPV) and the National Network of Spanish Railways (RENFE) is to offer assistance to help in the planning of train scheduling, to obtain conclusions about the maximum capacity of the network, to identify bottlenecks, to determine the consequences of changes, to provide support in the resolution of incidents, to provide alternative planning and real traffic control, etc. Besides of mathematical processes, a high level of interaction with railway experts is required to be able to take advantage of their experience.

Different models and mathematical formulations for train scheduling have been created by researchers [10, 4, 5, 9, 7, 3, 6, 2], etc. Several European companies are also working on similar systems. These systems include complex stations, rescheduling due to incidents, rail network capacities, etc. These are complex problems for which work in network topology and heuristic-dependent models can offer adequate solutions.

In this paper, we propose a topological constraint optimization technique for solving periodic train scheduling. This technique has been inserted in our system [1] and it is committed to solve this problem in order to obtain as good and feasible running map as possible. The system is able to plot the obtained running map. A running map contains information regarding railway topology (stations, tracks, distances between stations, traffic control features, etc.) and the schedules of the trains that use this topology (arrival and departure times of trains at each station, frequency, stops, junctions, crossing, etc,) (Figure 1). In our system, the railway running map problem is formulated as a Constraint Optimization Problem (COP). Variables are frequencies, arrival and departure times of trains at stations. Constraints are composed by user requirements and the intrinsical constraints (railway infrastructures, rules for traffic coordination, etc.). These constraints are composed by the parameters defined using user interfaces and database accesses. The objective function is to minimize the journey time of all trains. The problem formulation is (traditionally) translated into a formal mathematical model to be solved for optimality by means of mixed integer programming techniques. In our framework, the formal mathematical model is partitioned in two different subproblems: integer programming problem composed by the constraints with integer variables and linearized problem in which there are now variables of type real remaining to be assigned. Therefore, the problem constraints are classified such that most restricted constraints are studied first [11]. This is based on the *first-fail* principle, which can be explained as

"To succeed, try first where you are more likely to fail"

The most restricted constraints are considered to be composed of integer variables. In this way, our system studies first the integer programming problem and then it solves the linearized problem. The integer programming problem will be partitioned in a set of subproblems such that the solution of each subproblem will generate a traffic pattern. The partition is carried out through the stations that take part in the running map. Each block of the partition is composed by contiguous stations, so that each traffic pattern represents the running map corresponding to each block of constraints. In Figure 1, a possible block of the partition may be composed by the first four stations: *Malaga Cent, Malaga Renfe, Los Prados* and *Aeropuerto*. Each traffic pattern will be periodically repeated to composed the entire running-map.

2 Problem Topology

A sample of a running map is shown in Figure 1, where several train crossings can be observed. On the left side of Figure 1, the names of the stations are presented and the vertical line represents the number of tracks between stations (one-way or two-way). The objective of the system is to obtain a correct and optimized running map taking into account: (i) the railway infrastructure topology, (ii) user requirements (parameters of trains to be scheduled), (iii) traffic rules, (iv) previously scheduled traffic on the same railway network, and (v) criteria for optimization.

A railway network is basically composed of stations and one-way or two-way tracks. A dependency can be:

- *Station*: Place for trains to park, stop or pass through. Each station is associated with a unique station identifier. There are two or more tracks in a station where crossings.

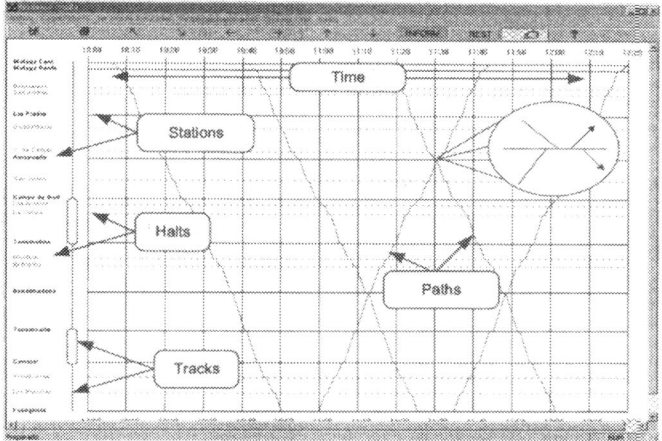

Figure 1: A sample of a running map

- *Halt*: Place for trains to stop, pass through, but not park. Each halt is associated with a unique halt identifier.

- *Junction*: Place where two different tracks fork. There is no stop time.

In Figure 1, horizontal dotted lines represent halts or junctions, while continuous lines represent stations. On a rail network, the user needs to schedule the paths of n trains going in one direction and m trains going in the opposite direction, trains of a given type and at a desired scheduling frequency.

The type of trains to be scheduled determines the time assigned for travel between two locations on the path. The path selected by the user for a train trip determines which stations are used and the stop time required at each station for commercial purposes. In order to perform crossing in a section with a one-way track, one of the trains should wait in a station. This is called a *technical stop*. One of the trains is detoured from the main track so that the other train can cross or continue. (Figure 2).

2.1 Railway Traffic Rules, topological and requirement constraints

A valid running map must satisfy and optimize the set of existing constraints in the periodic problem. Some of the main constraints to be considered are:

1. **Traffic rules** guarantee crossing operations. The main rules to take into account are:

   - *Crossing constraint*: Any two trains and going in opposite directions must not simultaneously use the same one-way track. The crossing of two trains can be performed only on two-way tracks and at stations, where one of the two trains has been detoured from the main track (Figure 2). Several crossings are shown in Figure 1.

   - *Expedition time constraint*. There exists a given time to put a detoured train back on the main track and exit from a station.

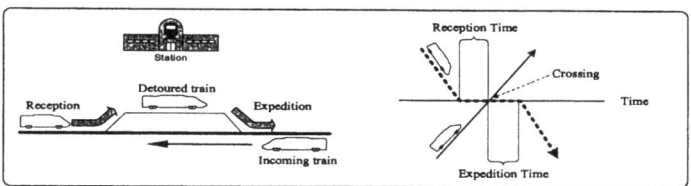

Figure 2: Constraints related to crossing in stations

- *Reception time constraint.* There exists a given time to detour a train from the main track so that crossing or overtaking can be performed.

2. **User Requirements**: The main constrains due to user requirements are:

   - *Type of train and Number of trains* going in each direction to be scheduled and *Travel time* between locations.
   - *Path of trains*: Locations used and *Stop time* for commercial purposed in each direction.
   - *Scheduling frequency.* The frequency requirements of the departure of trains in both directions. This constraint is very restrictive, because, when crossing is performed, trains must wait for a certain time interval at stations. This interval must be propagated to all trains going in the same direction in order to maintain the established scheduling frequency.

In accordance with user requirements, the system should obtain the best solutions available so that all constraints are satisfied. Several criteria can exist to qualify the optimality of solutions: minimize duration and/or number of technical stops, minimize the total time of train trips (span) of the total schedule, giving priority to certain trains, etc.

2.2 General System Architecture

The general outline of our system is presented in Figure 3. It shows several steps, some of which require the direct interaction with the human user to insert requirement parameters, parameterize the constraint solver for optimization, or modify a given schedule. First of all, the user should require the parameters of the railway network and the train type from the central database (Figure 3). This database stores the set of locations, lines, tracks, trains, etc. Normally, this information does not change, but authorized users may desire to change this information. With the data acquired from the database, the system generates the formal mathematical model. This model is composed by a large number of mixed-integer constraints. To translate the mixed-integer problem into a linear problem, a topological technique is carried out to assign value to each integer variable. This technique carries out a partition of the stations such that each block of stations represents a subproblem and a traffic pattern (solution) must be generated for each subproblem. This traffic pattern is generated based on the problem topology just as the number of stations, the train frequency, the type of stations, and mainly the distance among the stations. Once the traffic patterns are generated, the integer variables are instantiated and the linearized problem is straightforward solved returning the running map data. If the mathematical model is not feasible, the user must modify the parameters, mainly the most restrictive ones. If the running map is consistent, the graphic interface plots the scheduling. Afterwards, the user can graphically interact with the scheduling to modify the arrival or departure times. Each interaction is automatically checked by the constraint checker in order to guarantee the consistency of changes. The user can finally print out the scheduling, to obtain reports with the arrival and departure times of each train in each location, or graphically observe the complete scheduling topology.

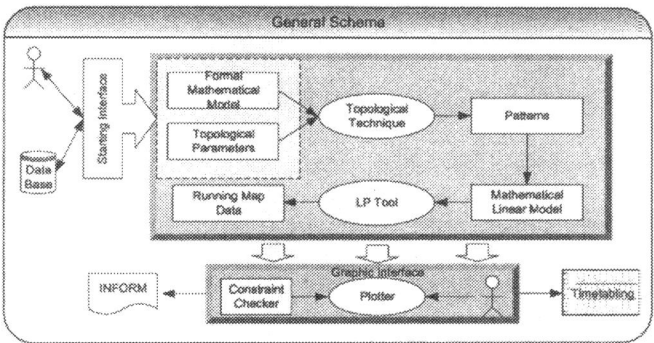

Figure 3: General scheme of our tool.

3   Topological Constraint Optimization Technique

The railway optimization problem is considered to be more complex than job-shop scheduling [8, 12]. Here, two trains, traveling in opposite directions use tracks between two locations for different durations, and these durations are causally dependent on how the scheduling itself is done (ie: order of tasks), due to the stopping, and starting time for trains in a non-required technical stop, expedition, reception times, etc. Some processes (detour from the main railway) may or may not be required for each train at each location. In our system, the problem is modeled as a COP, where finite domain variables represent frequency and arrival and departure times of trains of locations. Relations on these variables permit the management of all the constraints due to the user requirements, topological constraints, traffic rules, commercial stops, technical operations, maximum slacks, etc. Hundred of trains, of different types, in different directions, along paths of dozens of stations have to be coordinated. Thus, many variables, and many and very complex constraints arise. The problem turns into a mixed-integer programming problem, in which thousands of inequalities have to be satisfied and a high number of variables take only integer values. As is well known, this type of model is far more difficult to solve than linear programming models.

Our goal is focused on periodic train scheduling, where all the trains in the same direction are of the same type; they stop in the same stations; and no previously trains are scheduled. Therefore, our objective is to solve this problem previously assigning values to integer variables such that the mixed-integer programming problem is transformed into a linear programming problem. Then, the linearized problem is easily solved. In this way, the topological constraint optimization technique is committed to this goal.

The topological constraint optimization technique generates the traffic patterns based on several features as identification of bottlenecks, periodicity of running maps, number of stations, distance among stations, possible wide-paths for trains, etc.

3.1   Topological Technique

The main idea of this technique is to generate a traffic pattern for each set of stations such that the union of these contiguous traffic patterns determine the journey of each train. Figure 4 shows a possible set of stations (block).

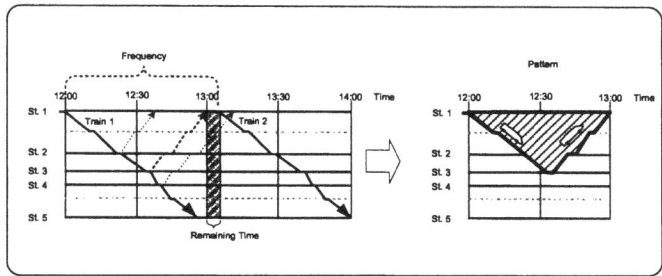

Figure 4: First traffic pattern generation.

The block of stations will be selected taking into account the speed of the trains, the distance among stations and the frequency inserted into the problem. Each traffic pattern covers the block of stations necessary for a train to go from the first station of the block to the last station of the block and return from the last station to the first one (round trip). This round trip must arrive to the first station (St.1) as close but before to the following train departure (Train 2) as possible. Thus, our objective is to minimize the remaining time between the frequency and the round trips. Each possible round trip will involve a different set of constraints. The round trip that minimize the remaining time will be selected as the *pattern*. This traffic pattern will be composed by a higher number of stations than the rest of possible round trips.

Once the first traffic pattern has been generated, we study the following pattern with the remaining stations. Figure 5 shows the generation of the second pattern using the same strategy.

Therefore, when the second traffic pattern is generated, the topological technique studies the following traffic pattern until there is no station left. In Figure 6, we can observe an example of running map with three complete traffic patterns and some stations without traffic pattern. However, it is usual that there are some stations left. These stations are not involved in any traffic pattern. We must take into account that the best traffic pattern in a block of stations implies to start the following block of stations in the last station of the previous block. We must check all traffic patterns together in order to obtain the journey. Moreover, the first combination of traffic patterns may not be the best solutions due to existence of some combinations of traffic patterns. This combination depends on the number of stations that are not involved in a traffic pattern. In this way, we explore all possible combinations in order to obtain the best set of traffic patterns.

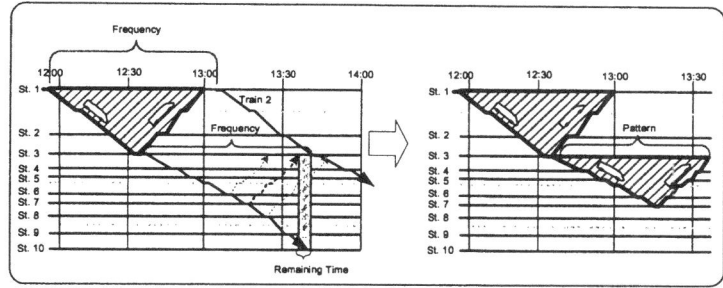

Figure 5: Second Pattern generation.

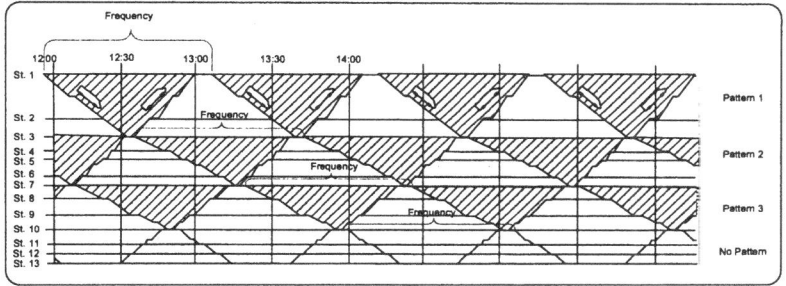

Figure 6: Periodic Pattern generation.

Figure 6 shows an example in which three stations are not involved in any traffic pattern. So, some combinations are possible and they are restricted to the set of stations involved in the first traffic pattern. Thus, these three stations can be sorted between the first and the last traffic pattern. In this way, the first traffic pattern may start at the second or third station and the last traffic pattern may finish in the penultimate or last but two station. However, due to efficient use of resources, or depending on the importance of the station, it is more appropriate the first traffic pattern (last traffic pattern) starts (finishes) at the first (last) station.

4   Evaluation

The application and performance of this system depends on several factors: Railway topology (locations, distances, tracks, etc.), number and type of trains (speeds, starting and stopping times, etc.), frequency ranges, initial departure interval times, etc.

In this section, we compare the performance of our topological technique with some well-known tools: LINGO as an Operational Research tool and ILOG Concert Technology (CPLEX) that combines techniques of constraint programming and mathematical programming. Both are appropriate tools for solving these types of problems. However, the system carried out important preprocessing heuristics [1] before executing these well-known tools in order to significantly reduce the size of these problems. Therefore, CPLEX and LINGO are combined with some heuristics, and they obtained the optimal solutions of their relaxed problems.

This empirical evaluation was carried out integrating both different types of problems: benchmark (real) problems and random problems. The computer used in our tests was a Pentium IV 2.8Mz with 512 Mb. of memory. Thus, we defined random instances over a real railway infrastructure that joins two important Spanish cities (La Coruña and Vigo). The journey between these two cities is currently divided by 40 dependencies between stations (23) and halts (17).

In our empirical evaluation, each set of random instances was defined by the 3-tuple $< n, s, f >$, where n was the number of trains in each direction, s the number of stations/halts and f the frequency. The problems were randomly generated by modifying these parameters. Thus, each of the tables shown sets two of the parameters and varies the other one in order to evaluate the algorithm performance when this parameter increases.

In Table 1, we present the running time in seconds and the journey time in problems where the number of trains was increased from 5 to 50 and the number of stations/halts and the frequency were set at 40 and 90, respectively: $< n, 40, 90 >$. The results shows that CPLEX obtained better running time and journey time than LINGO. However, it can be observed that the running time is lower using the topological technique than the other two COP tools. Furthermore, our technique always obtained the same journey time (lower than CPLEX and LINGO) due to the fact that it generates the corresponding traffic patterns and it is independent of the number of trains. Figure 7 shows the system interface executing our technique with the instance $< 10, 40, 90 >$. The first window shows the user parameters, the second window presents the best solution obtained in this moment, the third window presents data about the best solution found, and finally the last window show the obtained running map.

Table 1: Running time (sec.) and journey time in problems with different trains.

$< n, 40, 90 >$	CPLEX+heuristics		LINGO+heuristics		TOPOLOGICAL	
Trains	running time	journey time	running time	journey time	running time	journey time
5	5"	2:29:33	8"	2:30:54	3"	2:22:08
10	8"	2:26:04	17"	2:31:37	4"	2:22:08
15	13"	2:26:18	24"	2:31:51	5"	2:22:08
20	16"	2:26:25	35"	2:31:58	5"	2:22:08
50	55"	2:31:09	1302"	2:32:11	10"	2:22:08

Table 2 shows the running time in seconds and the journey time in problems where the number of stations was increased from 10 to 60 and the number of trains and the frequency were set at 10 and 90, respectively: $< 10, s, 90 >$. In this case, only stations were included to analyze the behavior of the techniques. It can be observed that the running time was lower using our technique in all instances. The journey time was also improved using our topological technique. It is important to realize the difference between the instance $< 10, 40, 90 >$ of the Table 1 and the instance $< 10, 40, 90 >$ of the Table 2. They represents the same instance, but in Table 2 we only used stations (no halts), so that the number of possible crossing between trains is much more larger. This item reduced the journey time from 2:22:08 to 2:20:22, but the number of combination increased the running time from 4" to 7". Furthermore, CPLEX and LINGO maintained similar behaviors.

In Table 3, we present the running time in seconds and the journey time in problems where the frequency was increased from 60 to 140 and the number of trains and stations were set at 20 and 40, respectively: $< 20, 40, f >$. It can be observed that the frequency the topological

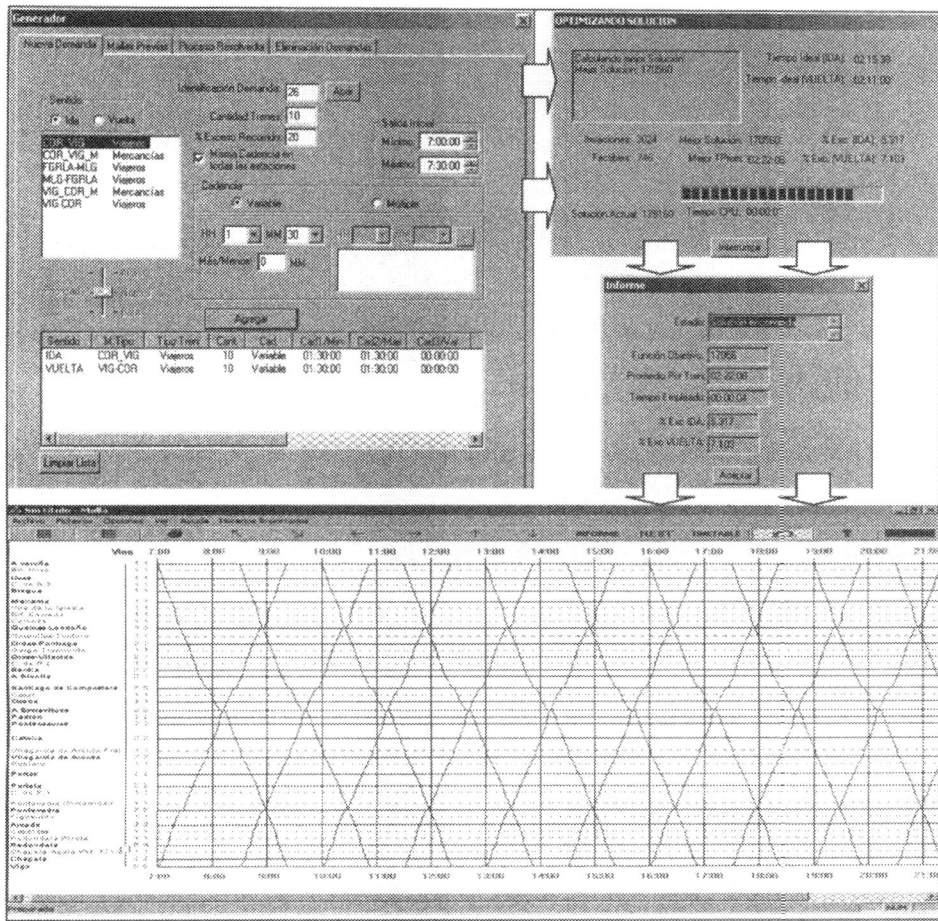

Figure 7: System Interface.

Table 2: Running time (sec.) and journey time in problems with different number of stations.

< 10, s, 90 >	CPLEX+heuristics		LINGO+heuristics		TOPOLOGICAL	
Stations	running time	journey time	running time	journey time	running time	journey time
10	2"	0:58:36	4"	0:58:06	1"	0:57:36
20	3"	1:04:11	20"	1:04:11	2"	1:04:11
30	15"	1:45:08	42"	1:45:38	4"	1:45:08
40	56"	2:23:16	28"	2:24:36	7"	2:20:22
60	340"	3:44:28	326"	3:44:22	40"	3:32:15

technique improved the journey time when the frequency increased. As in previous results, the running time of the topological technique was lower than CPLEX and LINGO.

Table 3: Running time (sec.) and journey time in problems with different cadencies.

< 20, 40, f >	CPLEX+heuristics		LINGO+heuristics		TOPOLOGICAL	
Frequency	running time	journey time	running time	journey time	running time	journey time
60	> 43200"	-	> 43200"	-	36"	2:32:11
90	17"	2:26:25	32"	2:31:58	5"	2:22:08
100	18"	2:23:10	34"	2:22:55	3"	2:19:09
120	16"	2:16:17	27"	2:18:47	4"	2:16:00
140	17"	2:20:18	27"	2:16:19	4"	2:17:03

5 Conclusions

We have proposed a topological constraint optimization technique for solving periodic train scheduling in collaboration with the National Network of Spanish Railways (RENFE). This technique has been inserted into the system to solve more efficiently periodic timetables. This system, at a current stage of integration, supposes the application of methodologies of Artificial Intelligence in a problem of great interest and will assist railways managers in optimizing the use of railway infrastructures and will help them in the resolution of complex scheduling problems.

References

[1] Barber, F., Salido, M.A., Ingolotti, L., Abril, M., Lova, A., Tormos, P. *An Interactive Train Scheduling Tool for Solving and Plotting Running Maps*, Current Topics in Artificial Intelligence LNAI 3040, (2004), To appear.

[2] Bussiecky, M.R., Winter, T., Zimmermann, U.T. *Discrete optimization in public rail transport*, Mathematical Programming 79(3), (1997), 415-444.

[3] Bussiecky, M.R., Zimmermann, U.T. *Combinatorial Optimization Methods for Optimal Lines in Real-World Railway Systems*, Technical Report TR-95-03, (1996).

[4] Caprara, A., Fischetti, M., Toth, P. *Modeling and Solving the Train Timetabling Problem*, Research Report OR/00/9 DEIS, (2000).

[5] Caprara, A., Fischetti, M., Guida, P., Monaci, M., Sacco, G., Toth, P. *Solution of Real-World Train Timetabling Problems*, 34th Annual Hawaii International Conference on System Sciences **3** (2001).

[6] Chiu, C.K., Chou, C.M., Lee, J.H.M., Leung, H.F., and Leung, Y.W., *A Constraint-Based Interactive Train Rescheduling Tool*, Constraints **7** (2002), 167–198.

[7] Kaas, A.H., *Methods to Calculate Capacity of Railways*, Ph. Dissertation (1998).

[8] Kreuger, P.; Carlsson, M.; Olsson, J.; Sjoland, T.; Astrom, E. *The TUFF train scheduler: Two duration trip scheduling on multi directional track networks*. Workshop on Tools and Environments for Constraint Logic Programming, (1997).

[9] Lindner, T., *Train schedule optimization in public rail transport*, Ph. Dissertation, Technische Universitat Braunschweig, Germany, (2000).

[10] Oliveira, E., Smith, B.M., *A Job-Shop Scheduling Model for the Single-Track Railway Scheduling Problem*, Research Report 2000.21, University of Leeds, (2000).

[11] Salido, M.A., Barber, F., *A Constraint Ordering Heuristic for Scheduling Problem*, 1st Multidisciplinary International Conference on Scheduling: Theory and Applications (MISTA 2003), (2) 476-491, (2003).

[12] Zuidwijk, R.A., Kroon, L.G., *Integer Constraints for Train Series Connections*, Erasmus Research Institute of Management (ERIM), Discussion Paper. (2002).

Planning, Scheduling and Constraint Satisfaction: From Theory to Practice
L. Castillo et al. (Eds.)
IOS Press, 2005

CPPlanner: extending Graphplan framework for optimal Temporal Planning

Tien Ba Dinh, and Barbara Smith
University of Huddersfield, UK
t.b.dinh@hud.ac.uk, b.m.smith@hud.ac.uk

Abstract. Since the introduction in 1995, Graphplan has been one of the most well-known approaches for optimal planning systems. It has been applied as the framework in many planners, such as FF [8], GP-CSP [2], TGP [11], TPSYS[7], LPGP [5], STAN [6]. In this paper, we presents our temporal planning system, CPPlanner, which extends the Graphplan approach to find an optimal solution in terms of time (*makespan*). In particular, the planner uses a "critical path" extracted from the expansion phase to improve the performance of the backtracking search in the solution extraction. It can deal with temporal planning domains in which actions can have effects at any time during their execution.

1   Introduction

In the past few years, many new techniques and algorithms have been introduced in AI Planning. Graphplan [1] is known as one of the best approaches for optimal planners. The original Graphplan is designed to deal with classical planning domains in which actions are performed simultaneously. Recently, in TGP and TPSYS, it has been extended to find an optimal solution for temporal planning domains.

In this paper, we present our planning system, CPPlanner, which applies the Graphplan approach to find an optimal solution in terms of time for temporal planning domains. Unlike TGP and TPSYS, CPPlanner uses "critical paths" which act as the backbone for the solution extraction to improve the performance of the system. In addition, CPPlanner is able to deal with richer temporal planning domains in which actions can have effects at any time during their execution. With this extension, the mutex relations of actions which have middle effects are built up as constraints in the graph expansion phase and they have to be re-checked in the solution extraction.

As other Graphplan-based planning systems, CPPlanner also has two stages: the expansion and the solution extraction. The expansion phase advances the planning graph in time until all the subgoals appear and are pairwise non-mutex. The solution extraction then searches for a solution in this graph based on the critical path which runs from a proposition in the initial state to a subgoal in the current state. This helps the backtracking search to eliminate actions and propositions which violate mutex relations, and so improves the performance.

2 Action representation

In CPPlanner, action representation has been designed to deal with temporal planning domains in which actions can have effects at any time during their execution. Our action representation is mainly influenced by PDDL+ [4] and the representation of the Sapa planner [3]. In this representation, each action A has Dur_A, a starting time Start_A, the list of conditions Cond_A, and the list of effects Eff_A. The duration Dur_A can be statically defined in the domain or dynamically calculated at the run time of the action. For example, the action *Fly* can be calculated based on the locations of the take-off airport, the landing airport, and the speed of the aircraft. The list of conditions which will allow the action A to perform is a conjunction of tuples $\langle \mathrm{Cond}_{A_i}, d_{A_i} \rangle$ (⟨condition, duration⟩). Each $\langle \mathrm{Cond}_{A_i}, d_{A_i} \rangle$ means that the Cond_{A_i} needs to hold (i.e. be true) from the starting time of the action A until $(\mathrm{Start}_A + d_{A_i})$. Similarly, the list of effects Eff_A is a conjunction of tuples $\langle \mathrm{Eff}_{A_j}, d_{A_j} \rangle$. Each tuple that represents the Eff_{A_j} will happen at the time $(\mathrm{Start}_A + d_{A_j})$ onwards. Briefly, the action representation for CPPlanner is described as follows:

An action A is presented as $\{\mathrm{Dur}_A, \mathrm{Cond}_A, \mathrm{Eff}_A\}$ in which:

- Dur_A: the duration of the action A. $(\mathrm{Dur}_A > 0)$.

- $\mathrm{Cond}_A = \{\langle \mathrm{Cond}_{A_1}, d_{A_1} \rangle, ..., \langle \mathrm{Cond}_{A_k}, d_{A_k} \rangle\}$ with $\forall i \in [1, k] : 0 \leq d_{A_i} \leq \mathrm{Dur}_A$.

- $\mathrm{Eff}_A = \{\langle \mathrm{Eff}_{A_1}, d_{A_1} \rangle, ..., \langle \mathrm{Eff}_{A_h}, d_{A_h} \rangle\}$ with $\forall i \in [1, h] : 0 \leq d_{A_i} \leq \mathrm{Dur}_A$.

3 Graph expansion

In AI planning, given the initial state, the goal state and a set of actions, a solution of the problem is a sequence of actions which takes the initial state to the goal state, i.e. a plan. In CPPlanner, we assume that the actions in the solution must be complete and the *makespan* is the ending time of the latest action in the plan, even if the goal state has been achieved as a result of effects taking place before the end of the action. With this assumption, the expansion phase is much more complicated than if plans can rely on uncompleted actions. In the expansion, the planner has to wait for the action to finish before taking its effects as conditions for other actions. Furthermore, when an action is applied, its starting time need not be the ending time of another action, but the maximum of the *timestamps* of its conditions.

Like TGP and TPSys, the graph expansion phase advances the planning graph in time by applying the earliest possible action at each time. Starting from the initial state in which all propositions are attached with *timestamps* 0, the graph is advanced in time by choosing the action which can use current propositions as conditions and has the earliest ending time. After applying this action, all of its effects are added to the graph with their corresponding *timestamps*. The mutex relations among those new actions and propositions with the old ones are also added. Then, the *examining timepoint t* is advanced to the next timepoint $t + \mathrm{Dur}_A$ if *examining timepoint* $t \leq t + \mathrm{Dur}_A$. Otherwise, it remains the same. This process is repeated until all the subgoals appear and are pairwise non-mutex. At this time, the solution extraction is tried to look for a solution. If a solution is found, it is also the optimal solution for the problem and the algorithm is terminated. Otherwise, the process will be performed again to move

// All initial props with timestamp 0 in the Queue
PropsQueue = $\{< p_1, 0 >, < p_2, 0 >, ..., < p_n, 0 >\}$
// *Props* - the propositions added to the graph
Props = $\{\}$
// *Actions* - the actions added to the graph
Actions = $\{\}$
// The examining timepoint starts at 0
t = 0

Loop

    while *PropsQueue* $\neq \emptyset$
        CurProp = the first prop in the *PropsQueue*
        Remove it from *PropsQueue*
        Create its mutex relations with *Props* and *Actions*
        PossibleActions={all actions having *CurProp* as one of their conditions,
                        and the others from Props}
        Apply *PossibleActions*
        TmpProps $\leftarrow$ *TmpProps* $\cup$ {effects of with *PossibleActions* with *timestamps*}
        // Add *CurProp* to the Graph
        Props $\leftarrow$ *Props* $\cup$ *CurProp*;
    end {while}

    // Move to the next possible timepoint where at least one action completes
    t = timestamp of the next ending effect in the *TmpProps*
    // add the completed actions to the Graph
    Actions $\leftarrow$ *Actions* $\cup$ {new completed actions after moving to the next timepoint}
    PropsQueue $\leftarrow$ *PropsQueue* + new props in *TmpProps* from completed actions at t
    Remove these propositions in *TmpProps*
    If goals $\subseteq$ {*Props* $\cup$ *PropsQueue*} & pairwise nonmutex **then** do solution extraction.
    If (solution extraction succeeds) **then** terminate the algorithm.

End {loop}

Table 1: Graph expansion algorithm

to the next possible *timepoint*. The *table 1* illustrates the details of the expansion algorithm.

In TGP, with the assumption that actions only have ending effects and conditions must be hold throughout the execution, the starting time of the possible action when applying is the examining time t. However, in CPPlanner, because actions can have middle effects, they can overlap partially. The starting time of the possible action is calculated by the maximum of the *timestamps* of its conditions instead of the examining time t. This leads to the fact that propositions will be stored in the list *Props* with new *timestamps* if they appear again.

For example, in TGP, it is very simple that if we are applying a possible action A at the examining time t, the starting time of A will be t and the effects will be attached with the *timestamp* = t + Dur$_A$. However, in CPPlanner, because actions can have effects at any time during the execution, an action X may take some intermediate effects of action Y as its conditions and start while action Y is still under way. Note that at the examining time t, Y has finished already. So when we apply the action X, if X has several conditions, the starting time of X will be calculated as max{$timestamp_{Cond_X}$}, not the examining time t. Note that this value may be less than t. The *timestamps* of X's effects are calculated based on this starting time.

4 Mutex relations

In TGP and TPSYS, because actions do not have effects in the middle, the mutex relations between actions show whether they can overlap or cannot overlap at all. The mutex relations are found in the expansion phase and can be re-used in the extraction phase. For example, suppose the mutex relation of action A and action B is calculated as true. It means that they cannot overlap with each other in the result plan, regardless of the time that these actions start. Therefore, in the solution extraction phase, when choosing actions and propositions for the plan, if the mutex checking is required, the planner just looks into the mutex relation that has been calculated in the expansion phase earlier. However, in our planner, because actions may have effects during their execution, the actions can overlap partially. Therefore, the mutex relations depend on the time when actions start or propositions become true. In the solution extraction phase, the mutex relations of some actions and propositions have to be re-checked with their assigned *timestamps* to know whether they are mutex or not. Thus, the mutex relations in CPPlanner are stored as constraints between actions and propositions, and must be re-checked in the extraction phase. The mutex relations of our planner are described as follows:

- **Proposition - proposition:** propositions p and q are mutex if (1) they are negations or (2) all actions supporting q are mutex with p and vice versa.

- **Action - proposition:** action A and proposition p are mutex if one of these holds

    - (p and q are mutex) $\land$ (q $\in$ Cond$_A$) $\land$ (p is true at t with $t \in$ [Start$_A$, Start$_A$+ d$_{A_q}$]).
    - (p and q are mutex) $\land$ (q $\in$ Eff$_A$) $\land$ (p is true at t with $t \in$ [Start$_A$ + d$_{A_q}$, End$_A$]).

- **Action - action:** action A, B are mutex if one of these holds

    - (p and q are mutex) $\land$ (p $\in$ Cond$_A$) $\land$ (q $\in$ Cond$_B$)
      $\land$ [Start$_A$, Start$_A$ + d$_{A_p}$] $\cap$ [Start$_B$, Start$_B$ + d$_{B_q}$] $\neq \emptyset$
    - (p and q are mutex) $\land$ (p $\in$ Cond$_A$) $\land$ (q $\in$ Eff$_B$)
      $\land$ (q is true at t with $t \in$ [Start$_A$, Start$_A$ + d$_{A_p}$]).
    - (p and q are mutex) $\land$ (p $\in$ Eff$_A$)$\land$ (q $\in$ Eff$_B$)
      $\land$ ((p is true at [Start$_B$ + d$_{B_q}$]) $\lor$ (q is true at [Start$_A$ + d$_{A_p}$])).

The mutex relation are stored as constraints between nodes in the graph. There are two types of mutex. One is the static mutex which we can know right after reading the planning domain. It is always mutex regardless of the time, e.g. negations of propositions. The other is the dynamic one which depends on the time of propositions or actions. The dynamic mutex relations have to be re-checked when new timestamps are assigned to actions or propositions in the extraction phase.

// Attach the goal propositions with timestamp t_G
$Goals = \{< p_1, t_G >, < p_2, t_G >, ..., < p_n, t_G >\}$
if *Goals* is a subset of initial state **then** stop the algorithm and print the solution.
Set $t = t_G$
Candidates = proposition-action paths leading to t_G

while *Candidates* $\neq \emptyset$

    CriticalPath $\leftarrow$ get one from *Candidates*
    Delete it from *Candidates*
    ActionPlan = all actions of the critical path with their timestamps
    Remove propositions supported by the critical path from *Goals*
    Add all conditions of actions in the critical path to *Goals* with their timestamps
    // Note: excluding the conditions are effects of other actions in the critical path

    while can choose (*NextAction* = one of the actions which supports p
                   such that p∈*Goals*, and doesn't mutex with *ActionPlan* and *Goals*).

        Slide *NextAction* as late as possible, but its ending time not exceeding t.
        Add *NextAction* into the *ActionPlan*.
        Delete its effects in the *Goals*.
        Add its conditions to the *Goals* with timestamps.
        if the timestamp of any propositions < 0 **then** fail and try another *NextAction*
        if *Goals* is a subset of initial state **then** print the solution and terminate the algorithm.
        Update the time t = ending time of the chosen action

    end {while}

end {while}

if cannot find a solution **then** graph expansion phase is run again by the *Loop*

Table 2: Solution extraction algorithm

5 Solution extraction

The solution extraction phase is called to extract a plan when the graph is expanded to the examining timepoint t_G where all the subgoals appear and are pairwise non-mutex. At first, the planner extracts all proposition-action paths in the graph which start from propositions in the initial state and end with subgoals at the time t_G. Because the planning graph is advanced step by step in time until all subgoals appear and are pairwise non-mutex at t_G, there must be at least one proposition-action path as described. These proposition-action paths are used as "critical path" candidates. The planner chooses one by one from these candidates and uses it as the critical path of the backtracking search. All the actions and propositions along this path will be chosen before we actually do the search. With the chosen actions and propositions, other actions or propositions will be quickly eliminated in the search later on if they are mutex.

As shown in table 2, the planner is looking for a solution at the time t_G. Firstly, to expand to t_G, the graph expansion phase has known actions finished at the time t_G. Based on the graph, starting from subgoals with timestamp t_G, the planner traces back to the initial state get all proposition-action paths. Note that we only trace proposition-action paths of sub-goals which have the timestamp t_G, because maybe there are other subgoals which have the timestamp less than t_G with which we failed to find a solution earlier. We consider these proposition-action paths as critical-path candidates. CPPlanner then takes the candidates one by one to look for a solution. With the critical path, some actions and propositions will be added to the *ActionPlan* before the backtracking search for solution extraction is actually performed. This helps to prune irrelevant branches in the search tree by stopping other propositions or actions which are mutex with *ActionPlan* from being selected.

In TGP and TPSYS, the subgoals are dequeued one by one following a predefined order. For each goal, each of the possible supporting actions is tried. The new subgoals which are preconditions of the action will be added to the list. This work continues until a solution is found or all possible cases have been explored. With this approach, in order to check all possible cases, the algorithm has to try all possible actions as well as their possible start times. It will lead to some redundant search because they cannot use any bound for the next step (next proposition) in searching. In CPPlanner, we are using the examining time t to act as a bound for the next choice of action in order to avoid some symmetry in searching for solutions. It means that chosen actions have a chronological order in their ending times, i.e. the chosen action has its ending time equal or earlier than the previous chosen one. In addition, conflict directed backjumping [10] [9] will be applied to speed up the search.

6   Improvements

The performance of Graphplan-based planning systems depends much on the solution extraction phase. Therefore, the improvement of the solution extraction will speed up the whole system significantly. In this section, we describe some improvements to avoid redundancy for the search:

6.1   Avoid some redundant solution extraction calls

In the expansion phase, in order not to miss any solution, the planner has to keep all the new timestamps for propositions if they appear again. This leads to the fact that the solution for the problem is a sub-graph of the planning graph. As the definition of the critical paths above, the sub-graph must contain one of them as the backbone (i.e the starting time and the ending time of the solution are those of the critical path chosen as the backbone). Therefore, at a certain timepoint, say t_G, all the goals are in the graph and pairwise non-mutex, but their timestamps are less than t_G. It means that all the timestamps of the goals are not updated from the last expansion. In this case, the planner does not need to run the solution extraction phase because no solution exists at this stage.

6.2   Conflict Directed Backjumping

In the algorithm described above, the solution extraction phase uses chronological backtracking search. In order to improve the search, we can exploit the structure of the planning graph and apply conflict-directed backjumping [10] [9] to avoid getting into irrelevant branches and jump back to the conflict source. In our extraction algorithm, because actions are chosen one by one supporting the current sub-goal propositions, we can store the conflict list for the

k^{th} action, called as level k. For example, we are looking for the kth action in the extraction phase. We try action a_i and see whether it is mutex with any previous chosen propositions and actions, if we find out that it is mutex with another action a_x that we have chosen in an earlier level, we will store the level of a_x in the conflict-list for the level k. Then, we will try another action a_j. Also, if this action a_j is mutex with another action, say a_y, we add its level to the conflict-list. At this time, supposing that all the actions have been tried, the planner sorts the conflict list according to the values of levels stored and backtrack to the previous level appearing next in the list. This will help the planner to jump directly back to the source of the conflict instead of wasting time looking around.

7   Preliminary results

We have implemented and tested the planner on some data extracted from the last International Planning Competition (IPC 2002). The planner runs on a Pentium 4 2.2GHz with 1GB RAM. Since the system is still being developed, we have not done much about optimization for the source code. The table below shows some preliminary results on some temporal planning domains provided by CPPlanner:

Problem	Time (s)
Depotprob1818	3.72
Depotprob7512	15.56
Att-log0	0.22
Att-log1	0.40
Att-log3	5.30
ZenoTravel-1	0.02
ZenoTravel-2	0.03

Since CPPlanner has been implemented on MS Windows, it is quite difficult for us to compare it with TGP and TPSYS at this time. We plan to have some relative comparisons with TGP and TPSYS by running them on the same hardware configuration or using terminal software which allows the system to run under Unix or Linux.

8   Conclusion and Future Work

The paper has described our Graphplan-based optimal temporal planning system, CPPlanner. It extends the Graphplan framework to deal with richer temporal planning domains to find an optimal solution in time. The planner has applied the critical paths provided by the expansion phase to act as the backbone for the search in the extraction phase. This helps to prune irrelevant branches in the search tree if there is any violation of mutex relations. In addition, the backtracking search has been improved to avoid redundant search calls and applied conflict directed backjumping. However, since this work has just been implemented and tested, we only have some preliminary results and the source code has not been optimized yet. In addition, due to the complexity of the planning domains, the planner has to re-check some of the mutex relations for actions and propositions in the extraction phase, which slows down the performance of the system.

We plan to investigate ways of avoiding rechecking mutex relations as such as possible. In addition, we will attempt to encode the backtracking search as a Constraint Satisfaction Problem (CSP) and use standard CSP solvers to carry on the search.

References

[1] A. L. Blum and M. L. Furst. Fast planning through Planning Graph Analysis. *Artificial Intelligence*, 90:281–300, 1997.

[2] M. B. Do and S. Kambhampati. Planning as Constraint Satisfaction: Solving the planning graph by compiling it into CSP. *Artificial Intelligence*, 132:151–182, 2001.

[3] M. B. Do and S. Kambhampati. Sapa: A Domain-Independent Heuristic Metric Temporal Planner. In *Proceedings of European Conference on Planning*, 2001.

[4] M. Fox and D.Long. PDDL+: An extension to PDDL2.1 for modelling planning domains with continuous time-dependent effects. In *Technical Report, Dept of Computer Science, University of Durham*, 2001.

[5] M. Fox and D.Long. Exploiting a Graphplan Framework in Temporal Planning. In *Proceedings of ICAPS*, 2003.

[6] M. Fox and D. Long. Hybrid STAN: Identifying and Managing Combinatorial Optimisation Sub-problems in Planning. In *Proceedings of IJCAI*, 2001.

[7] A. Garrido, M. Fox, and D. Long. Temporal Planning with PDDL2.1. In *Proceeding of ECAI'02*, 2002.

[8] J. Hoffmann and B. Nebel. The FF Planning System: Fast Plan Generation Through Heuristic Search. *Journal of Artificial Intelligence Research*, 14:253–302, 2001.

[9] S. Kambhampati. Planning Graph as a (dynamic) CSP: Exploiting EBL, DDB, and other CSP search techniques in Graphplan. *Artificial Intelligence Research*, 12:1–34, 2000.

[10] P. Prosser. Domain filtering can degrade intelligent backtracking search. In *Proceedings of IJCAI*, pages 262–267, 1993.

[11] D. Smith and D. Weld. Temporal Planning with Mutual Exclusion Reasoning. In *Proceedings of IJCAI*, pages 326–337, 1999.

Planning, Scheduling and Constraint Satisfaction: From Theory to Practice
L. Castillo et al. (Eds.)
IOS Press, 2005

Reversed Planning Graphs for Relevance Heuristics in AI Planning

Mats Petter PETTERSSON

Department of Computer Science, Lund University, Sweden
matsp@cs.lth.se

Abstract.
Most AI planning heuristics are reachability heuristics, in the sense that they estimate the minimum plan length from the initial state to a search state. Such heuristics
are best suited for use in regression state-space planners, since a progression planner
would have to reconstruct the heuristic function at each new search state. However,
some domains (or problem instances within a certain domain) are better suited for
progression search, motivating the need for relevance heuristics that estimate the distance from a search state to the goal state.

In this paper we show how to construct reversed planning graphs that can be used
for computing new relevance heuristics, based on the work on extracting reachability heuristics from planning graphs, and a general framework for reversing planning
domains.

1 Introduction

During the last decade, AI planning has been dominated by constraint-based methods (e.g.,
Graphplan [1], heuristic distance-based methods (e.g., HSP [2], and FF [4]), and combinations thereof. One common combination is to use a distance-based heuristic method, combined with binary constraints (e.g., planning graph mutexes) adding some extra pruning
power to it.

A common approach to heuristic planning is to do regression search (searching back-
wards), from the goals towards the initial state, using a reachability heuristic, i.e., a heuristic
that estimates the cost of reaching a given search state from the initial state. This heuristic
is generally precomputed, in the sense that the cost estimate is easily computed, given some
data structure which only needs to be computed once per planning task. However, this data
structure is based on the initial state, so only reachability from the initial state can be cheaply
computed in this way.

Regression search is not always the best option. Although the differences are not very
well understood, it seems that some domains, and even problem instances within domains,
are better suited for progression (forward) search [5]. However, if we want to do progression
search, using a heuristic function that does not have to be recomputed at each search state, we
need a relevance heuristic, i.e., one that estimates the cost of reaching the goal from a given
search state.

We are aware of only a few such pure relevance heuristics, [7, 8]. The construction of relevance heuristics is complicated by partially defined states, for example open goal states, and

the time-directionality of STRIPS [3] actions. There are systematic methods for creating a STRIPS representation for reversed planning problems [5], so that plans in the original problem correspond directly (through inversion) to plans in the reversed problem. This could be useful, in order to compute relevance heuristics, since these would correspond to reachability heuristics in the reversed problem. The idea is simple: instead of inventing a new, relevance heuristic, we change the problem and use our old reachability heuristic on the reversed problem.

Of course, there are some complications. The reversal scheme introduces new facts, and reversed actions will be a bit different from their original counterparts. The effect of this can be expected to vary between heuristics. One recent interesting approach for computing reachability heuristics is based on planning graphs [6], from which several different heuristics, admissible and inadmissible, can be extracted. Planning graphs can be built based on the domain reversal mentioned above, and seem to suffer little from the changes due to problem reversal. This is the motivation for this work on relevance heuristics based on reversed planning graphs.

This paper is organized in the following way: Section 2 contains an introduction to planning problem reversal, followed by the introduction of the planning graph reversal method in Section 3. Some experimental results are presented in Section 4. Related work is discussed in Section 5. Section 6 outlines future work, followed by conclusions in Section 7.

2 Planning Problem Reversal

In this section, we will introduce a method for reversing a planning problem, i.e., reformulating it as a planning problem from the goal towards the initial state. We will use the method introduced by Massey in [5], but will partly use a different notation.

Massey's reversal scheme allows negative preconditions. This will lead directly to the scheme that we here call *extended reversal* (we do not include negative preconditions however). As we only deal with standard STRIPS representations, which do not allow negative preconditions, we will also have an intermediary scheme, here simply called *reversal*.

2.1 STRIPS Planning

A planning problem in STRIPS is a triple $P = (A, S_{init}, S_{goal})$, consisting of a set of ground actions, and two sets of ground facts. Implicitly, the specification of P also defines the set of all ground facts, F. An action, a, is a triple $(pre(a), add(a), del(a))$ of sets of ground facts. (We will assume, without loss of generality, that $add(a) \cap del(a) = \emptyset$, and $add(a) \cap pre(a) = \emptyset$.) A world state is represented by a set of positive ground facts – the set of facts that hold in the world state. We say that an action, a, is applicable in world state S iff $pre(a) \subseteq S$. In this case, the world state resulting from applying a is $res(S, a) = (S \cup add(a)) \setminus del(a)$. We also use this notation for recursively defining the result of applying a sequence of actions: $res(S, a_0 \ldots a_n) = res(res(S, a_0), a_1 \ldots a_n)$. This of course assumes that all actions are applicable in their respective intermediate states. A state, S, is a goal state iff $S_{goal} \subseteq S$, and a valid plan p is a sequence of action s.t. $res(S_{init}, p)$ is a goal state.

In STRIPS planning, there is a one-to-one relationship between sets of facts and world states – a set of facts can be interpreted as describing a world state. Note however that the set of facts S_{goal} does not represent a single state, but indirectly defines a *set* of goal states.

2.2 Progression Search States

In our analysis of planning problem reversal, we will use the concept of search state, rather than that of world state. A search state is defined by a sequence of actions, p, (the path chosen in the search tree), and a resulting set of world states $\mathcal{W}$. Thus, formally a search state is a pair $(\mathcal{W}, p)$.

In progression search, p will be a plan prefix, and $\mathcal{W}$ will be the singleton set $\mathcal{W} = \{S\}$, where $S = res(S_{init}, p)$. Note however that other search modes than progression will have non-singleton $\mathcal{W}$. We will often use a simpler notation for search states, better suited to the search mode we are dealing with. In the case of progression search states, we will write $(S, p)^{pro}$ instead of $(\mathcal{W}, p)$.

We say that $(S', pa)^{pro}$ is an expansion of $(S, p)^{pro}$ through a iff $S' = res(S, a)$. This is denoted $(S, p)^{pro} \rightarrow (S', pa)^{pro}$. In the same way as with world states, we always have an initial search state and a set of goal search states. The initial progression search state is $(S_{init}, \epsilon)^{pro}$, and $(S, p)^{pro}$ is a progression goal state iff $S_{goal} \subseteq S$.

2.3 Regression Search States

We can define regression search states in a similar way. Here, $\mathcal{W}$ is the set of world states in which applying the action sequence p will lead to a goal state. Thus, p will always be a valid plan suffix in a regression state.

It turns out that $\mathcal{W}$ has a very simple structure in regression search. Given a regression search state, $(\mathcal{W}, p)$, if we consider each fact in isolation, it is clear that it will belong to one of two categories: those that are necessary to execute p and reach the goal state, and those who are not. A fact is necessary, either beacause it is a precondition of some action in p and not produced earlier in p, or because it is a goal fact, and not produced by p. If we consider the set, S, of necessary facts, it is clear that $\mathcal{W} = \{X \mid S \subseteq X \subseteq F\}$. This means that the set S can be used to represent $\mathcal{W}$. Here, we will use this notation, $(S, p)^{reg}$, for regression search states, where S is the set of necessary facts.

The start state in regression search is (S_{goal}, ϵ), and we define the set of goal states to be states $(S, p)^{reg}$ where $S \subseteq S_{init}$, i.e., states for which p is a valid plan. We also have the concept of expanding a regression state through an action, $(S, p)^{reg} \rightarrow (S', ap)^{reg}$. The rules for expansion in regression search are the following:

1. An action a can expand a regression search state $(S, p)^{reg}$ iff $del(a) \cap S = \emptyset$.
2. If a is applicable, $S' = (S \setminus add(a)) \cup pre(a)$.
3. When actually using regression search, we are only interested in expansions for which $add(a) \cap S \neq \emptyset$. If this is not the case, we will have $S \subseteq S'$, meaning that $(S', ap)^{reg}$ allows a subset of the world states that $(S, p)^{reg}$ allows. There is no point in the expansion, from the point of view of efficiency, but it is perfectly legal, and we will not use this extra condition, thus using a definition of regression that differs from the standard one.

The second rule preserves the property that S' represents all world states that will lead to a goal state through the action sequence ap.

2.4 Reversed Search States

We can think of regression search as solving a reversed planning problem in a STRIPS-like formalism. It is natural to ask if there is a way of expressing this reversed planning problem in STRIPS. More specifically, given our original planning problem P, we are looking for a planning problem, $P^{rev} = (A^{rev}, S_{init}^{rev}, S_{goal}^{rev})$, where valid plans in P^{rev} are the reversal of valid plans in P, after some one-to-one mapping from A^{rev} to A.

We will show that the regression search problem can be expressed as such a reversed planning problem, by modifying the regression search states. The modified version of a regression search state $(S, p)^{reg}$ is called a reversed search state, $(S', p)^{rev}$, where $S' = \overline{S}$, the complement taken with F as the universe. The interpretation of a reversed search state $(S, p)^{rev}$ is that S is the set of all facts that are not necessary in a world state to have p lead to a goal world state.

Regression search, as defined above, and reversed search are completely equivalent, i.e., there is a one-to-one relation between search states and between expansion relations. The only difference lies in how the rules for expansion are expressed. The key is rewriting the rules for regression search state expansions in terms of $\overline{S}$ instead of S:

1. $del(a) \cap S = \emptyset \Leftrightarrow del(a) \setminus \overline{S} = \emptyset \Leftrightarrow del(a) \subseteq \overline{S}$
2. $S' = (S \setminus add(a)) \cup pre(a) \Leftrightarrow \overline{S'} = \overline{(S \setminus add(a)) \cup pre(a)}$ and thus
   $\overline{S'} = \overline{(S \setminus add(a))} \cap \overline{pre(a)} = (S \cap \overline{add(a)}) \setminus pre(a) = (\overline{S} \cup add(a)) \setminus pre(a)$

The goal criterion for $(S, p)^{reg}$ is also rewritten: $S \subseteq S_{init} \Leftrightarrow \overline{S_{init}} \subseteq \overline{S}$. Thus $(S, p)^{rev}$ is a goal state in the reversed search iff $\overline{S_{init}} \subseteq S$, and the first reversed search state is $(\overline{S_{goal}}, \epsilon)^{rev}$.

Note that the rules above, expressed using reversed search states, look very much like those for progression search. The only difference is that the sets $pre(a)$ and $del(a)$ have changed places. Also note that the goal criterion requires that some set, in this case $\overline{S_{init}}$, should be the subset of the search state's set representation. As a consequence, reversed search in P is equivalent to progression search in $P^{rev} = (A^{rev}, \overline{S_{goal}}, \overline{S_{init}})$, where for each action a in A, there is a reversed action a^{rev} in A^{rev}, defined in the following way:

$$add(a^{rev}) = add(a)$$
$$del(a^{rev}) = pre(a)$$
$$pre(a^{rev}) = del(a)$$

Valid plans in P^{rev} will be reversed versions of valid plans in P, after mapping each a^{rev} to its corresponding a.

2.5 Planning Graphs

Before introducing the extended reversal scheme, some background on planning graphs is needed. A (serial) planning graph [1] can be thought of as a sequence of relaxed search states, $(\mathcal{W}_0, 0), \ldots, (\mathcal{W}_n, n)$, where $\mathcal{W}_i$ is an upper bound estimate on the set of world states that can be reached from the initial state, using i or fewer actions. (In a sense, the integer i stands for all plan prefixes p of length i.) Clearly, we have $\mathcal{W}_0 = \{S_{init}\}$. In planning graph terminology, these sets are called *fact layers*, so $\mathcal{W}_i$ corresponds to the ith fact layer. Note that exact computation of the fact layers would be at least as hard as the planning problem itself.

The fact layers are specified using constraints on single facts, $C_P(\{f\}, i)$, and pairs of facts (called fact mutexes), $C_P(\{f_1, f_2\}, i)$. These constraints are interpreted as follows:

$C_P(X, i)$: All world states in P in which all facts in X hold require a plan prefix of at least i actions to be reached.

$\mathcal{W}_i$ is the set of all world states that satisfy every constraint $C_P(X, k)$ for which $i < k$. It is constructed based on $\mathcal{W}_{i-1}$, by considering the effects of all actions that are applicable in at least one world state of $\mathcal{W}_{i-1}$. Thus, the constraints are used for limiting action applica- bility as the planning graph is built, and constructing a new layer means updating the set of constraints. Eventually, for some n, the nth level of the planning graph will be equivalent to the previous one. We then say that the planning graph has levelled off. At this point there will usually be fact mutexes remaining. These are called *static mutexes*, and usually represent domain invariants.

2.6 Extended Reversed Search States

The problem with regression search is that it produces many irrelevant search states, $(S, p)^{reg}$, in which S only represents world states that cannot be reached by a progression search. As reversed search in P and progression search in P^{rev} are equivalent to regression search in P, these suffer from the same problem.

One approach to excluding such states is to use external or derived knowledge about what world states are possible. We will assume that this information is based on the static mutexes of a serial planning graph, but of course other sources of information, like human-defined domain knowledge, could be used.

The method used here, which makes the reversal scheme equivalent to that of [5], is to include in the search states information about what facts can possibly be included. One way to do this is to extend $(S, p)^{rev}$ to include two components: $((S^+, S^-), p)^{rev}$, where $S^- = S$, i.e., the set of facts that can be excluded, and S^+ is the set of facts that can be included. S^+ works as an upper bound on $\mathcal{W}$, i.e., we have $\mathcal{W} = \{X \mid \overline{S^-} \subseteq X \subseteq S^+\}$.

A more compact representation, used in [5], introduces two new facts, f^+ and f^- for each ground fact f in P. We will use this to represent our extended reversed search states, $((S^+, S^-), p)^{rev}$, as $(S, p)^{revx}$, where $S = \{f^+ \mid f \in S^+\} \cup \{f^- \mid f \in S^-\}$.

Extended reversed search is equivalent to progression search for a planning problem P^{revx} that is related to P^{rev}, and has its actions defined based on actions in P in the following way:

$f^- \in add(a^{revx}) \Leftrightarrow f \in add(a)$

$f^- \in del(a^{revx}) \Leftrightarrow f \in pre(a)$

$f^- \in pre(a^{revx}) \Leftrightarrow f \in del(a)$

$f^+ \in add(a^{revx}) \Leftrightarrow f \in del(a)$

$f^+ \in pre(a^{revx}) \Leftrightarrow (f \in add(a) \lor f \in pre(a)) \land f \notin del(a)$

f^+s are never deleted, i.e., $f^+ \notin del(a^{revx})$

Without using any constraints, the goal state of the forward problem does not rule out any facts, and thus we will have $f^+ \in S_{init}^{revx}$ for all ground facts f in P. As we never delete positive facts, the same will hold for all other extended reversed search states as well. On the other hand, assume that we have a static mutex between facts f_1 and f_2 in P, and that

$f_1 \in S_{goal}$. In this case we can rule out f_2 in any goal state of P, i.e., $f_2^+ \notin S_{init}^{revx}$. (Note that we will always have at least one of $f^+ \in S_{init}^{revx}$ and $f^- \in S_{init}^{revx}$, and that this property is preserved by the definition of expansion).

The natural extension of the reversed goal is to set $f^+ \in S_{goal}^{revx} \Leftrightarrow f \in S_{init}$. This preserves the property that the goal test is a subset test: $(S, p)^{revx}$ is a goal state iff $S_{goal}^{revx} \subseteq S$.

3 Planning Graph Reversal

Like for any other STRIPS planning problem, we can use the extended reversed planning problem, P^{revx}, to build a planning graph. This planning graph will encode constraints on (single and pairs of) f^+s and f^-s. In the context of the original planning problem, P, we will call this the *reversed planning graph*, since it is the planning graph based on the reversal of P.

3.1 Interpretation of the Constraints of the Reversed Planning Graph

It is clear what the interpretation of the constraints encoded in the reversed planning graph are in P^{revx}. But what about P? To see what the reversed planning graph tells us about P, we need to go back to the definition of the extended reversed search state $(S, p)^{revx}$, and the interpretation of $f^+ \in S$ and $f^- \in S$. In fact, the interpretation becomes clearer if we consider the cases when f^+ or f^- does not belong to S:

- $f^+ \notin S$: There are no world states in which f holds that lead to a goal state through the action sequence p.
- $f^- \notin S$: There are no world states without f that lead to a goal state through the action sequence p.

Consider the constraint $C_{P^{revx}}(\{f^+\}, k)$. We have a number of equivalent statements:

1. All world states in P^{revx} in which f^+ holds require a plan prefix of at least k actions to be reached.
2. No plan prefix in P^{revx} of length less than k will lead to a state in which f^+ holds.
3. f is not possible in any world state in P for which there is a plan suffix of less than k actions that leads to a goal world state.
4. All world states in P in which f holds require a plan suffix of at least k actions to reach the goal.

The step between the second and the third statement is based on the fact that there is a one-to-one relationship between plan prefixes in P^{revx} and plan suffixes in P. Reasoning similarly for the constraint $C_{P^{revx}}(\{f^-\}, k)$, the corresponding final statement becomes:

All world states in P in which f does not hold require a plan suffix of at least k actions to reach the goal.

This reasoning can be extended to fact mutexes as well. For example, the interpretation of the constraint $C_{P^{revx}}(\{f^+, g^-\}, k)$ is:

All world states in P in which f holds and g does not hold require a plan suffix of at least k actions to reach the goal.

Thus, we can use the reversed planning graph while doing progression search in P in the same way that we use the normal planning graph in regression search. For example, if we are in the progression search state $(S, p)^{pro}$, and $C_{Prevx}(\{f^+, g^+\}, k)$, where $\{f, g\} \subseteq S$, we know that we need to add at least k actions to p to get a valid plan. This information can be used for pruning or as a basis for heuristics.

If we have the constraint $C_{Prevx}(\{f^-\}, k)$ and $f \notin S$, we also know that we need to add at least k more actions to get a valid plan. However, using constraints on negative facts (f^-s) would require checking all facts that are not in the search state. This is probably computationally too expensive in most cases. In our experiments, we have based the heuristics only on the constraints on positive facts (f^+s).

3.2 Enforced Static Mutexes

When we build the reversed planning graph, we will use an extra set of enforced static mutexes. These mutexes will be enforced at all fact layers in the graph, meaning that if the mutex is not present after building a fact layer, it will be added to that fact layer before building the next one.

There is no guarantee that this process does not introduce constraints in the reversed planning graph that are not valid in P^{revx}. However, we are only going to use these constraints in P, where they will be valid. We use two kinds of enforced static mutexes:

- Static mutexes from the forward planning graph, which we assume has been built before we build the reversed planning graph.
- Logic mutex relations between all pairs of opposite facts (f^+, f^-)

Preliminary experimental results indicate that enforcing static mutexes significantly improves the reversed planning graph, while the logic mutexes seem to be of little importance.

4 Experimental Results

To demonstrate that reversed planning graphs provide useful constraints, we have built a planner that can be run in two modes: progression search, using the reversed planning graph as its source of heuristic information, and regression search, using the normal planning graph as its source of heuristic information.

Most parts of the implementation are common to the two modes, and we believe that the tests performed here gives a fair comparison. The planner is based on standard A* search, with $f(s) = g(s) + h(s)$, i.e., no weighting of the heuristic estimate. Two different heuristics, set-level and partition-2, both from [6], are tested.

The results are presented in table 1. Tests were stopped after 600 seconds if they had not reached a solution. The number of states is reported as e/g, where e is the number of expanded states and g is the total number of generated states, where g may count each unique state more than once. We believe that the running times provide the best basis for comparison, as the implementation is fairly optimized. Note that planning graph construction is not included in the times reported. The tests were done on an Intel P4 2.40 GHz machine with 1GB RAM, running Linux. We draw the following conclusions from the tests:

- Progression search is in many cases significantly superior to regression search, and in no case significantly worse. It seems that this is mostly due to the fact that the regression

Table 1: Results for some planning problems.

PROBLEM	HEURISTIC	PROGRESSION			REGRESSION		
		Search time (s)	Number of states exp/gen	Plan length	Search time (s)	Number of states exp/gen	Plan length
hanoi-3	set-level	0.08 s	11 / 32	7	0.07 s	15 / 211	7
	partition-2	0.07 s	12 / 35	7	0.08 s	18 / 256	7
hanoi-4	set-level	0.08 s	41 / 122	15	0.08 s	45 / 1022	15
	partition-2	0.07 s	42 / 125	15	0.08 s	47 / 1071	15
hanoi-5	set-level	0.08 s	153 / 458	31	0.13 s	157 / 5133	31
	partition-2	0.08 s	127 / 380	31	0.14 s	144 / 4703	31
hanoi-6	set-level	0.11 s	531 / 1592	63	0.41 s	535 / 23394	63
	partition-2	0.10 s	452 / 1355	63	0.42 s	455 / 19908	63
hanoi-7	set-level	0.20 s	1741 / 5222	127	1.96 s	1745 / 97553	127
	partition-2	0.14 s	1452 / 4355	127	2.02 s	1493 / 83478	127
hanoi-8	set-level	0.58 s	5595 / 16784	255	9.46 s	5599 / 387260	255
	partition-2	0.35 s	4984 / 14951	255	10.18 s	4981 / 344750	255
8-puzzle-1	set-level	3.47 s	39545 / 106902	31	36.25 s	45264 / 1819753	31
	partition-2	0.10 s	450 / 1257	39	0.28 s	226 / 9229	33
8-puzzle-2	set-level	2.41 s	26279 / 71152	30	21.38 s	26279 / 1057603	30
	partition-2	0.17 s	1427 / 3948	34	1.50 s	1527 / 62047	34
8-puzzle-3	set-level	0.11 s	380 / 1042	20	0.65 s	695 / 28015	20
	partition-2	0.08 s	118 / 328	20	0.65 s	640 / 26143	24
bw-large-a	set-level	0.20 s	376 / 1607	12	0.32 s	133 / 5182	12
	partition-2	0.08 s	15 / 65	12	0.13 s	27 / 1054	12
bw-large-b	set-level	16.52 s	31110 / 150916	18	37.50 s	9498 / 511218	18
	partition-2	0.12 s	148 / 571	18	2.56 s	667 / 33703	26
bw-large-c	set-level	>600 s	-	-	>600 s	-	-
	partition-2	25.74 s	61709 / 279947	42	99.47 s	9718 / 735636	46
bw-large-d	set-level	>600 s	-	-	>600 s	-	-
	partition-2	41.10 s	41886 / 223616	80	252.65 s	10182 / 1084674	66

search produces a lot of irrelevant and unreachable states that have to be pruned, which takes considerable time.

- Progression search can take advantage of inadmissible heuristics in the same problems as regression search. This suggests that the constraints encoded by the reversed planning graph are of comparable strength to those of the normal planning graph.

5 Related Work

5.1 GRT

GRT [8] is a planning system which is based on a relaxation-based relevance heuristic, very similar to the reachability heuristic in HSP [2]. In the h_{HSP} heuristic, the cost of a state is the sum of the costs of the individual facts in the state, and the cost of a fact is one more than the lowest cost of a set of preconditions of an action that produces the fact:

$$h_{HSP}(S) = \sum_{f \in S} h_{HSP}(f)$$
$$h_{HSP}(f) = 0, \text{ if } f \in S_{init}$$
$$h_{HSP}(f) = 1 + min_{f \in add(a)} h_{HSP}(pre(a)), \text{ otherwise.}$$

On top of this, to get more accurate estimates, GRT also takes interaction between pairs of facts into account, when it constructs its heuristic function. In order to make this a relevance heuristic, it is necessary to have some definition of a reversed action. In GRT, each action a

has a reversed version a', defined by the adds, deletes, and preconditions of a in the following way:

$$pre(a') = add(a) \cup pre(a) \setminus del(a)$$
$$del(a') = add(a)$$
$$add(a') = del(a)$$

This definition of reversed actions is based on the assumption that we start applying them at a complete goal state. There are different ways to make an open goal state complete. A simple one, and the one that was used in the version of GRT described in [8], is to add to the goal state all possible facts that are not static mutex with it – the same method that we used for the extended reversed search.

5.2   Bsr-graphplan

Bsr-graphplan [7] is a planning system that uses a structure which is a bit like Graphplan's planning graph, but reversed, thus representing relevance information instead of reachability information. This is done by using regression to create fact layers, the first layer being equal to the goal state. In addition to this unary reasoning, a so called "constraint tree" is built, defining a partial order between actions. This partial order is based on a notion of interference between facts at different levels. The structure is used to guide a search process similar to that of Graphplan.

Even though the way that the reversed planning graphs in Bsr-graphplan are built looks very different, it is not clear exactly how the information they represent differs from that of our approach. We believe that our planning graphs are able to discover stronger constraints, yielding more informed heuristics. This assumption is based on the fact that Bsr-graphplan uses regression for the unary constraints, which imposes less restriction on what facts and actions will be added to the next level. However, to fully support this statement, it would be necessary to either analyze or test the power of the binary interference concept in Bsr-graphplan, relative to that of the static mutexes in our reversed planning graphs.

5.3   AltAlt

Planning graph constraints were originally used for pruning purposes in optimal planners such as Graphplan, and for generating binary mutexes to be used together with relaxation-based heuristics. Nguyen et. al. [6] have shown how to make wider use of planning graphs, constructing a family of heuristics, based on both the unary and binary information about the facts in a given search state.

The heuristic computation in AltAlt is similar to that of h_{HSP} in the sense that it is based on combining the costs of single facts, but also uses binary constraints. The main difference, as we see it, lies in the recursive definition of costs, where the planning graph always encodes *true* constraints, and h_{HSP} does not.

It is however worth mentioning that the most successful heuristics of AltAlt are actually based on both h_{HSP} and the constraints of the planning graph. We have not been able to make use of these heuristics, but restricted ourselves to working only with those that are entirely based on the planning graph. However, we believe that the heuristic of GRT could be used with reversed planning graphs in a way similar to how h_{HSP} is used in AltAlt.

6 Future Work

We would like to investigate more directly the strength of the constraints encoded by the reversed planning graphs – how they are affected by open goal states, how important the enforced mutexes are, and compare them to the constraints of the normal planning graph (especially in symmetric domains).

Further experiments could be made, on harder problems, and comparing results to other planners, e.g., GRT.

Possibly, the heuristic of GRT could be used with reversed planning graphs, in the same way that the heuristic of HSP is used in AltAlt.

Recently, we have discovered that $f^+ \in del(a^{revx})$ can be inferred, if f and g are static mutex and $g \in pre(a)$, i.e., $g^- \in del(a^{revx})$. We are currently investigating the effect this has on the reversed planning graph.

7 Conclusions

We have introduced a method for constructing reversed planning graphs, that can be used to compute relevance heuristics for progression planners. The strength of this approach is that it makes it possible to use any planning graph-based reachability heuristic for progression planning as well. We have also shown experimentally that progression planning using reversed planning graph-based relevance heuristics can perform at least as good as regression planning with corresponding reachability heuristics based on normal planning graphs.

Acknowledgements

The author would like to thank Patrik Haslum, Peter Jonsson, Krzysztof Kuchciński, and Jacek Malec, for helpful comments at different stages of this work.

References

[1] A. Blum and M. Furst. Fast planning through planning graph analysis. In *Proceedings of the 14th International Joint Conference on Artificial Intelligence (IJCAI 95)*, pages 1636–1642, 1995.

[2] B. Bonet and H. Geffner. Planning as heuristic search. *Artificial Intelligence*, 129(1-2):5–33, 2001.

[3] R. E. Fikes and N. J. Nilsson. STRIPS: A new approach to the application of theorem proving to problem solving. *Artificial Intelligence*, 2:189–208, 1971.

[4] J. Hoffmann and B. Nebel. The FF planning system: Fast plan generation through heuristic search. *JAIR*, 14:253–302, 2001.

[5] B. Massey. Directions in planning: Understanding the flow of time in planning. *Dissertation, available at http://www.cs.pdx.edu/ bart/papers.html*, 1999.

[6] X. Nguyen, S. Kambhampati, and R. S. Nigenda. Planning graph as the basis for deriving heuristics for plan synthesis by state space and CSP search. *Artificial Intelligence*, 135(1-2):73–123, 2002.

[7] E. Parker. Making graphplan goal-directed. In *ECP*, pages 333–346, 1999.

[8] I. Refanidis and I. Vlahavas. The GRT planning system: Backward heuristic construction in forward state-space planning. *Journal of Artificial Intelligence Research*, 15:115–161, 2001.

Planning, Scheduling and Constraint Satisfaction: From Theory to Practice
L. Castillo et al. (Eds.)
IOS Press, 2005

A Flexible Constraint Model for Validating Plans with Durative Actions

Roman BARTÁK

Charles University, Malostranské nám. 2/25, 118 00 Praha, The Czech Republic
roman.bartak@mff.cuni.cz

Abstract. Planning problems with durative actions represent one of the hot research topics in AI planning. Durative actions introduce numerical aspects to planning and so constraint satisfaction technology is becoming more popular in solving this new type of planning problems. The paper describes a constraint programming approach for validating and finishing partially ordered plans with durative actions. In particular, we propose a Boolean constraint model of the planning graph, a numerical constraint model of durative actions and precedence relations, and channeling constraints connecting both models. We also briefly discuss solving techniques for such integrated model, in particular using binary decision diagrams versus constraint propagation.

1. Introduction

AI Planning is an area dealing with finding plans that convert some initial state of the world into a desired state. Probably the most widely used formulation of the planning problem is a STRIPS model [5]. The *state of the world* is described there as a conjunction of propositions that are either valid – *positive propositions* – or invalid – *negative propositions*. The state can be changed by *actions* that make some propositions valid – an *add effect* – and other propositions invalid – a *delete effect*. The action can be applied to a given state only if an action precondition is satisfied. The *action precondition* is expressed as a propositional formula over the state propositions. Together, the standard STRIPS formulation of the planning problem consists of a finite set of actions, a finite set of propositions describing the initial state, and a finite set of propositions describing the desired state. The planning task is to find a sequence of actions converting the initial state into a desired state.

Sometimes, a set of actions in encapsulated into an abstract task that is often decomposable to several sets of actions (and tasks). Then, the planning task is to find the right decomposition of given abstract tasks into primitive actions that form a valid plan in terms of the STRIPS model. This is called Hierarchical Task Network (HTN) planning [4]. We call the decomposition of the abstract task a *task network* because the actions and tasks in the decomposition are often connected, for example they are partially ordered.

The above purely logical formulation of the planning problem has been recently updated to cover numerical features [6]. In particular, durative actions and numerical preconditions and effects modeling resources are assumed. In this paper, we cover durative actions with logical preconditions that must be satisfied when the action starts, and the logical effects that become valid when the action finishes. Moreover, we allow specifying an invariant condition that must be valid during execution of the action. Naturally, when durative actions are assumed then overlapping of actions is allowed to obtain shorter plans in terms of time.

In this paper, we address the problem of validating task networks with durative actions. Such a task network, i.e., a decomposition of the abstract task into actions and other abstract tasks, is given by the user. Before using this task network by the planner, it is better to check, whether the task network can form a valid plan. If it cannot form a valid plan then the decomposition of the abstract task into such task network should be avoided during planning because it leads to a dead end. The plan validation consists of finding a time allocation for the actions respecting the precedence relations and the logical dependencies between the actions. By logical dependencies we understand the relations between the actions expressed in preconditions and effects. We can see this problem from a more general perspective as a plan validation problem where the plan is given by a partially ordered set of actions. In addition to checking validity of the task network, we may require some additional information about the task network that can be used during planning. For example, one may ask what the minimal makespan of the task network is, which can be used as the minimal duration of the corresponding abstract task. Moreover, it is possible to deduce what the required precondition of the task network is as well as what the necessary effect of the task network is (independently of the particular time allocation and ordering of the actions). Again, this information can be encoded in the abstract task to allow better co-ordination of the abstract tasks before they are decomposed into actions. Last but not least, the planners producing partially ordered plans may use the same tool to finish the plan by allocating the actions to time. We propose to use constraint satisfaction technology for the above described plan validation because this technology can naturally model logical features via Boolean constraints as well as durations and precedence relations via numerical constraints. Moreover, the proposed constraint model is flexible enough to allow addition of other features like numerical preconditions and effects.

The main contribution of the paper is twofold. First, an extended version of the planning graph is proposed to handle durative actions. Second, a new constraint model for this extended planning graph is designed. We also discuss various constraint satisfaction techniques to solve the proposed model, namely binary decision diagrams versus singleton consistency.

The paper is organized as follows. First, we will give more details about the plan validation problem. Then, we will survey the models supporting durative actions and constraint-based approaches to planning. The main part of the paper will be devoted to a description of the constraint model for the extended planning graph that will also be introduced there. After that we will briefly discuss the solving techniques and we will conclude with a description of possible extensions of the proposed model.

2. Plan Validation Problem

In this paper we study the problem of validating partially ordered plans with durative actions. We use a propositional representation of the world states there. It means that a finite set of propositions is given and we describe the state by specifying which propositions are valid. The propositions which are not valid are invalid. The *initial state* is specified by a propositional formula that is built over the propositions using conjunction, disjunction, and negation. In planning, the initial state is usually described as a list of valid propositions which is a description equivalent to a conjunction of positive (valid) and negative (invalid) propositions. We use a more general formula to describe the initial state mainly because of the task networks where the initial state is equivalent to the initial precondition of the task network so it could be a general formula. The *goal state* is described using a propositional formula too. In case of task networks, the goal is equivalent to the effect of the task network. One of the tasks that we are solving is to find out which propositions must or must not hold in the initial state and in the goal state. This information may be used to fine tune the description of the precondition and effect of the abstract task that is decomposable to a given task network. We also allow specification of another propositional formula – a so called *invariant condition* – that must be satisfied by all the states inside the task network. The invariant condition substitutes axioms from PDDL. For example, it is possible to describe axioms like "if doors 1 or doors 2 are open then the room A is accessible". Notice also that both the initial state and the goal state can be specified incompletely meaning that the propositional formula does not force validity or invalidity of all the propositions. For example, the formula *(1 and (not 2) and (3 or 4))* sets the proposition 1 to be valid and the proposition 2 to be invalid but it does not force validity of 3 and 4 (one of them must be valid, but the formula does not specify which one). The formula also says nothing about validity of propositions other than 1, 2, 3, and 4.

The input plan to be validated is given by a finite set of partially ordered actions. Each action has assigned a duration that could be either a positive integer or an interval starting with a positive integer. Durative actions have a start time and an end time that we call *action time points*. Action duration equals to the difference between the action time points. We expect discrete time so time points are represented by integers. Some planning problems are formulated over the continuous time but there is always some ε describing the minimal resolution of the plan so actually the time is discrete there too.

The action has a *precondition* that is a propositional formula built from the propositions using conjunction, disjunction, and negation. The precondition must be satisfied when the action starts. Formally, if *st* is the start time of the action A then the world state at time *st* must satisfy the precondition of A. The action has an *effect* that is a list of added and deleted propositions. If *p* is an add effect of some action finishing at the time *et* then *p* becomes valid at time *et*. If *p* is a delete effect of some action finishing at the time *et* then *p* becomes invalid at time *et*. Finally, it is possible to specify an *action invariant condition* that is a propositional formula that must hold when the action is executed. Formally, if an action A starts at time *st* and finishes at time *et* then the world states at times ⟨*st,et*-1⟩ must satisfy the invariant condition of A. The invariant condition of A prevents the actions that interfere with A to overlap with A.

As we already mentioned, there is a partial order specified among the actions. We allow specifying the order of action time points, for example to say that the action A starts before the action B finishes or that the action A starts at the same time as the action B. Moreover these simple ordering constraints can be connected via disjunction and conjunction (negation is not necessary there). Thus, one may specify a shared unary resource using the familiar disjunctive relation – either A finishes before B starts or B finishes before A starts. We call all these relations *precedence constraints*.

The plan validation problem is to decide whether the plan is feasible. The feasible plan means that there exist times for the activity time points in such a way that the precedence constraints are satisfied and the plan is valid with respect to all the logical relations. In particular, the given plan transfers the initial state into the goal state, all intermediate states satisfy the invariant condition, and the actions are applied correctly. For example an action deleting some proposition cannot precede directly another action that uses this proposition as its precondition. Recall that the activities may overlap in time so it might be useful to find the shortest plan in terms of total duration. It might be also interesting to find out which propositions must be valid or invalid in the initial and goal states. This information can be used to specify better the minimal duration, precondition, and effect of the task network.

The plan validation problem differs from the planning problem because the set of actions is known in the plan validation problem. The basic task is to find out a proper timing of the known actions which is a task closer to the scheduling problem. However, the difference from the traditional scheduling problem is that the interaction of actions is more complex via preconditions and effects.

3. Related Works

Probably the most widely used approach to planning is based on a so called *planning graph* by Blum and Furst [1]. The planning graph is a layered graph starting with a propositional layer, continuing with an action layer, followed by another propositional layer and so on until the final propositional layer. The propositional layer consists of nodes representing the propositions that describe the world state. The action layer consists of nodes representing the actions that change the world state. Each action is connected to its preconditions in the preceding propositional layer and to add effects in the next propositional layer. The delete effects are modeled via a so called mutex that describes activities (and propositions) that cannot be active together in the same layer. Planning is done by constructing the planning graph of a given size and extracting the plan from the graph. If no plan exists then a longer planning graph is constructed until a plan is found.

The traditional planning graph expects instantaneous actions which have no duration (or unit duration). Smith and Weld [12] proposed a temporal planning graph to handle durative actions. They use a directed graph with nodes representing propositions and actions. The arcs connect the preconditions with the action and the action with its effects. Moreover a time stamp is assigned to each node indicating the first time point at which the proposition or the action appears. The plan is constructed by backward-chaining search through the temporal planning graph. Note that even if the action appears just once in the graph, it may be added several times to the plan because of the cycles in the graph. Moreover, because there are no explicit layers in the graph, the actions may have real duration. The difficulty of this approach (from a CSP view) is that the plan is built dynamically.

Fox and Long [7] proposed a different way of handling durative actions. Their idea was to split the durative action into a set of instantaneous actions, in particular to start, invariant, and end actions. Instead of attaching duration to the actions, the duration is attached to the propositional layers. Then, the duration of the action equals to the sum of durations of the propositional layers between the start and end actions. The invariant actions are used to pass information between the start and end actions as well as to ensure the possible invariant condition of the action. The disadvantage of this approach is that more actions are necessary.

A static formulation of constraint satisfaction problems complicates usage of constraints in planning because of a dynamic character of planning (the number of planned actions is unknown). Nevertheless, as pointed out by Kautz and Selman [8] it is possible to start planning with some lower bound on the plan size and to formulate this sub-problem statically. They used a SAT formulation but it is possible to use a constraint formulation too.

Do and Kambhampati [3] proposed a constraint encoding of the planning graph so the plan extraction stage can be done using a constraint satisfaction technology. They used variables for propositions in the propositional layers and the domain of these variables was a set of actions that have a given proposition among add effects. The constraints were used to model mutexes as well as to model preconditions of the actions. The difficulty of this approach is a large number of constraints.

Lopez and Bacchus [9] proposed a different constraint model of the planning graph that uses binary variables both for propositions and for actions. The values of the variables are *true* and *false* and they indicate whether a given node is active in the layer or not. The constraints connect actions with preconditions and effects. It is also possible to specify mutexes as constraints.

In this paper, we propose an extension of the encoding by Lopez and Bacchus [7] to handle durative actions. Actually, we use the same Boolean variables and constraints to model preconditions and effect. However, we propose an extension of the planning graph such that the action may lie in several layers. In some sense, we also use the idea of Fox and Long [7] of splitting the action into start, middle, and end part. However, the action is not really split, there will be a timetable indicating in which stage the action is. Keeping the action as a single object simplifies modeling of action duration and other relations between the actions like the precedence relations. In particular, we use numerical constraints over the actions to model these features. Note also that all the above surveyed approaches are used for planning while we are solving a plan validation problem. In particular, we expect that the actions are known and the task is to find out a proper timing of the actions respecting the logical and precedence relations between the actions.

4. Constraint Model

To solve the plan validation problem, we use an extended version of the planning graph covering durative actions. In this section we will present this extension together with its constraint representation. Recall that the constraint representation consists of the set of variables, their domains, and the set of constraints.

Because the actions may overlap, we do not know the number of propositional layers in the planning graph in advance. However, we know the number of actions in the plan, say N. Each action requires the state when the action starts and the state when the action ends so we can deduce that the maximal number of states in the plan and hence the maximal number of propositional layers in the planning graph is 2*N.

4.1 Logical constraints

The propositional layer consists of a set of binary variables – one variable per proposition. Let us use a 0-1 variable $Prop_{L,i}$ to denote the validity of proposition i in the layer L. Recall, that the actions may overlap so before an action finishes another action may start. Thus, an action may spread through several consecutive layers because we need to capture the states inside the duration of the action when another action starts or stops. To model this situation, we use three types of the action layers: start, middle, and stop layer. The action layer consists of a set of 0-1 variables – one variable per action – that indicate when the action starts, runs, and ends. Let us denote these variables $Start_{L,a}$, $Middle_{L,a}$, and $End_{L,a}$ for the layer L and the action a. Figure 1 shows how these variables are used to describe the position of an action.

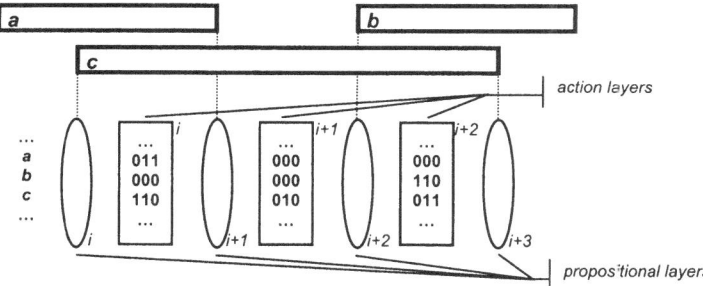

Figure 1. Extended planning graph. The 0/1 numbers in the action layers indicate the values of *Start*, *Middle*, and *End* variables for actions a, b, and c.

Notice that an action starts in exactly one layer and stops in exactly one layer. This can be modeled using the following constraints:

$$\forall a: \; (\Sigma_{L=1,...,2*N-1} \; Start_{L,a} = 1)$$
$$\forall a: \; (\Sigma_{L=1,...,2*N-1} \; End_{L,a} = 1)$$

We can see the 0-1 variables as Boolean variables where 1 indicates *true* and 0 is *false*. This view simplifies the notation of the following logical constraints.

An action is processed in all layers between the start layer and the end layer. It means that an action is being processed in a given action layer if it starts here or if it has been processed in the previous layer and it did not stop here:

$$\forall a: \; Middle_{1,a} = Start_{1,a}$$
$$\forall a \; \forall L \in \{2,..,2*N-1\}: \; Middle_{L,a} = (Start_{L,a} \lor (Middle_{L-1,a} \land \neg \, End_{L-1,a}))$$

We use propositional formulas to describe the initial state, the goal state, and the invariant condition. These formulas can be directly converted to the constraints over the first propositional layer for the initial state, over the final propositional layer for the goal state, and over all the layers for the invariant condition. We also use the propositional formulas for the action preconditions and for the action invariant conditions. Let us denote $Precondition_{L,a}$ the precondition for the action a defined over the propositions in the layer L and $Invariant_{L,a}$ the action invariant condition for the action a over the propositional layer L. Then we can describe satisfaction of the action precondition and the action invariant condition using the following constraints:

$$\forall a \; \forall L \in \{1,..,2*N-1\}: \; Start_{L,a} \Rightarrow Precondition_{L,a}$$
$$\forall a \; \forall L \in \{1,..,2*N-1\}: \; Middle_{L,a} \Rightarrow Invariant_{L,a}$$

The actions have add and delete effects that change validity of propositions. Because the validity of propositions is not changing between the propositional layers, the only possibility for change is when some action finishes in the preceding action layer. Assume that $Add(i)$ is a set of actions that make the proposition i valid – the proposition i is an add effect of these actions – and $Del(i)$ is a set of actions that make the proposition i invalid – the proposition i is a delete effect of these actions. The proposition is valid in some layer if it is an add effect of some action finishing in the preceding action layer or if the proposition is already valid in the preceding propositional layer and there is no action deleting it and finishing in the preceding action layer. Formally:

$$\forall i \; \forall L \in \{1,..,2*N-1\}: \; Prop_{L+1,i} = ((\lor_{a \in Add(i)} \; End_{L,a}) \lor ((\land_{a \in Del(i)} \neg \, End_{L,a}) \land Prop_{L,i})).$$

Note that the above constraint allows the proposition to be true if it is added by some action and deleted by another action at the same time. Such situation is not valid so we use the following constraint to forbid this situation:

$$\forall i \; \forall L \in \{1,..,2*N-1\}: \; Prop_{L+1,i} \Rightarrow (\land_{a \in Del(i)} \neg \, End_{L,a}).$$

The above constraint model fully describes the logical relations in the plan. It means that we have a valid plan if all the variables are assigned and all the constraints are satisfied. Recall that we use the upper estimate on the number of layers so it is possible that some of the layers are not necessary because the actions may share some layers. Basically, action layers may exist such that no action is starting or finishing in them – let us call them *empty action layers*.

These empty action layers may appear anywhere in the planning graph which increases the number of valid but equivalent solutions and also increase the size of the search space to be explored when solving the problem. We propose to collect these empty layers to the end of the planning graph. The following constraint ensures that if there is a non-empty action layer then all the preceding action layers are also non-empty:

$$\forall L \in \{1,..,2*N\text{-}2\}: (\vee_a (Start_{L+1,a} \vee End_{L+1,a})) \Rightarrow (\wedge_{K=1,..,L} (\vee_a (Start_{K,a} \vee End_{K,a}))).$$

4.2 Numerical constraints

The propositional layer models the state at some time so a numerical time variable $Time_L$ is attached to each propositional layer L. Assume that we measure time from zero so the initial state is in time zero hence $Time_1 = 0$. Moreover, the layers describe how the state evolves in time. We do not know the actual time distance between the layers so we can post only the following constraints:

$$\forall L \in \{1,..,2*N\text{-}1\}: Time_L < Time_{L+1}.$$

We use only the simple temporal relations between the actions so we can estimate the upper bound for the plan length by a sum of durations of all the actions. This upper bound defines the upper bound for domains of the variables T_L.

Each action starts at some time, stops at another time, and has a duration specified by the user. All these attributes could be variable so let us denote by $StartTime_a$, $EndTime_a$, and $Duration_a$ the start time, the end time and the duration of the action a. There is a constraint connecting these variables:

$$StartTime_a + Duration_a = EndTime_a.$$

The precedence constraints from the problem specification can now be directly expressed as equalities or inequalities ($=$, $<$, $\leq$) over the *StartTime* and *EndTime* variables. Note that in a constraint satisfaction framework it is possible to use more general constraints, for example to specify that the action A finishes 5 time units before the action B starts.

4.3 Channeling constraints

To connect the logical and numerical parts of the constraint model we need to identify the layers where the action starts and stops. Let us use the following two variables to identify the action layers where the action starts – $StartLayer_a$ – and stops – $EndLayer_a$. Visibly, the following constraint must hold:

$$StartLayer_a \leq EndLayer_a.$$

The connection between the logical variables describing the position of the action in the planning graph and *StartLayer* and *EndLayer* variables is established using the constraints:

$$\forall a: Start_{StartLayer_a,a} = 1$$
$$\forall a: End_{EndLayer_a,a} = 1.$$

Note that such constraints can be easily modeled in existing constraint satisfaction packages using the element constraint [11]. The semantics of the element constraint is as follows: element(X,List,Y) is true if and only if the X-th element of List is Y. X, Y, and the elements of List could be variables with finite domains.

Finally, it is necessary to connect the action time points with the times of the propositional layers. This connection can be realized in the same way as above. Just note that the end propositional layer for the action has a one unit larger index than the index of the end action layer (see Figure 1).

$$\forall a: \quad Time_{StartLayer_a,a} = StartTime_a$$
$$\forall a: \quad Time_{EndLayer_a+1,a} = EndTime_a$$

5. Solver

One of the advantages of constraint programming is a specification of the constraint model independently of a particular constraint solver. We have implemented the above described constraint model using constraint satisfaction packages in SICStus Prolog [11]. First, we tried a Boolean constraint solver to implement the logical constraints and a finite domain solver to implement the numerical constraints. Note that the integration of the solvers is natural via shared variables. The Boolean solver is based on Binary Decision Diagrams (BDDs) [1] and it can produce a solution (for the logical constraints) without search. However, this solver requires a lot of memory and it crashed even for small problems. Therefore, we decided to use a finite domain solver for the logical constraints as well. Instead of logical operations corresponding arithmetical operations over the 0-1 variables are used (Table 1).

Table 1. Conversion between logical and arithmetical operations.

logical operation	arithmetical operation
A∨B	min(1,A+B)
A∧B	A*B
¬A	1-A
A⇒B	A≤B

The finite domain constraint solver uses the techniques of constraint propagation, in particular generalized arc consistency, to remove inconsistent values from variables' domains. Not surprisingly, constraint propagation is weaker than BDDs. To achieve better pruning, we have applied singleton arc consistency [10] to the Boolean variables modeling the planning graph. There exist some studies comparing the power of BDDs with constraint propagation and search [13,14] but we are not aware about any work comparing BDDs to singleton arc consistency. Anyway, in our test models, we have achieved the same pruning as BDDs without the memory consumption of BDDs. Thus, singleton consistency seems to be an appropriate method for initial domain pruning of Boolean variables modeling the planning graph. The reason could be that the domains of Boolean variables consist of two elements so if a value is removed from the domain due to inconsistency then the remaining value is assigned immediately to the variable. Note that after making the problem consistent, it is possible to deduce some information for the task network. In particular, the propositions that are known to be valid or invalid (the respective variable is instantiated) in the initial layer form a more specific precondition of the task network. Similarly, it is possible to deduce add and delete effects of the task network from the propositions in the last layer. This additional information can then be used during planning.

Constraint propagation can prune the domains but it does not guarantee existence of the solution. Thus, it is usually combined with search that attempts to assign values to the variables – this is often called labeling. We have decided that only the numerical variables will participate in labeling, namely *StartLayer*, *EndLayer*, *StartTime*, and *EndTime*. If these variables are assigned, constraint propagation ensures that the relevant Boolean variables in the action layers are assigned as well. In our models, we use action preconditions in the form of conjunction only (which is the case of most planning problems) so the Boolean variables in the proposition layers are decided as well. If this is not the case, these variables should be labeled as well. We decided to use numerical variables in labeling because then the generic variable ordering heuristics, like first-fail, play a role and they can improve efficiency of search. Actually deciding a value for the *StartLayer* variable is equivalent to finding values for 2*N-1 Boolean variables *Start*. We first label the layer variables *StartLayer* and *EndLayer*. This ensures that the actions are located to layers so all the logical relations between them are valid. In the second round, we label the time variables *StartTime* and *EndTime*. The labeling procedure is wrapped into a branch-and-bound algorithm that minimizes the completion time of the last action to obtain a plan with the minimal makespan.

6. Example

Assume that the task network consists of three actions A, B, and C such that the actions A and B cannot overlap in time (end(A)≤start(B) ∨ end(B)≤start(A)), all actions have duration 1 and there are three predicates p, q, and r. Action A has a precondition (p ∧ r) and a delete effect {p,r}, action B has a precondition (p) and an add effect {q}, and action C has a precondition (q ∧ ¬r) and a delete effect {q}. Then the proposed plan validator deduces (using constraint propagation combined with singleton consistency, i.e., no search is used) that the ordering of actions in the network is B<<A<<C, the precondition of the network is (p ∧ r), the delete effect of the network is {p,q,r}, and the minimal duration of the network is 3 (see Figure 2).

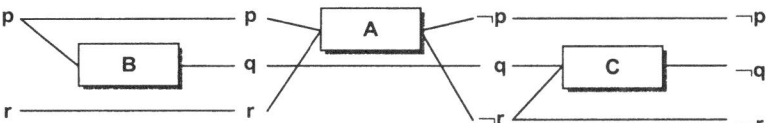

Figure 2. A simple task network.

7. Conclusions

In this paper, we proposed a new constraint-based approach for validating task networks and finishing plans with durative actions. Its main advantages are clarity and extendibility. It is easy and fast to implement the model in existing constraint packages like SICStus Prolog. Moreover, the constraint satisfaction technology allows painless extensions of the model. We have already integrated Boolean and numerical constraints there and it is possible to add other constraints for example modeling numerical effects of the actions or resource consumption and production. Also, the solving technology can be changed without necessity to modify the constraint model. We have tried a Boolean solver based on Binary Decision Diagrams (BBDs) to solve the Boolean part of the model. It has the advantage of providing solutions without search but it consumes a lot of memory (note that search is still necessary to resolve the numerical part of the model). Therefore, we have converted the Boolean constraints into numerical ones and we used standard generalized arc consistency for the whole model improved by singleton consistency for the original Boolean part. We did only a few preliminary experiments that showed that using singleton consistency achieves the same domain pruning as BBDs without horrible memory consumption. However, a further theoretical study is necessary there which could be based on works [13,14]. Our future research will go in the direction of generalizing the proposed approach to do full planning. After this generalization we will be able to do comparison with existing approaches for temporal modeling.

Acknowledgements

Research is supported by the Czech Science Foundation under the contract no. 201/04/1102 and by the project LN00A056 of the Ministry of Education of the Czech Republic. The author has been awarded an ECCAI Travel Grant to present the paper during ECAI'04. My thanks go also to Susanne Biundo and her team, namely Hartmut Jungholt, for introducing me to the problem of task network validation and for providing data sets for experiments.

References

[1]   Blum, A., Furst, M.: Fast planning through planning graph analysis. Artificial Intelligence 90 (1997) 281–300

[2]   Bryant, R.E.: Graph-Based Algorithms for Boolean Function Manipulation. IEEE Transactions on Computers C-38-8 (1986) 677–691

[3]   Do, M.B., Kambhampati, S.: Planning as Constraint Satisfaction: Solving the planning graph by compiling it into CSP. Artificial Intelligence 132 (2001), 151–182

[4]   Erol K., Hendler J., and Nau, D.: UMCP: A Sound and Complete Procedure for Hierarchical Task-Network Planning. In Proceedings of Second International Conference on AI Planning Systems (1994) 249–254

[5]   Fikes, R. E. and Nilsson, N. J.: STRIPS: A New Approach to the Application of Theorem Proving to Problem Solving. Artificial Intelligence 3–4 (1971) 189–208

[6]   Fox, M., Long, D.: PDDL 2.1: An extension to PDDL for expressing temporal planning domains. Journal of Artificial Intelligence Research (2003)

[7]   Fox, M., Long, D.: Fast Temporal Planning in a Graphplan Framework, AIPS workshop on Temporal Planning, Toulouse, France (2002)

[8]   Kautz, H. and Selman, B.: Planning as satisfiability. Proceedings of the European Conference on Artificial Intelligence (1992), 359-363.

[9]   Lopez, A., Bacchus, F.: Generalizing GraphPlan by Reformulating Planning as a CSP. In Gottlob, G., Walsh, T. (eds.): Proceedings of the Eighteenth International Joint Conference on Artificial Intelligence. Morgan Kaufmann Publishers (2003), 954–960

[10] Prosser P., Stergiou K., Walsh T.: Singleton Consistencies. In Principles and Practice of Constraint Programming (CP). LNCS. Springer-Verlag (2000) 353–368

[11] SICStus Prolog 3.11.0 User's Manual, SICS (2003)

[12] Smith, D., Weld, D.: Temporal Graphplan with mutual exclusion reasoning, In Proceedings of International Joint Conference on Artificial Intelligence (1999)

[13] Uribe, T., Stickel, M.E.: Ordered Binary Decision Diagrams and the Davis-Putnam Procedure. In Jouannaud J.P. (ed.): Proceedings of the First International Conference on Constraints in Computational Logics. LNCS, Vol. 845. Springer-Verlag (1994), 34–49

[14] Walsh, T.: SAT v CSP. In Proceedings of CP-2000. LNCS, Vol. 1894. Springer-Verlag (2000) 441–456

Planning, Scheduling and Constraint Satisfaction: From Theory to Practice
L. Castillo et al. (Eds.)
IOS Press, 2005

Differential Anti-Chain Algorithms for the Generalized Resource-Envelope Problem

T. K. Satish Kumar

Knowledge Systems Laboratory
Stanford University
tksk@ksl.stanford.edu

Abstract.
Interleaved planning and scheduling employs the idea of extending partial plans by regularly heeding to the scheduling constraints during search. One of the techniques used to analyze scheduling and resource consumption constraints is to compute the so-called *resource-envelopes*. These envelopes can then be used in a variety of ways to guide the search for a good plan. In this paper, we will define a generalized version of the resource-envelope problem, and provide efficient algorithms for solving it.

1 Introduction

Interleaved planning and scheduling employs the idea of extending partial plans by regularly heeding to the scheduling constraints during search. One of the techniques used to analyze scheduling and resource consumption constraints is to compute the so-called *maximum (upper)* and *minimum (lower) resource consumption envelopes*. These envelopes can be used to the guide search for a good plan in a variety of ways (see [3], [5] and [6]). First, they provide sanity checks for early backtracking when it is possible to examine the lower envelope and determine that no consistent schedule for the current set of constraints could possibly satisfy all the resource conflicts. Second, they provide a heuristic value for estimating the "constrainedness" of a partial plan. Third, they provide a search termination criterion when it is possible to examine the envelopes and determine that any consistent schedule for the current set of constraints would succeed in satisfying the resource conflicts. Fourth, they provide potential subroutines in designing approximation algorithms for optimal plan dispatching.

The *generalized resource-envelope* problem is as follows. A directed graph $\mathcal{G} = \langle \mathcal{X}, \mathcal{E} \rangle$ has $\mathcal{X} = \{X_0, X_1 \ldots X_n\}$ as the set of nodes corresponding to events (X_0 is the "beginning of the world" node and is assumed to be set to 0), and $\mathcal{E}$ as the set of directed edges between them. A directed edge $e = \langle X_i, X_j \rangle$ in $\mathcal{E}$ is annotated with the simple temporal information $[LB(e), UB(e)]$ indicating that a consistent schedule must have X_j scheduled between $LB(e)$ and $UB(e)$ ($LB(e) \leq UB(e)$) seconds after X_i is scheduled. Some edges (called *action edges*) correspond physically to actions and have $LB(e), UB(e) > 0$. An action edge A can consume a resource in a variety of ways: (Type 1) A claims w_A amount of the resource at the beginning of its execution and returns it at the end, (Type 2) A claims w_A amount of the resource at the beginning of its execution and does not return it at the end, or (Type 3) A consumes the resource according to a positive rate function

$u_A(t)$. Given a consistent schedule s for all the events, the amount of resource consumed by time t is denoted by $C_s(t)$. The goal is to build the upper envelope function $g(t)$ and the lower envelope function $h(t)$ such that $g(t) = \max_{\{s \text{ is a consistent schedule}\}} C_s(t)$ and $h(t) = \min_{\{s \text{ is a consistent schedule}\}} C_s(t)$.

Some attempts for estimating $g(t)$ have been made in [3], [5] and [6]. This paper improves upon them in a number of ways. First, the estimation of $g(t)$ provided in [5] is conservative, while it is tight in [3], [6] and in the algorithm provided in this paper. Tightness in the estimates of $g(t)$ and $h(t)$ is extremely important because a tight bound can save a potentially exponential amount of search through early backtracking and solution detection when compared to a looser bound. Tight bounds also provide better heuristic estimates for the "constrainedness" of a problem during search. Second, [3], [5] and [6] deal only with producer-consumer models, whereas the algorithm presented in this paper efficiently handles the most general case where some actions can be of Type 1, others of Type 2 and still others of Type 3. We note that although it is unlikely that any particular resource is consumed by actions of all possible types (Types 1, 2 and 3), the chosen model is extremely important in reasoning about plans (schedules) that require multiple resources to execute. Building the resource envelopes separately for every resource does not ensure that the schedules that achieve $g(t)$ or $h(t)$ (for different resources) are the same (for any given t). Instead, converting the resource requirements to *costs* and building a single profile function is often more useful. This would however, then require us to reason about all possible ways of consuming all possible resources, which the chosen model justifiably allows. Third, we provide algorithms for the computation of both $g(t)$ and $h(t)$ (even when there are Type 3 actions). Fourth, our algorithms are constructive in the sense that we can determine a flexible schedule s that achieves $g(t)$ or $h(t)$. This is better than determining an arbitrary fixed schedule (as in [6]) because flexible schedules tend to be robust in dealing with uncertainty of execution.[1]

We assume that the constraints specified in $\mathcal{E}$ are consistent, and throughout the paper, we will refer to a Type 1 action A being *active* when it holds w_A amount of resource, a Type 2 action B being *active* when it has consumed w_B amount of resource, and a Type 3 action C being *active to a degree* d when it has consumed d amount of resource. Moreover, for a Type 3 action C, we will assume that $LB(C) = UB(C)$.

2   Computing $g(t)$ for Type 1 Action Edges

In this section, we will restrict all actions to be of Type 1. Figure 1 presents the algorithm for the computation of $g(t)$ and a flexible schedule s that achieves it for a given time instant t. Figure 2 presents the algorithm for computing $g(t)$ for all t.

Lemma 1: A consistent schedule exists for $X_0, X_1 \ldots X_n$ in $\mathcal{G} = \langle \mathcal{X}, \mathcal{E} \rangle$ if and only if the distance graph $D(\mathcal{G})$ does not contain any negative cycles (see Figure 1).

Proof: (see [2]).

Lemma 2: A Type 1 action $A = \langle X_i, X_j \rangle$ can be made active at time t if it is possible to add the two edges $\langle X_0, X_i \rangle$ and $\langle X_j, X_0 \rangle$ annotated with t with $-t$ respectively to $D(\mathcal{G})$ without introducing any negative cycles.

Proof: A Type 1 action edge $\langle X_i, X_j \rangle$ is active at time t if and only if X_i is scheduled before t and X_j is scheduled after t. Using the semantics of the distance graph—that a constraint $X_b - X_a \leq w$ is specified as the edge $\langle X_a, X_b \rangle$ annotated with w—this corresponds to the addition of the two edges $\langle X_0, X_i \rangle$ and $\langle X_j, X_0 \rangle$

---

[1][3] provides constructive and incremental algorithms for determining flexible consistent schedules in producer-consumer models (in addition to computing the envelopes themselves).

ALGORITHM: UPPER-ENVELOPE-TYPE-1-AT-T
INPUT: An instance of the resource-envelope problem with all actions of Type 1, and a time instant t.
OUTPUT: $g(t)$ and a flexible schedule s achieving it.
(1) Construct the distance graph $D(\mathcal{G})$ on $X_0, X_1 \ldots X_n$ as:
  (a) Every edge $e = \langle X_i, X_j \rangle \in \mathcal{E}$ is compiled to two edges: $\langle X_i, X_j \rangle$ annotated with $UB(e)$, and $\langle X_j, X_i \rangle$ annotated with $-LB(e)$.
  (b) Let $dist(X_a, X_b)$ = distance from X_a to X_b in $D(\mathcal{G})$.
(2) FOR actions $A_1 = \langle X_{i_1}, X_{j_1} \rangle$ and $A_2 = \langle X_{i_2}, X_{j_2} \rangle$:
  (a) Construct a (directed) size-2 conflict from A_1 to A_2 (denoted $A_1 \rightarrow A_2$) iff $dist(X_{i_2}, X_{j_1}) < 0$.
(3) Construct a node-weighted directed graph $E(\mathcal{G})$ as follows:
  (a) The nodes of $E(\mathcal{G})$ correspond to the actions.

(b) The weight on a node corresponding to action A, is w_A.
(c) A directed edge $\langle A_1, A_2 \rangle$ in $E(\mathcal{G})$ encodes a size-2 conflict $A_1 \rightarrow A_2$.
(4) Construct a node-weighted directed graph $M(\mathcal{G})$ from $E(\mathcal{G})$ by removing a node corresponding to action $A = \langle X_i, X_j \rangle$ iff $t + dist(X_i, X_0) < 0$ or $dist(X_0, X_j) - t < 0$ (such actions are referred to as size-1 conflicts).
(5) Compute $Q = \{A_{q_1}, A_{q_2} \ldots A_{q_k}\}$ as the largest weighted anti-chain in $M(\mathcal{G})$.
(6) RETURN:
  (a) $g(t) = |Q| = \sum_{p=1}^{k} w_{A_{q_p}}$.
  (b) $s = D(\mathcal{G}) \cup \{\langle X_0, X_i^{q_p} \rangle$ annotated with t, and $\langle X_j^{q_p}, X_0 \rangle$ annotated with $-t \mid A_{q_p} = \langle X_i^{q_p}, X_j^{q_p} \rangle \in Q\}$.

Figure 1: $g(t)$ for Type 1 actions for a specified t.

ALGORITHM: UPPER-ENVELOPE-TYPE-1-ALL-T
INPUT: An instance of the resource-envelope problem with all actions of Type 1.
RESULT: $g(t)$ for all t.
(1) FOR all action edges $A = \langle X_i, X_j \rangle$:
  (a) Insert $-dist(X_i, X_0)$ into list L.
  (b) Insert $dist(X_0, X_j)$ into list L.

(2) Sort L in ascending order $\langle d_1, d_2 \ldots d_{|L|} \rangle$.
(3) FOR $i = 1, 2 \ldots |L| - 1$:
  (a) Compute $g(d_i) =$ UPPER-ENVELOPE-TYPE-1-AT-T at time d_i.
  (b) Set $g(t) = g(d_i)$ for all t in the interval $[d_i, d_{i+1})$.
(4) Set $g(t) = 0$ for all t in the intervals $[-\infty, d_1)$ and $(d_{|L|}, +\infty]$.

Figure 2: $g(t)$ for Type 1 actions for all t.

---

annotated with t with $-t$ respectively. Further, since any inconsistency in the constraints is reflected by the presence of a negative cycle in $D(\mathcal{G})$ (Lemma 1), the truth of the Lemma follows.

Definition 1: A *conflict* is a set of action edges all of which cannot be simultaneously active at a given time t. A *minimal conflict* is a conflict no proper subset of which is also a conflict.

Lemma 3: A set of action edges can be made simultaneously active at time t if and only if there is no subset of them that constitutes a minimal conflict.

Proof: A set of action edges can be made simultaneously active at time t if and only if there is no subset of them that constitutes a conflict. Further, the truth of the Lemma follows from the fact that there exists a subset of actions that constitutes a conflict if and only if there exists a subset of actions that constitutes a minimal conflict.

Lemma 4: The size of a minimal conflict is ≤ 2.

Proof: A set of action edges $A_1 = \langle X_{i_1}, X_{j_1} \rangle, A_2 = \langle X_{i_2}, X_{j_2} \rangle \ldots A_k = \langle X_{i_k}, X_{j_k} \rangle$ can be attempted to be made simultaneously active at time t by the addition of the edges $\langle X_0, X_{i_m} \rangle$ and $\langle X_{j_m}, X_0 \rangle$ (for $m = 1, 2 \ldots k$) annotated with t and $-t$ respectively to the distance graph $D(\mathcal{G})$. Let these edges be referred to as *special* edges and let $D'(\mathcal{G})$ refer to the resulting distance graph. Knowing that $D(\mathcal{G})$ does not contain any negative cycles (because $\mathcal{E}$ is consistent), a negative cycle can occur in $D'(\mathcal{G})$ only if it involves a special edge. Since all special edges have X_0 as an end point, a negative cycle must involve X_0. Further, since a fundamental cycle can have any node repeated at most once, at most 2 special edges can be present in a negative cycle in $D'(\mathcal{G})$. Finally, since special edges correspond to the activation of Type 1 actions, the size of a minimal conflict is ≤ 2.

Lemma 5: A size-2 conflict is independent of t.

Proof: Continuing the above arguments, when the size of a minimal conflict is 2, the negative cycle in $D'(\mathcal{G})$ must involve an incoming special edge to X_0—say $\langle X_{j_d}, X_0 \rangle$—with weight $-t$, and an outgoing special edge from X_0—say $\langle X_0, X_{i_c} \rangle$—with weight t. The weight of the negative cycle containing exactly these two special edges is therefore $t + dist(X_{i_c}, X_{j_d}) - t$. This is independent of t and is < 0 if and only if $dist(X_{i_c}, X_{j_d}) < 0$.

Lemma 6: The relation $\succeq$ defined on Type 1 actions as follows forms a POSET (partially ordered set)— $A_1 \succeq A_2$ if and only if $A_1 = A_2$ or there is a size-2 conflict $A_1 \rightarrow A_2$ (see Figure 1).

Proof: We will show that the relation $\succeq$ is *reflexive, antisymmetric* and *transitive*. By definition, $\succeq$ is reflexive since $A_1 \succeq A_1$. For the antisymmetry property, we will show that when $A_1 \neq A_2$, $A_1 \succeq A_2$ and $A_2 \succeq A_1$

cannot hold simultaneously. Assuming the contrary, let $A_1 \neq A_2$, and let the size-2 conflicts $A_1 \to A_2$ and $A_2 \to A_1$ hold. If $A_1 = \langle X_{i_1}, X_{j_1} \rangle$ and $A_2 = \langle X_{i_2}, X_{j_2} \rangle$, $dist(X_{i_2}, X_{j_1}) < 0$ and $dist(X_{i_1}, X_{j_2}) < 0$. Further since $D(\mathcal{G})$ contains the edges $\langle X_{j_1}, X_{i_1} \rangle$ and $\langle X_{j_2}, X_{i_2} \rangle$ annotated with $-LB(A_1)$ and $-LB(A_2)$ respectively (for $LB(A_i)$ known to be positive for all actions A_i), we would have the negative cycle $dist(X_{j_1}, X_{i_1}) + dist(X_{i_1}, X_{j_2}) + dist(X_{j_2}, X_{i_2}) + dist(X_{i_2}, X_{j_1})$. This contradicts that $D(\mathcal{G})$ does not contain any negative cycle, hence establishing the antisymmetry property. To prove the transitivity property, suppose $A_1 = \langle X_{i_1}, X_{j_1} \rangle$, $A_2 = \langle X_{i_2}, X_{j_2} \rangle$ and $A_3 = \langle X_{i_3}, X_{j_3} \rangle$ are 3 different actions such that $A_1 \to A_2$ and $A_2 \to A_3$. This means that $dist(X_{i_2}, X_{j_1}) < 0$ and $dist(X_{i_3}, X_{j_2}) < 0$. Since $dist(X_{j_2}, X_{i_2}) \leq -LB(A_2)$ (for $LB(A_2)$ known to be positive), $dist(X_{i_3}, X_{j_1}) \leq dist(X_{i_3}, X_{j_2}) + dist(X_{j_2}, X_{i_2}) + dist(X_{i_2}, X_{j_1}) < 0$. This makes $dist(X_{i_3}, X_{j_1}) < 0$, hence establishing the conflict $A_1 \to A_3$ and proving the transitivity property.

Lemma 7: An action edge $A = \langle X_i, X_j \rangle$ constitutes a size-1 conflict at time t when $t + dist(X_i, X_0) < 0$ or $dist(X_0, X_j) - t < 0$.

Proof: Continuing the arguments in the proof of Lemma 4, a negative cycle in $D'(\mathcal{G})$ can also involve just one special edge (referred to as a size-1 conflict). In the case that it involves an incoming special edge to X_0—say $\langle X_j, X_0 \rangle$ for the action $A = \langle X_i, X_j \rangle$—$dist(X_0, X_j) - t$ needs to be < 0 to create a negative cycle. In the case that it involves an outgoing special edge from X_0—say $\langle X_0, X_i \rangle$ for the action $A = \langle X_i, X_j \rangle$—$t + dist(X_i, X_0)$ needs to be < 0 to create a negative cycle.

Lemma 8: If $Q = $ largest weighted anti-chain in $M(\mathcal{G})$, $g(t) = |Q|$ and $s = D(\mathcal{G}) \cup \{\langle X_0, X_i^{q_p} \rangle$ annotated with t, and $\langle X_j^{q_p}, X_0 \rangle$ annotated with $-t \mid A_{q_p} = \langle X_i^{q_p}, X_j^{q_p} \rangle \in Q\}$.

Proof: By construction (step 4 in Figure 1), $M(\mathcal{G})$ incorporates the deletion of all size-1 conflicts. Further, by definition, an anti-chain in $M(\mathcal{G})$ chooses a set of actions no two distinct ones of which are comparable using $\succeq$. This means that no two distinct actions exhibit a size-2 conflict. Together, all minimal conflicts are removed in any anti-chain of $M(\mathcal{G})$ and the maximum weighted anti-chain targets the maximum possible resource demand at time t over all consistent schedules. The required flexible schedule s corresponds to the addition of edges required to activate the qualifying actions, and is appropriately given as above.

Lemma 9: $g(t)$ is piecewise constant and changes only at a polynomial number of time points.

Proof: By the previous Lemma, $g(t)$ is the largest weighted anti-chain in the graph $M(\mathcal{G})$. Since $M(\mathcal{G})$ is computed from $E(\mathcal{G})$ by deleting all size-1 conflicts at time t, the number of times $g(t)$ changes is equal to the number of times the set of size-1 conflicts changes. Further, since $dist(X_0, X_j)$ and $-dist(X_i, X_0)$ mark the membership of an action $\langle X_i, X_j \rangle$ in this set, the potential number of transition points for the piecewise constant function $g(t)$ is $O(K)$ where K is the number of Type 1 actions.

The largest weighted anti-chain in a POSET having B nodes can be efficiently computed in time $O(B^{2.5})$ using *max-flow* techniques (see [1] and [4]).

The complexity of the steps in UPPER-ENVELOPE-TYPE-1-AT-T that are independent of t (and can therefore be done just once) is referred to as its *static complexity* ($|sc|$). The time dependent complexity is referred to as its *dynamic complexity* ($|dc|$). The analysis of these two complexities is subsumed in the analysis presented for the most general version of the problem. The complexity of UPPER-ENVELOPE-TYPE-1-ALL-T (by Lemma 9) is equal to $O(|sc| + K|dc|)$, where K is the number of Type 1 actions.

3 Computing $g(t)$ for Type 2 Action Edges

In this section, we will restrict all actions to be of Type 2. Figure 3 presents the algorithm for the computation of $g(t)$ and a flexible schedule s that achieves it for a given time instant t. Figure 4 presents the algorithm for computing $g(t)$ for all t.

Lemma 10: A Type 2 action edge $A = \langle X_i, X_j \rangle$ can be made active at time t if and only if it is possible to add

---

ALGORITHM: UPPER-ENVELOPE-TYPE-2-AT-T
INPUT: An instance of the resource-envelope problem with all actions of Type 2, and a time instant t.
OUTPUT: $g(t)$ and a flexible schedule s achieving it.
(1) FOR all actions $A = \langle X_i, X_j \rangle$:

(a) Compute $dist(X_i, X_0)$ in the distance graph $D(\mathcal{G})$.
(2) RETURN:
(a) $g(t) = \sum_A \{w_A$ (s.t. $A = \langle X_i, X_j \rangle$ has $dist(X_i, X_0) + t \geq 0)\}$.
(b) $s = D(\mathcal{G}) \cup \{\langle X_0, X_i \rangle$ annotated with $t \mid A = \langle X_i, X_j \rangle$ and has $dist(X_i, X_0) + t \geq 0\}$.

Figure 3: $g(t)$ for Type 2 actions for a specified t.

ALGORITHM: UPPER-ENVELOPE-TYPE-2-ALL-T
INPUT: An instance of the resource-envelope problem with all actions of Type 2.
RESULT: $g(t)$ for all t.
(1) FOR all action edges $A = \langle X_i, X_j \rangle$:
(a) Insert $-dist(X_i, X_0)$ into list L.
(2) Sort L in ascending order $\langle d_1, d_2 \ldots d_{|L|} \rangle$.

(3) FOR $i = 1, 2 \ldots |L| - 1$:
(a) Compute $g(d_i)$ = UPPER-ENVELOPE-TYPE-2-AT-T at time d_i.
(b) Set $g(t) = g(d_i)$ for all t in the interval $[d_i, d_{i+1})$.
(4) Set $g(t) = 0$ for all t in the interval $[-\infty, d_1)$.
(5) Set $g(t) = \sum_{\text{all actions } A} w_A$ for all t in the interval $[d_{|L|}, +\infty]$.

Figure 4: $g(t)$ for Type 2 actions for all t.

the edge $\langle X_0, X_i \rangle$ annotated with t to $D(\mathcal{G})$ without introducing any negative cycles.

Proof: (similar to that of Lemma 2).

Lemma 11: The size of a minimal conflict is $= 1$.

Proof: (similar to that of Lemma 4).

Lemma 12: An action edge $A = \langle X_i, X_j \rangle$ constitutes a size-1 conflict at time t when $t + aist(X_i, X_0) < 0$.

Proof: (similar to that of Lemma 7).

Lemma 13: $g(t) = \sum_A \{w_A$ (such that $A = \langle X_i, X_j \rangle$ has $dist(X_i, X_0) + t \geq 0)\}$ and $s = D(\mathcal{G}) \cup \{\langle X_0, X_i \rangle$ annotated with $t \mid A = \langle X_i, X_j \rangle$ and has $dist(X_i, X_0) + t \geq 0\}$.

Proof: The only minimal conflicts are of size 1 and are removed in the summation $\sum_A \{w_A$ (such that $A = \langle X_i, X_j \rangle$ has $dist(X_i, X_0) + t \geq 0)\}$—which is the required $g(t)$ since all w_As are known to be positive. The required flexible schedule s corresponds to the addition of edges required to activate the qualifying actions.

Lemma 14: $g(t)$ is piecewise constant and changes only at a polynomial number of time points.

Proof: (similar to that of Lemma 9).

The analysis of $|sc|$ and $|dc|$ of UPPER-ENVELOPE-TYPE-2-AT-T is subsumed in the analysis presented for the most general version of the problem. The complexity of UPPER-ENVELOPE-TYPE-2-ALL-T (by Lemma 14) is equal to $O(|sc| + K|dc|)$, where K is the number of Type 2 actions.

4   Computing $g(t)$ for Type 3 Action Edges

In this section, we will restrict all actions to be of Type 3. Figure 5 presents the algorithm for the computation of $g(t)$ and a flexible schedule s that achieves it for a given time instant t. Figure 6 presents the algorithm for computing $g(t)$ for all t.

Lemma 15: A Type 3 action edge $A = \langle X_i, X_j \rangle$ can be made active at time t to a degree $\geq d$ if and only if it is possible to add the edge $\langle X_0, X_i \rangle$ to $D(\mathcal{G})$ without introducing any negative cycles—where $\langle X_0, X_i \rangle$ should be annotated with $t' \leq t$ and t' is such that $\int_0^{t-t'} u_A(x)dx = d$.

Proof: A Type 3 edge contributes a resource consumption of $\int_0^{t-X_i} u_A(x)dx$ by time t when X_i is scheduled before t. To ensure that A consumes $\geq d$ of resource by time t, we must have $\int_0^{t-X_i} u_A(x)dx \geq d$. Since $u_A(x) > 0$, and t' is such that $\int_0^{t-t'} u_A(x)dx = d$, we require $X_i \leq t'$. Using the semantics of the distance graph, this corresponds to the addition of the edge $\langle X_0, X_i \rangle$ annotated with t'. Also, since $d > 0$, $t' \leq t$.

Lemma 16: The size of a minimal conflict is $= 1$.

Proof: (similar to that of Lemma 4).

Lemma 17: An action edge $A = \langle X_i, X_j \rangle$ constitutes a size-1 conflict at time t when attempted to be activated

---

ALGORITHM: UPPER-ENVELOPE-TYPE-3-AT-T
INPUT: An instance of the resource-envelope problem with all actions of Type 3, and a time instant t.
OUTPUT: $g(t)$, the set of actions Q constituting it, and a flexible schedule s achieving it.
(1) FOR all actions $A = \langle X_i, X_j \rangle$:

(a) Compute $dist(X_i, X_0)$ in the distance graph $D(\mathcal{G})$.
(2) RETURN:
(a) $Q = \{A \mid A = \langle X_i, X_j \rangle$ and $dist(X_i, X_0) + t \geq 0\}$.
(b) $g(t) = \sum_{A \in Q} \{ \int_0^{t+dist(X_i, X_0)} u_A(x) dx \}$.
(c) $s = D(\mathcal{G}) \cup \{\langle X_0, X_i \rangle$ annotated with $- dist(X_i, X_0) \mid A = \langle X_i, X_j \rangle \in Q\}$.

Figure 5: $g(t)$ for Type 3 actions for a specified t.

ALGORITHM: UPPER-ENVELOPE-TYPE-3-ALL-T
INPUT: An instance of the resource-envelope problem with all actions of Type 3.
RESULT: $g(t)$ for all t.
(1) FOR all action edges $A = \langle X_i, X_j \rangle$:
  (a) Insert $-dist(X_i, X_0)$ into list L.

(2) Sort L in ascending order $\langle d_1, d_2 \ldots d_{|L|} \rangle$.
(3) FOR $i = 1, 2 \ldots |L|$:
  (a) Compute $Q = $ UPPER-ENVELOPE-TYPE-3-AT-T at time d_i.
  (b) Set $g(t) = \sum_{A \in Q} \{ \int_0^{t+dist(X_i, X_0)} u_A(x) dx \}$ for all t in the interval $[d_i, d_{i+1})$ (treat $d_{|L|+1} = +\infty$).
(4) Set $g(t) = 0$ for all t in the interval $[-\infty, d_1)$.

Figure 6: $g(t)$ for Type 3 actions for all t.

---

to a degree $\geq d$ if $t' + dist(X_i, X_0) < 0$ where t' is such that $\int_0^{t-t'} u_A(x) dx = d$.

Proof: (similar to that of Lemma 7).

Lemma 18: $g(t) = \sum_A \{ \int_0^{t+dist(X_i, X_0)} u_A(x) dx$ (such that $A = \langle X_i, X_j \rangle$ has $dist(X_i, X_0) + t \geq 0$)$\}$ and $s = D(\mathcal{G}) \cup \{\langle X_0, X_i \rangle$ annotated with $- dist(X_i, X_0) \mid A = \langle X_i, X_j \rangle \in Q\}$ (see Figure 5).

Proof: The only minimal conflicts are of size 1 and are appropriately removed in $\sum_A \{ \int_0^{t-t'} u_A(x) dx$ (s.t. $A = \langle X_i, X_j \rangle$ has $dist(X_i, X_0) + t' \geq 0$)$\}$. Since each term in this summation is maximized with decreasing t', the smallest value of t' that does not introduce a negative cycle, together with the conditions that $t' + dist(X_i, X_0) \geq 0$ and $t' \leq t$, is $-dist(X_i, X_0)$ provided that $t + dist(X_i, X_0) \geq 0$. Put together, this means that $g(t) = \sum_A \{ \int_0^{t+dist(X_i, X_0)} u_A(x) dx$ (such that $A = \langle X_i, X_j \rangle$ has $dist(X_i, X_0) + t \geq 0$)$\}$. The required flexible schedule s corresponds to the addition of edges required to activate the qualifying actions.

Lemma 19: $g(t)$ is piecewise continuous and is discontinuous only at a polynomial number of time points.

Proof: By the previous Lemmas, $g(t)$ is the summation of integrals over all actions $\langle X_i, X_j \rangle$ that have $t + dist(X_i, X_0) \geq 0$. Assuming that $u_A(x)$ is continuous, all integrals of the form $\int_0^{t+dist(X_i, X_0)} u_A(x) dx$ are continuous and the number of times $g(t)$ becomes discontinuous is bounded by the number of times the set of actions having $t + dist(X_i, X_0) \geq 0$ changes. Since $-dist(X_i, X_0)$ marks the membership of an action $\langle X_i, X_j \rangle$ in this set, the number of discontinuities in $g(t)$ is $O(K)$ where K is the number of Type 3 actions.

The analysis of $|sc|$ and $|dc|$ of UPPER-ENVELOPE-TYPE-3-AT-T is subsumed in the analysis presented for the most general version of the problem. The complexity of UPPER-ENVELOPE-TYPE-3-ALL-T (by Lemma 19) is equal to $O(|sc| + K\Im|dc|)$, where K is the number of Type 3 actions and $\Im$ is the complexity of symbolic integration.

5   Computing $g(t)$ for Hybrid Action Edges

We will now deal with the most general version of the resource-envelope problem—allowing for Type 1, Type 2 and Type 3 actions. Figure 9 presents an algorithm that discretizes a Type 3 action into a series of Type 2 actions such that a solution for the latter can be easily translated to a solution for the former. Interestingly, the discretization depends on the Type 1 actions present in the problem instance, and the time instant t. Figure 7 presents the algorithm for the discretization, and Figure 8 presents the algorithm for solving the modified problem. A series of Lemmas are presented that prove the correctness of these algorithms. The correctness of Figure 8 follows directly from the arguments presented in previous sections.

Lemma 20: The size of a minimal conflict is ≤ 2 (in attempting to make various actions active).

ALGORITHM: DISCRETIZE-TYPE-3-TO-TYPE-2
INPUT: An instance of the generalized resource-envelope problem, and a time instant t.
RESULT: Discretization of all Type 3 actions.
(1) FOR all Type 3 action edges $C = \langle X_i^c, X_j^c \rangle$:
   (a) FOR all Type 1 action edges $A = \langle X_i^a, X_j^a \rangle$:
      (i) Insert $dist(X_i^c, X_j^a)$ into List D iff it is ≥ 0.
   (b) Insert $t + dist(X_i^c, X_0)$ into List D iff it is ≥ 0.
   (c) Insert $UB(C)$ into List D.
   (d) Sort D in ascending order $\langle d_1, d_2 \ldots d_{|D|} \rangle$.

(e) FOR $h = 1, 2 \ldots |D|$:
   (i) Create a Type 2 action $B_h = \langle X_i^{B_h}, X_j^{B_h} \rangle$ so that:
      (A) $X_i^{B_h}$ and $X_j^{B_h}$ are new nodes in $D(\mathcal{G})$.
      (B) $\langle X_i^{B_h}, X_j^{B_h} \rangle$ and $\langle X_j^{B_h}, X_i^{B_h} \rangle$ are edges annotated with ϵ and $-\epsilon$ respectively (for any $\epsilon > 0$).
      (C) $\langle X_i^c, X_i^{B_h} \rangle$ and $\langle X_j^{B_h}, X_i^c \rangle$ are edges annotated with d_h and $-d_h$ respectively.
      (D) Set $w_{B_h} = \int_{d_{h-1}}^{d_h} u_C(t) dt$ (use $d_0 = 0$ when $h = 1$).
(f) Set $u_C(t) = 0$ (i.e. remove action C from further consideration).

Figure 7: Discretizing Type 3 actions to Type 2 actions in the context of the Type 1 actions and t.

ALGORITHM: UPPER-ENVELOPE-TYPE-1-2-AT-T
INPUT: An instance of the resource envelope problem with all actions of Type 1 or Type 2, and a time instant t.
OUTPUT: $g(t)$ and a flexible schedule s achieving it.
(1) FOR all pairs of Type 1 actions $A = \langle X_{i_1}, X_{j_1} \rangle$ and Type 1 or Type 2 actions $B = \langle X_{i_2}, X_{j_2} \rangle$:
   (a) Construct a (directed) size-2 conflict $A \rightarrow B$ iff $dist(X_{i_2}, X_{j_1})$ in the distance graph $D(\mathcal{G})$, is < 0.
(2) Construct a node-weighted directed graph $E(\mathcal{G})$ as follows:
   (a) The nodes of $E(\mathcal{G})$ correspond to actions.
   (b) The weight on a node corresponding to action A, is w_A.
   (c) A directed edge $\langle A, B \rangle$ in $E(\mathcal{G})$ encodes a size-2 conflict $A \rightarrow B$.
(3) Construct a node-weighted directed graph $M(\mathcal{G})$ from

$E(\mathcal{G})$ as follows:
   (a) Remove a node $A = \langle X_i, X_j \rangle$ if $\{ t + dist(X_i, X_0) < 0 \vee dist(X_0, X_j) - t < 0 \}$ and A is of Type 1.
   (b) Remove a node $A = \langle X_i, X_j \rangle$ if $t + dist(X_i, X_0) < 0$ and A is of Type 2.
(4) Compute $Q = \{A_{q_1}, A_{q_2} \ldots A_{q_k}\}$ as the largest weighted anti-chain in $M(\mathcal{G})$.
(5) RETURN:
   (a) $g(t) = |Q| = \sum_{p=1}^{k} w_{A_{q_p}}$.
   (b) $s = D(\mathcal{G}) \cup \{\langle X_0, X_i^{q_p} \rangle$ annotated with t and $\langle X_j^{q_p}, X_0 \rangle$ annotated with $-t \mid \langle X_i^{q_p}, X_j^{q_p} \rangle$ is of Type 1 and is in $Q\}$
$\cup \{\langle X_0, X_i^{q_p} \rangle$ annotated with $t \mid \langle X_i^{q_p}, X_j^{q_p} \rangle$ is of Type 2 and is in $Q\}$.

Figure 8: $g(t)$ for Type (1,2) actions for a specified t.

Proof: (similar to that of Lemma 4).

Lemma 21: The size-2 conflicts may not be independent of t.

Proof: A size-2 conflict should involve an incoming edge (to X_0) of a Type 1 action and an outgoing edge (from X_0) of either a Type 1, Type 2 or Type 3 action. It is only in the final case that the weights on the incoming and outgoing edges do not cancel each other, but are $-t$ and t' (required to activate a Type 3 action to a certain degree) respectively. In such a case, a size-2 conflict arises between a Type 1 action $A = \langle X_i^a, X_j^a \rangle$ and a Type 3 edge $C = \langle X_i^c, X_j^c \rangle$ when $t' + dist(X_i^c, X_j^a) - t < 0$.

Lemma 22: For a Type 3 action $C = \langle X_i^c, X_j^c \rangle$, the schedule achieving $g(t)$ must either have $t + dist(X_i^c, X_0) < 0$ or incorporate the addition of the edge $\langle X_0, X_i^c \rangle$ annotated with t'_{opt} such that $t - t'_{opt} \in D$ (see Figure 7).

Proof: When $t + dist(X_i^c, X_0) < 0$, C cannot contribute to the total amount of resource consumed by time t because the addition of $\langle X_0, X_i^c \rangle$ annotated with t'_{opt} constrained to be $\leq t$ causes a size-1 conflict. When this does not happen, we will show that $t'_{opt} \in D'$ where $d'_i \in D'$ is $t - d_i$. Suppose $t'_{opt} \notin D'$. Let L be in D' such that it is closest to t'_{opt} and smaller than it. L exists because D is known to contain $t + dist(X_i^c, X_0)$ and it cannot be the case that $t'_{opt} < t - (t + dist(X_i^c, X_0))$ as this would cause the size-1 conflict $t'_{opt} + dist(X_i^c, X_0) < 0$. The set of Type 1 actions that C conflicts with are the same whether $\langle X_0, X_i^c \rangle$ is annotated with t'_{opt} or L. This is because if there is any Type 1 action $A = \langle X_i^a, X_j^a \rangle$ such that $t'_{opt} + dist(X_i^c, X_j^a) - t \geq 0$ but $L + dist(X_i^c, X_j^a) - t < 0$, then $t - dist(X_i^c, X_j^a)$ is $> L$ but $\leq t'_{opt}$. Further, since $t'_{opt} \leq t$, $dist(X_i^c, X_j^a) \geq 0$, and by construction, $t - dist(X_i^c, X_j^a)$ belongs to D'. This contradicts that L is the closest element in D' that is lesser than t'_{opt}. It also cannot be the case that annotating $\langle X_0, X_i^c \rangle$ with L causes a size-1 conflict when annotating it with t'_{opt} does not cause one. Suppose this were possible, then $dist(X_i^c, X_0) + L < 0$ and $dist(X_i^c, X_0) + t'_{opt} \geq 0$. Since $t \geq t'_{opt}$, $dist(X_i^c, X_0) + t \geq 0$ and belongs to D. This implies that $-dist(X_i^c, X_0)$ is present in D' and is required to be $> L$ but $\leq t'_{opt}$—contradicting the construction of L. Finally, since the conflicts remain the same in both cases, the POSET remains the same except that in the case where $\langle X_0, X_i^c \rangle$ is annotated with L, the contribution of C is $\int_0^{t-L} u_C(x) dx$, which is greater than $\int_0^{t-t'_{opt}} u_C(x) dx$. The size of the largest weighted anti-chain will therefore be necessarily greater in the case of L, proving that $t'_{opt} \in D'$.

```
ALGORITHM: UPPER-ENVELOPE-HYBRID-AT-T       (b) s_{[P]} = s_{[P']} with the modification that if the series of
INPUT: An instance P of the generalized resource envelope   Type 2 actions B_1, B_2 ... B_{|D|} (B_k = ⟨X_i^{B_k}, X_j^{B_k}⟩)
problem, and a time instant t.                              in P' corresponds to the discretization of the Type 3 action
OUTPUT: g(t) and a schedule s that achieves it.            C = ⟨X_i^c, X_j^c⟩ in P, then s_{[P]} contains ⟨X_0, X_i^c⟩ annotated
(1) DISCRETIZE-TYPE-3-TO-TYPE-2 to obtain instance P'.     with t − d_h, where h is the highest number such that
(2) RETURN:                                                 ⟨X_0, X_i^{B_h}⟩ is annotated with t in s_{[P']}.
   (a) g(t)_{[P]} = g(t)_{[P']}.
```

Figure 9: $g(t)$ for the most general version of the problem.

Lemma 23: For a Type 3 action C and its discretization into the Type 2 actions $B_1, B_2 \ldots B_{|D|}$ (see Figure 7), $\int_0^{UB(C)} u_C(x)dx = \sum_{h=1}^{|D|} w_{B_h}$.

Proof: We know that $\sum_{h=1}^{|D|} w_{B_h} = \int_0^{d_1} u_C(x)dx + \int_{d_1}^{d_2} u_C(x)dx \ldots \int_{d_{|D|-1}}^{d_{|D|}} u_C(x)dx = \int_0^{d_{|D|}} u_C(x)dx$. Since D is known to contain $UB(C)$, $\sum_{h=1}^{|D|} w_{B_h} = \int_0^{UB(C)} u_C(x)dx$.

Lemma 24: For a given time instant t, the discretization of the Type 3 action C to the Type 2 actions $B_1, B_2 \ldots B_{|D|}$ produces equivalent results for the computation of $g(t)$ (see Figure 7).

Proof: We have to prove the equivalence of C and $B_1, B_2 \ldots B_{|D|}$ with respect to both size-1 conflicts and size-2 conflicts. By previous Lemmas, no higher order conflicts need to be considered. First, consider the equivalence with respect to size-1 conflicts. We have to prove that for the given time t, the sum of the weights on B_h ($h = 1, 2 \ldots |D|$) that do not exhibit a size-1 conflict is equal to the maximum degree to which we can activate C without allowing it to exhibit a size-1 conflict. By the previous Lemma, this would also prove that the sum of weights on B_h ($h = 1, 2 \ldots |D|$) that exhibit a size-1 conflict at time t is equal to the conflicting part of C. Consider the sum of all w_{B_h} such that $B_h = \langle X_i^{B_h}, X_j^{B_h} \rangle$ can have the successful addition of $\langle X_0, X_i^{B_h} \rangle$ annotated with t. This is possible only when $dist(X_i^{B_h}, X_0) + t \geq 0$. But we know that $dist(X_i^{B_h}, X_0) = dist(X_i^{B_h}, X_i^c) + dist(X_i^c, X_0)$ because the only node that $X_i^{B_h}$ is connected to is X_i^c. By construction, $dist(X_i^{B_h}, X_i^c)$ is $-d_h$. Therefore, we need to qualify all B_h such that $-d_h + dist(X_i^c, X_0) + t \geq 0$—i.e. $d_h \leq t + dist(X_i^c, X_0)$. For the activation of C, we require the lowest t' such that $t' \geq -dist(X_i^c, X_0)$. The corresponding resource consumption by C would be $\int_0^{t-t'} u_C(x)dx = \int_0^{t+dist(X_i^c, X_0)} u_C(x)dx$. By construction, $t + dist(X_i^c, X_0)$ is present in D (if $t + dist(X_i^c, X_0) < 0$, C and $B_1, B_2 \ldots B_{|D|}$ are trivially equivalent). Let this be d_g. The required weight of all w_{B_h} such that $d_h \leq d_g$ is $\int_0^{d_1} u_C(x)dx + \int_{d_1}^{d_2} u_C(x)dx \ldots \int_{d_{g-1}}^{d_g} u_C(x)dx = \int_0^{d_g} u_C(x)dx = \int_0^{t+dist(X_i^c, X_0)} u_C(x)dx$ as required. Now consider the equivalence of C and $B_1, B_2 \ldots B_{|D|}$ with respect to size-2 conflicts. It suffices to prove that for any Type 1 action edge $A = \langle X_i^a, X_j^a \rangle$, and a given time t, the sum of the weights of w_{B_h} ($h = 1, 2 \ldots |D|$) that do not conflict with A is equal to the maximum value of $\int_0^{t-t'} u_C(x)dx$ such that $t' - t + dist(X_i^c, X_j^a) \geq 0$. By the previous Lemma, this would also prove that the sum of weights on B_h ($h = 1, 2 \ldots |D|$) that exhibit a size-2 conflict with A at time t is equal to the conflicting part of C with A. Consider the sum of all w_{B_h} that do not exhibit a size-2 conflict with A. This happens when $B_h = \langle X_i^{B_h}, X_j^{B_h} \rangle$ is such that we can have a successful addition of the edge $\langle X_0, X_i^{B_h} \rangle$ annotated with t satisfying $t + dist(X_i^{B_h}, X_j^a) - t \geq 0$. We have $dist(X_i^{B_h}, X_j^a) = dist(X_i^{B_h}, X_i^c) + dist(X_i^c, X_j^a)$ because the only node that $X_i^{B_h}$ is connected to is X_i^c. Also, by construction, $dist(X_i^{B_h}, X_i^c) = -d_h$. Therefore, we require to qualify all w_{B_h} such that $dist(X_i^c, X_j^a) - d_h \geq 0$—i.e. $d_h \leq dist(X_i^c, X_j^a)$. Now consider the value of t' that allows for the maximum resource consumption made by C without conflicting with A. This happens when we have the least possible value of t' such that $t' - t + dist(X_i^c, X_j^a) \geq 0$—i.e. $t - t' = dist(X_i^c, X_j^a)$. By construction, $dist(X_i^c, X_j^a)$ is present in D (if $dist(X_i^c, X_j^a) < 0$, C and $B_1, B_2 \ldots B_{|D|}$ are trivially equivalent). Let this be d_g. The maximum resource consumption made by C before it conflicts with A is then $\int_0^{t-t'} u_C(x)dx = \int_0^{dist(X_i^c, X_j^a)} u_C(x)dx$. The required weight of all w_{B_h} such that $d_h \leq d_g$ is $\int_0^{d_1} u_C(x)dx + \int_{d_1}^{d_2} u_C(x)dx \ldots \int_{d_{g-1}}^{d_g} u_C(x)dx = \int_0^{d_g} u_C(x)dx = \int_0^{dist(X_i^c, X_j^a)} u_C(x)dx$, hence establishing the truth of the Lemma.

Lemma 25: UPPER-ENVELOPE-HYBRID-AT-T is correct (see Figure 9).

ALGORITHM: LOWER-ENVELOPE-HYBRID
INPUT: An instance of the generalized resource-envelope problem P.
OUTPUT: $h(t)$ and a flexible schedule s achieving it.
(1) Construct P_1 from P as follows:
  (a) FOR all Type 3 action edges $C = \langle X_i, X_j \rangle$:
    (i) Compute $w_C = \int_0^{UB(C)} u_C(t) dt$.
  (b) FOR all action edges (Type 1, 2 or 3) $A = \langle X_i, X_j \rangle$:
    (i) Add the two complementary edges $\langle X_{-\infty}, X_i \rangle$ and $\langle X_j, X_{+\infty} \rangle$ ($X_{-\infty} = -\infty$ and $X_{+\infty} = +\infty$).
    (ii) Make $\langle X_{-\infty}, X_i \rangle$ a Type 1 action with weight w_A.
    (iii) Make $\langle X_j, X_{+\infty} \rangle$ a Type 1 action edge with weight w_A only if A is of Type 1.

(iv) Set the weight of A to 0 if it is of Type 1 or Type 2 and assign the rate function $u_A^{P_1}(t)$ if it is of Type 3. $u_A^{P_1}(t)$ satisfies $\int_0^t u_A^{P_1}(x) dx = \int_0^{UB(A)} u_A(x) dx - \int_0^t u_A(x) dx$.
(2) Construct P_2 from P_1 as follows:
  (a) FOR all temporal edges $\langle X_i, X_j \rangle$ in P_1 annotated with t:
    (i) Reverse $\langle X_i, X_j \rangle$ in P_2 to get $\langle X_i', X_j' \rangle$ annotated with t.
  (b) FOR a Type 3 action edge $C = \langle X_j', X_i' \rangle$ (originally $\langle X_i, X_j \rangle$ in P_1):
    (i) Reassign rate function $u_C^{P_2}(t) = u_C(UB(C) - t)$.
(3) RETURN:
  (a) $h(t)_{[P]} = \sum_{\text{all actions } A} w_A - g(-t)_{[P_2]}$.
  (b) $s_{[P]} = -s_{[P_2]}$.

Figure 10: $h(t)$ for the most general version of the problem.

Proof: The previous Lemma proves that $g(t)_{[P]} = g(t)_{[P']}$ and it remains to prove the correctness of $s_{[P]}$. If $B_h = \langle X_i^{B_h}, X_j^{B_h} \rangle$ is active in P', it must incorporate the addition of the edge $\langle X_0, X_i^{B_h} \rangle$ annotated with t without causing a negative cycle. This means that $dist(X_i^{B_h}, X_0) \geq -t$. Since X_i^c is the only node that $X_i^{B_h}$ is connected to, and this edge is annotated with $-d_h$, we have $dist(X_i^{B_h}, X_i^c) + dist(X_i^c, X_0) \geq -t$ or equivalently $dist(X_i^c, X_0) \geq -t + d_h$. This implies that C incorporates the addition of the edge $\langle X_0, X_i^c \rangle$ annotated with $t - d_h$ without creating any negative cycle. Since this is true for any active B_h, the maximum activation of C is obtained by considering the largest such h (assuming increasing order of $d_1, d_2 \ldots d_{|D|}$).

The $|sc|$ of UPPER-ENVELOPE-HYBRID-AT-T is dominated by the computation of integrals and the computation of shortest paths in $D(\mathcal{G})$. If K_1, K_2 and K_3 are respectively the number of Type 1, Type 2 and Type 3 actions, integrals are computed $O((K_1+1)K_3)$ times and there are $O((K_1 + 1)(K_1 + K_2 + K_3))$ pairs of nodes between which shortest paths are computed. Since $D(\mathcal{G})$ can have negative edges, the complexity of shortest path computation using the Bellman-Ford algorithm is $O(|\mathcal{X}||\mathcal{E}|)$. Hence, $|sc| = O((K_1 + 1)K_3\Im + (K_1 + 1)(K_1 + K_2 + K_3)|\mathcal{X}||\mathcal{E}|)$. Here, $\Im$ is the complexity of symbolic integration. The $|dc|$ of UPPER-ENVELOPE-HYBRID-AT-T is dominated by the time dependent discretization of Type 3 actions, and the computation of the largest weighted anti-chain in a POSET having at most $O(K_1 + K_2 + K_1K_3)$ nodes. Since the latter is related to a staged *max-flow* in a bipartite graph (see [1] and [4]), $|dc| = O(K_3\Im + (K_1 + K_2 + K_1K_3)^{2.5})$.

6 Computing the Lower Envelope $h(t)$

Given an instance P of the generalized resource-envelope problem, we show how to construct an instance Q such that a solution for $g(t)$ (and a flexible schedule that achieves it) on Q can be translated to a solution for $h(t)$ (and a flexible schedule that achieves it) on P. Figure 10 presents this idea, and a series of Lemmas are presented that prove its correctness.

Lemma 26: $h(t)_{[P]} = \sum_{\text{all actions } A} w_A - g(t)_{[P_1]}$ (see Figure 10).
Proof: For every schedule s, if $A = \langle X_i, X_j \rangle$ is a Type 1 action edge that is active in P, then it contributes a weight of 0 in P_1, and if it is not active in P, exactly one of its complementary edges $\langle X_{-\infty}, X_i \rangle$ or $\langle X_j, X_{+\infty} \rangle$ is active in P_1 and contributes a weight of w_A. Similarly, if A is a Type 2 action edge that is active in P, it contributes a weight of 0 in P_1, and if it is not active in P, its complementary edge $\langle X_{-\infty}, X_i \rangle$ contributes w_A in P_1. Again, if A is a Type 3 action edge that is not active in P, it contributes w_C in P_1, and if it is active to the degree d in P, it contributes $w_C - d$ in P_1. The foregoing statements imply that for a given schedule s, $(C_s(t))_{[P]} = \sum_A w_A - (C_s(t))_{[P_1]}$. Also, a schedule is consistent for P if and only if it is so for P_1 (because they have the same temporal constraints). Together, we can conclude that $h(t)_{[P]} = \sum_{\text{all actions } A} w_A - g(t)_{[P_1]}$.

However, $g(t)$ cannot be computed directly in P_1 because $u_A^{P_1}(t)$s defined on its Type 3 edges are negative, and the discretization of Type 3 edges for computing $g(t)$ was performed under the assumption that these rates are positive. P_1 is therefore transformed to P_2 such that $g(t)_{[P_1]} = g(-t)_{[P_2]}$ and yet, $u_C^{P_2}(t)$s defined on the Type 3 edges of P_2 are positive, hence making the application of the discretization procedure possible.

Lemma 27: $g(t)_{[P_1]} = g(-t)_{[P_2]}$ (see Figure 10).

Proof: For a constraint $X - Y \leq r$ in P_1, we would have $Y' - X' \leq r$ in P_2. These two constraints are equivalent if $Y' = -Y$ and $X' = -X$. Hence, s is a consistent schedule in P_1 if and only if $-s$ is a consistent schedule in P_2. If a Type 1 action $\langle X_i, X_j \rangle$ is active at time t in P_1, then the Type 1 action $\langle X_j', X_i' \rangle$ is active at time $-t$ in P_2. This is because the conditions $X_i \leq t$ and $X_j \geq t$ in P_1 and $X_j' \leq -t$ and $X_i' \geq -t$ in P_2 are equivalent when $X_i' = -X_i$ and $X_j' = -X_j$. Similarly, if a Type 3 action $\langle X_i, X_j \rangle$ is active at time t to a degree d in P_1, then the Type 3 action $\langle X_j', X_i' \rangle$ is active at time $-t$ to the same degree d in P_2. This can be established if we can prove that $\int_0^{t-X_i} u_C^{P_1}(x)dx = d$ is equivalent to $\int_0^{-t-X_j'} u_C^{P_2}(x)dx = d$. We have $\int_0^{t-X_i} u_C^{P_1}(x)dx = \int_0^{UB(C)} u_C(x)dx - \int_0^{t-X_i} u_C(x)dx = \int_{t-X_i}^{UB(C)} u_C(x)dx$. Since $X_j = X_i + UB(C)$ (because $LB(C) = UB(C)$ for any Type 3 action C), we have $\int_{t-X_i}^{UB(C)} u_C(x)dx = \int_{t-(X_j-UB(C))}^{UB(C)} u_C(x)dx = \int_{UB(C)-(X_j-t)}^{UB(C)} u_C(x)dx$. In P_2, since $X_j' = -X_j$, we have $\int_0^{-t-X_j'} u_C^{P_2}(x)dx = \int_0^{X_j-t} u_C^{P_2}(x)dx = \int_0^{X_j-t} u_C(UB(C) - x)dx = \int_{UB(C)-(X_j-t)}^{UB(C)} u_C(x)dx$ as required. Finally, since there are no Type 2 actions in the transformation of P to P_1, the truth of the Lemma is established.

Lemma 28: $h(t)_{[P]} = \sum_{\text{all actions } A} w_A - g(-t)_{[P_2]}$ and $s_{[P]} = -s_{[P_2]}$.

Proof: Follows directly from the arguments presented in the proofs of the previous two Lemmas.

The complexity of LOWER-ENVELOPE-HYBRID is dominated by the computation of $g(-t)_{[P_2]}$ and is therefore equal to that of UPPER-ENVELOPE-HYBRID-AT-T.

7 Conclusions and Future Work

We described efficient algorithms for variants of the resource-envelope problem (including the generalized version) by reducing them to largest weighted anti-chain computations in a POSET. The algorithms are constructive—producing flexible schedules that actually achieve the upper or lower bounds. We expect that this will potentially help us to save exponential amounts of work during search, along with providing good heuristic values to guide search, when compared to looser bounds (see [3], [5] and [6]). We are currently working on algorithms for plan dispatching that employ the resource-envelope computations as subroutines.

References

[1] Cormen T. H., Leiserson C. E. and Rivest R. L. 1990. Introduction to Algorithms. *Cambridge, MA, 1990.*

[2] Dechter R., Meiri I. and Pearl J. 1991. Temporal Constraint Networks. *AI Journal 49. 1991.*

[3] Kumar T. K. S. 2003. Incremental Computation of Resource-Envelopes in Producer-Consumer Models. *Proceedings of CP 2003.*

[4] Kumar T. K. S. 2004. A Polynomial-time Algorithm for Simple Temporal Problems with Piecewise Constant Domain Preference Functions. *Proceedings of AAAI 2004.*

[5] Laborie P. 2001. Algorithms for Propagating Resource Constraints in AI Planning and Scheduling: Existing Approaches and New Results. *Proceedings of ECP 2001.*

[6] Muscettola N. 2002. Computing the Envelope for Stepwise-Constant Resource Allocations. *CP 2002.*

Planning, Scheduling and Constraint Satisfaction: From Theory to Practice
L. Castillo et al. (Eds.)
IOS Press, 2005

Extending Allen Algebra to Manage Numeric and Metric Temporal Information

Malek Mouhoub

Department of Computer Science, University of Regina
3737 Wascana Parkway, Regina SK, Canada, S4S 0A2

Abstract. Representing and reasoning about numeric and symbolic aspects of time is crucial in many real-world applications such as planning, scheduling, language processing, molecular biology and temporal database. We present in this paper a modeling framework capable of representing these two types of information, in addition to activity constraints and composite variables, into a unique CSP-based constraint network that we call Conditional Composite Temporal Constraint Satisfaction Problem (CCTCSP). Activity constraints allow some constraint variables to be added dynamically to the problem to be solved. Composite variables are variables whose values are the possible constraint variables each composite variable can take. Dealing with activity constraints and composite variables is a challenging task since, in this particular case, the set of variables involved by the constraint problem to be solved are not known in advance. To solve a CCTCSP, we propose a method based on constraint propagation at both the symbolic and numeric levels. More precisely, this is achieved through arc consistency, path consistency and backtrack search using a forward check strategy.

1 Introduction

A well-know approach to managing the symbolic and numeric aspects of time is to view them as Constraint Satisfaction Problems (CSPs)[1][12, 9, 6]. We talk then about temporal constraint networks [1, 18, 4, 16]. In a temporal constraint network, variables, corresponding to temporal objects, are defined on a set of time points or time intervals while constraints can restrict the domains of the variables and/or represent the relative position between variables. The relative positions between variables can be qualitative or quantitative relations. Quantitative relations are temporal distances between temporal variables while qualitative relations represent incomplete and less specific symbolic information between variables. Constraint propagation techniques and backtrack search are then used to check the consistency of the temporal network and to infer new temporal information. While a considerable research work has been recently proposed to reasoning on the metric or the symbolic aspects of time (respectively through metric and qualitative networks) little work has been developed to manage both types of information. Meiri[10] has proposed a model based on a single network (time map) managing both constraints: metric constraints that restrict the distance between time points, and symbolic constraints that specify the relative positions between temporal objects (either

---

[1]A CSP involves a list of variables defined on discrete domains of values and a list of relations constraining the values that the variables can simultaneously take.

points or intervals). Kautz and Ladkin[7] have proposed a model allowing the representation and processing of metric temporal information in the form of a system of simple linear inequalities to encode metric relations between time points, and systems of binary constraints in Allen's qualitative temporal calculus to encode qualitative relations between time points. In Kautz and Ladkin approach, both kinds of constraints are independently processed in separate networks.

In a previous work [14, 13], we have developed a temporal model, TemPro, based on Allen's interval algebra [1] and a discrete representation of time to express numeric and symbolic time information in terms of qualitative and quantitative temporal constraints. More precisely, TemPro translates an application involving temporal information into a binary Constraint Satisfaction Problem[2] where variables are temporal events defined on domains of numeric intervals and binary constraints between variables correspond to disjunctions of Allen primitives. We call it Temporal Constraint Satisfaction Problem (TCSP)[3]. The resolution method for solving the TCSP is based on constraint propagation and requires two stages. In the first stage, local consistency is enforced by applying the arc consistency on variable domains and the path consistency on symbolic relations. A backtrack search algorithm is then performed in the second stage to check the consistency of the TCSP by looking for a feasible solution. Note that for some TCSPs, local consistency implies the consistency of the TCSP network [10]. The backtrack search phase can be avoided in this case. In order to deal with a large variety of real world applications, we present in this paper an extension of the modeling framework TemPro including:

- Representing numeric relative distance between temporal events. This is the case where the relation between two temporal events is expressed by a symbolic and a numeric value. For example, the sentence: *John arrives at work 5 minutes before Lisa*, includes both the symbolic relation *before* and the numeric distance between the end of the first event and the beginning of the second one.

- Handling conditional temporal constraints. This is the case where temporal variables can have either active or non active status. Only active variables require an assignment from their domain of values. Non active variables will not be considered during the resolution of the temporal network until they are activated . A temporal variable can be activated by default (in the initial problem) or via an activity constraint. Here, an activity constraint having the following form: $Ev_i, \cdots , Ev_j \overset{condition}{\rightarrow} Ev_q, \cdots , Ev_r$, is fired if *condition* holds and the events $Ev_i, \cdots , Ev_j$ are active. This activity constraint will then activate the events $Ev_q, \cdots , Ev_r$.

- Managing composite temporal variables. Composite temporal variables are those variables whose values are temporal events. In other words, the temporal events are the possible values the composite variables can take.

In the following section we will introduce, through an example, how we represent numeric and symbolic information into a Temporal Constraint Satisfaction Problem (TCSP) using our

---

[2]A binary CSP is a CSP where the constraints are binary relations between variables.

[3]Note that this name and the corresponding acronym was used in [4]. The TCSP, as defined by Dechter et al, is a quantitative temporal network used to represent only numeric temporal information. Nodes represent time points while arcs are labeled by a set of disjoint intervals denoting a disjunction of bounded differences between each pair of time points.

modeling framework TemPro. In Section 3 we present the different methods based on constraint propagation for solving TCSPs. Section 4 is dedicated to the management of composite variables and conditional constraints. Finally, concluding remarks and possible perspectives are listed in Section 5.

2   Managing Symbolic and Numeric Information

2.1   Representation of Symbolic Information

In TemPro, temporal objects are called events. An event has a uniform reified representation made up of a proposition and its temporal qualification: $Ev = OCCUR(p, I)$ defined by Allen [1] and denoting the fact that the proposition p occurred over the interval I. For the sake of notation simplicity, an event is used in this paper to denote its temporal qualification. Qualitative constraints specify the relative temporal position of an event with respect to other events. The qualitative constraint between two events ev_1 and ev_2 can take the following forms : $Ev_1\ r_1\ r_2 \dots r_n\ Ev_2$ where each of the r_i 's is one of the thirteen Allen primitives [1]. Figure 1 presents the definition of these primitives augmented by numeric distances as we will show in subsection 2.2.2.

2.2   Representation of Numeric Information

There are two types of numeric information that can be handled by our model. The first one constrains each event to occur within a temporal window while the second one specifies the relative numeric position between events.

2.2.1   Temporal Windows: SOPOs

Restricting an event to occur within a temporal window can be expressed by the fourfold $[begintime, endtime, duration, step]$ where $begintime$ and $endtime$ are respectively the earliest start time and latest end time of the corresponding event, $duration$ is the duration of the event and $step$ defines the distance between the starting time of two adjacent intervals within the temporal window. $begintime, endtime, duration$ and $step$ can be constant values or variables taking values from a discrete and finite domain. We can also use constraints in the form of equations or inequalities in order to restrict the values these variables can take. The fourfold is called a SOPO, i.e, the Set Of Possible Occurrences where the given event can take place. Thus, if e_i is an event numerically constrained by the SOPO $[inf_i, sup_i, d_i, s_i]$, then the set of possible occurrences of e_i is defined as follows:
$I = \{occ_j \mid begin(occ_j) = inf_i + k * s_i, end(occ_j) = begin(occ_j) + d_i, end(occ_j) <= sup_i, k \in [0, \frac{sup_i - inf_i - d_i}{s_i}] \cap \aleph\}$. $begin$ and end are functions on intervals that return the begin and the end points of a given interval, respectively.

2.2.2   Numeric Distances Between Events

As mentioned before, the symbolic relation between each pair of events is represented by the disjunction of Allen primitives. In order to represent the numeric relative information between events we have added a numeric information (distance between time points) to some of the Allen primitives as shown in figure 1. This allows us to represent temporal information

Relation	Symbol	Inverse	Meaning
X precedes(n) Y	P(n)	P-(n)	X ←—n—→ Y
X equals Y	E	E	X / Y
X meets Y	M	M-	X Y
X overlaps(n) Y	O(n)	O-(n)	X ←—n—→ Y
X during(n) Y	D(n)	D-(n)	Y X n
X starts(n) Y	S(n)	S-(n)	X / Y n
X finishes(n) Y	F(n)	F-(n)	Y X n

Figure 1: Extension of Allen Relations

such as: *"Mike arrives to work **3 minutes before Lisa**"*. This information will be represented
as follows. The symbolic relation that can hold between Mike and Lisa is $M \vee D \vee O \vee S \vee P$. When adding the numeric information (3 minutes), the relation will be: $M \vee D\,(3) \vee O\,(duration(Lisa) - 3) \vee S\,(3) \vee P\,(3 - duration(Lisa))$.

2.3   Example 1

To illustrate the concepts presented in previous subsections, let us see how we can transform
the following scheduling problem[4] into a TCSP using our model TemPro.

The production of five items A, B, C, D and E requires three mono processor machines M_1, M_2 and M_3. Each item can be produced using two different ways depending on the order in which the machines are used. The process time of each machine is variable and depends on the task to be processed. The following lists the different ways to produce each of the five items (the process time for each machine is mentioned in brackets):

item A:	$M_2(3), M_1(3), M_3(6)$ *or*
	$M_2(3), M_3(6), M_1(3)$
item B:	$M_2(2), M_1(5), M_2(2), M_3(7)$ *or*
	$M_2(2), M_3(7), M_2(2), M_1(5)$
item C:	$M_1(7), M_3(5), M_2(3)$ *or*
	$M_3(5), M_1(7), M_2(3)$
item D:	$M_2(4), M_3(6), M_1(7), M_2(4)$ *or*
	$M_2(4), M_3(6), M_2(4), M_1(7)$
item E:	$M_2(6), M_3(2)$ *or*
	$M_3(2), M_2(6)$

The goal here is to find a possible schedule of the different machines to produce the five
items and respecting all the constraints of the problem. Figure 2 illustrates the graph representation of the TCSP corresponding to the constraints needed to produce items A and B. We
assume that items A and B should be produced within 25 and 30 units of time respectively.
A temporal event corresponds here to the contribution of a given machine to produce a certain item. For example, the event AM_1 corresponds to the use of the machine M_1 to produce

---

[4]This problem is taken from [8].

the item A, ..., etc. Sixteen events are needed in total to produce the five items. The events required to produce items A and B are as follows:

item A: $AM_2(3), AM_1(3), AM_3(6)$ or
          $AM_2(3), AM_3(6), AM_1(3)$
item B: $BM_{21}(2), BM_1(5), BM_{22}(2), BM_3(7)$ or
          $BM_{21}(2), BM_3(7), BM_{22}(2), BM_1(5)$

The binary constraints between the different events are expressed by the disjunctions of the Allen primitives we presented in figure 1. For example, the relation $P \vee P^\smile \vee M \vee M^\smile$ between AM_3 and BM_3 are executed in a mutual exclusion since these two events are executed by the same mono processor machine. The translation to Allen primitives of the disjunction of the two sequences required to produce item B needs a 3-ary relation involving BM_1, BM_{22} and BM_3. This relation states that BM_{22} should occur between BM_1 and BM_3. Since our temporal network handles only binary relations, the way we use to represent this kind of 3-ary relations is as follows: we create an additional event (Ev_1) and represent the constraints for producing item B as shown in figure 2. The duration X of Ev_1 is greater (or equal) than the sum of the durations of BM_1, BM_{22} and BM_3. Thus, the SOPO corresponding to Ev_1 will be: $[0,30,X,1]$ where $X \geq 14$ (14 is the sum of the durations of BM_1, BM_{22} and BM_3). Note that we will not consider the symbolic information at this stage to adjust the earliest start and latest end of the different events. This will be handled at the resolution level.

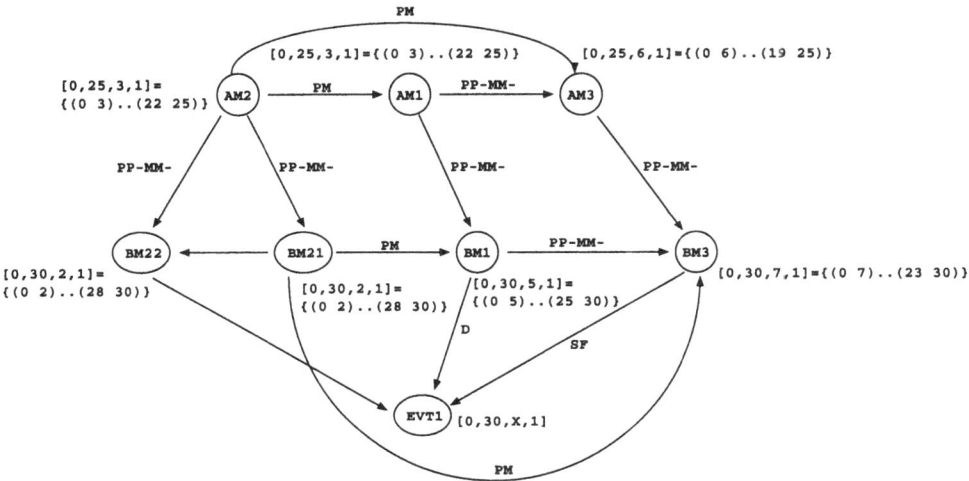

Figure 2: TCSP corresponding to a subset of the problem presented in example 1.

3 Resolution Techniques Based on Constraint Propagation

We present here a resolution method based on constraint propagation for solving TCSPs. The method involves two main stages. A filtering stage in which local consistency techniques and a numeric → symbolic conversion method are used to reduce the size of the search space by removing some inconsistent values. Backtrack search phase is then used to look for a possible solution. More precisely, our solving method works as follows.

Numeric → Symbolic Conversion. Perform the numeric → symbolic conversion on all the constraints. If one symbolic relation becomes empty then the constraint network is not consistent. The numeric → symbolic conversion works as follows: from the numeric information, we can extract the corresponding symbolic relation. An intersection of this relation with the given qualitative information will reduce the size of the latter which simplifies the size of the original problem. Although the exact algorithm that converts numeric to symbolic time information requires $O(e(Max(\frac{sup_i - inf_i - d_i}{s_i}))^2)$ in time where e is the number of qualitative constraints, we have defined a method that extracts most of the primitives within a relation between each pair of events in constant time reducing the complexity to $O(e)$. The method consists of using the information concerning the lower bound, upper bound and duration of the event temporal window instead of its occurrences. The pseudo-code of the method can be found in [13].

Path Consistency. Perform the path consistency algorithm PC-2 [17] on the symbolic relations. If the resulting graph is not path consistent then it is not consistent.

Arc Consistency. Perform the arc consistency algorithm AC-3 [19, 2] on the temporal windows. If the new graph is not arc consistent then it is not consistent.

Backtrack Search. Perform a backtrack search algorithm in order to look for a possible solution to the problem. The arc consistency algorithm is used here during the backtrack search in order to prevent earlier later failure.

Figure 3 illustrates the solution to the problem of example 1, provided by the above solving method. Note that this solution is optimal[5] but not unique.

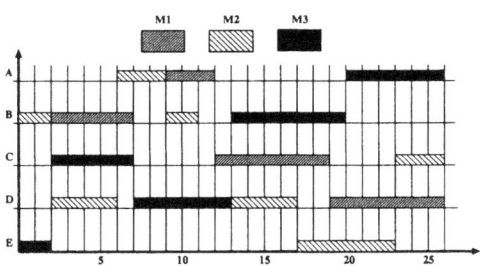

Figure 3: Optimal solution provided by the constraint propagation based method.

4 Managing Composite Variables and Conditional Constraints

Dealing with conditional and composite CSPs has already been reported in the literature [11, 15, 3, 5]. [11] introduced the notion of *Dynamic Constraint Satisfaction Problems* for configuration problems (renamed *Conditional Constraint Satisfaction Problems (CCSPs)* later).

---

[5]The total processing time of all machines needed to produce the five items, 26 seconds, is minimal

In contrast with the standard CSP paradigm, in a CCSP the set of variables requiring assignment is not fixed by the problem definition. A variable has either *active* or *nonactive* status. An activity constraint enforces the change of the status of a given variable from *nonactive* to *active*. In [15], Freuder and Sabin have extended the traditional CSP framework by including the combination of three new CSP paradigms: *Meta CSPs, Hierarchical Domain CSPs, and Dynamic CSPs*. This extension is called *composite CSP*. In a composite CSP, the variable values can be entire sub-CSPs. A domain can be a set of variables instead of atomic values (as it is the case in the traditional CSP). The domains of variable values can be hierarchically organized. The participation of variables in a solution is dynamically controlled by activity constraints.

We adopt the above two paradigms (CCSPs and composite CSPs) and extend our modeling framework TemPro by including conditional temporal constraints and composite temporal events. We call conditional TCSP (CTCSP) a TCSP augmented by activity constraints. Solving a CTCSP can be seen like solving a TCSP dynamically i.e. when some of the variables and their corresponding constraints are added dynamically during the resolution of the TCSP. We call a composite CTCSP (CCTCSP) a CTCSP including composite temporal variables. A CCTCSP represents a finite set of possible CTCSPs where each CTCSP corresponds to a complete assignment of values (temporal events) to composite variables. Solving a CCTCSP consists of finding a feasible scenario for one of its possible CTCSPs. Let us consider the following examples illustrating a given CCTCSP.

Example 2

> *John, Mike and Lisa work for a company. It takes John **20 minutes**, Mike **25 minutes** and Lisa **30 minutes** to get to work. Every day, John left home **between 7:20 and 7:26**. Mike arrives at work **between 7:55 and 8** and Lisa arrives at work **between 7:50 and 8**. We also know that John and Mike meet on their way to work, that Mike arrives to work before Lisa and that Lisa and John go to work at the same time.*

The above example is translated to the TCSP represented by the graph in figure 4a. Let us assume now that we have the following new information.

> *John may stop at a gas station. It takes him **10 minutes** to drive to the gas station and fill up the gas. If John stops at the gas station, it takes him **15 minutes** to arrive at work **between 7:50 and 7:55**. However John will not stop at the gas station if he is late. John will not meet Mike if he stops at the gas station.*

John's event will be represented here as a composite temporal event whose domain contains the following values: $JWork$ and $JGas$ which represent respectively the events *John goes directly to work* and *John goes to the gas station*. In addition we define the following activity constraint: $JGas \longrightarrow GWork$. $GWork$ represents the event: John goes from the gas station to work. Figure 4b describes the CCTCSP corresponding to the above example and including composite events and activity constraints. In the figure, temporal events are represented by rectangle solid line nodes while composite events are represented by rectangle dash line nodes. The activity constraint is denoted by a solid arrow with a small diamond in the middle and is labeled with the condition and the temporal constraint that will link the two events if the activity constraint is fired. A temporal constraint between two temporal events is represented by a solid arrow while a temporal constraint involving at least one composite event has one of the following forms:

Case 1: the temporal constraint involves 1 event Ev and a composite variable X.

- A solid arrow labeled with a temporal relation R, in the case where all the temporal events in the domain of X have the same temporal relation R with Ev. This is, for example, the case of the relation "$ESS^\smile$" between the event Lisa and the composite variable John.

- A dash arrow labeled with a list of temporal constraints, $R_1, \ldots, R_n$, where each of the R_is denotes respectively a temporal constraint between Ev and each temporal event in the domain of X. This is the case of the relations "$EOO^\smile SS^\smile FF^\smile DD^\smile$" and "I" between the event Mike and the composite variable John. "I" denotes here the disjunction of the 13 Allen primitives.

Case 2: the temporal constraint involves 2 composite variables X and Y.

- A solid arrow labeled with a temporal relation R, in the case where all the temporal events in the domain of X have the same temporal relation with all the temporal events in the domain of Y.

- A dash line labeled with the list: Ev_{X_1} R_{11} $Ev_{Y_1}, \ldots, Ev_{X_n}$ R_{nm} Ev_{Y_m} where $\{Ev_{X_1}, \ldots, Ev_{X_n}\}$ and $\{Ev_{Y_1}, \ldots, Ev_{Y_m}\}$ are respectively the domains of X and Y, and each of the R_{ij}s is a temporal constraint between Ev_{X_i} and Ev_{Y_j}.

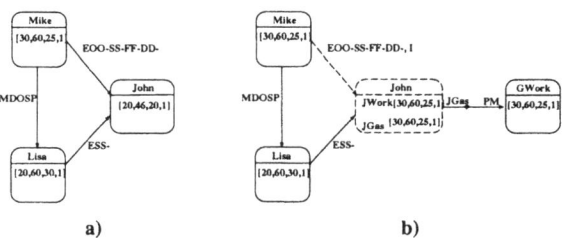

Figure 4: CCTCSP representing the example 2.

Solving a CTCSP requires a backtrack search algorithm with exponential complexity in time, $O(D^N)$, where N is the number of temporal events and D the domain size of each event. The possible number of CTCSPs the CCTCSP involves is d^M where d is the domain size of composite variables and M the number of composite variables. Thus solving a CCTCSP requires a backtrack search algorithm of complexity $O(D^N \times d^M)$. To overcome this difficulty in practice, we propose a solving method based on constraint propagation techniques and backtrack search. The backtrack search is used here for both the generation of the possible CTCSPs and the resolution of each CTCSP. The algorithm will stop if a consistent CTCSP has been found. Constraint propagation through arc and path consistencies is used here before and during the backtrack search to detect earlier any inconsistent CTCSP. This will save a lot of efforts needed to check the consistency of the CCTCSP. More precisely, the resolution method includes the following steps.

1. The method starts with an initial problem containing a list of initially activated temporal events and composite variables. Numeric $\rightarrow$ symbolic conversion and Local consistency (path and arc consistency) are applied on the initial temporal events in the same way as described in Section 2. If the temporal events are not consistent then the method will stop. The CCTCSP is inconsistent in this case.

2. Activate any variable if the activating condition is true. Use numeric $\rightarrow$ symbolic conversion, path and arc consistency to maintain the local consistency of the old and the new activated events. The method will stop if a local inconsistency is detected since the CCTCSP in inconsistent in this case.

3. Pick a variable from the list of composite variables.

4. Assign a value (temporal event) to the chosen composite variable. In other words we replace the composite variable with a chosen event from its domain. Run numeric $\rightarrow$ symbolic conversion, arc and path consistencies on the old events and the new one. If an inconsistency is detected backtrack and choose another temporal event for the composite variable. This process will continue until we find an event from the domain of the composite variable which is consistent with the old events. If such event is not found, backtrack to the previously assigned composite variable and goto step 4.

5. Activate any variable generated by the added event of the last step and run numeric $\rightarrow$ symbolic conversion and local consistency in the same way as shown in step 2. If a local inconsistency is detected, backtrack to step 4 and choose another value for the current composite variable.

6. Repeat steps 3, 4 and 5 until all the composite variables are processed. As a result, an arc and path consistent TCSP will be generated.

7. Perform a backtrack search algorithm on the generated TCSP. Return a solution if it is found otherwise backtrack to step 4 and choose another event for the last assigned composite variable. If all events of all composite variables have been tried without success then the CCTCSP is inconsistent.

5 Conclusion

In this paper we propose a modeling framework for representing numeric and symbolic time information, conditional constraints and composite variables within a single constraint network that we call CCTCSP. Solving a CCTCSP consists of finding a solution to one of its possible TCSPs. This requires an exponential time algorithm to go through the different TCSPs in addition to the exponential time cost for solving each TCSP. To overcome this difficulty in practice, we have defined a solving method based on constraint propagation in order to prevent any inconsistencies at the earlier stage of the resolution process.

In order to evaluate in practice the performance of the method we propose, we intend to implement it and test it on randomly generated CCTCSPs as well as on real world applications.

References

[1] J.F. Allen, 'Maintaining knowledge about temporal intervals', *CACM*, **26**(11), 832–843, (1983).

[2] C. Bessière and J. C. Régin, 'Refining the basic constraint propagation algorithm', in *Seventeenth International Joint Conference on Artificial Intelligence (IJCAI'01)*, pp. 309–315, Seattle, WA, (2001).

[3] E. C. Freuder D. Sabin and R. J. Wallace, 'Greater efficiency for conditional constraint satisfaction', *Proc., Ninth International Conference on Principles and Practice of, Constraint Programming - CP 2003*, **2833**, 649–663, (2003).

[4] R. Dechter, I. Meiri, and J. Pearl, 'Temporal constraint networks', *Artificial Intelligence*, **49**, 61–95, (1991).

[5] E. Gelle and B. Falting, 'Solving mixed and conditional constraint satisfaction problems', *Constraints*, **8**, 107–141, (2003).

[6] R.M. Haralick and G.L. Elliott, 'Increasing tree search efficiency for Constraint Satisfaction Problems.', *Artificial Intelligence*, **14**, 263–313, (1980).

[7] H.A. Kautz and P.B. Ladkin, 'Integrating metric and qualitative temporal reasoning', in *AAAI'91*, pp. 241–246, Anaheim, CA, (1991).

[8] P. Laborie, *Une approche intégrée pour la gestion de ressources et la synthèse de plans*, Ph.D. dissertation, École Nationale Supérieure des Télécommunications, 1995.

[9] A. K. Mackworth, 'Consistency in networks of relations', *Artificial Intelligence*, **8**, 99–118, (1977).

[10] I. Meiri, 'Combining qualitative and quantitative constraints in temporal reasoning', *Artificial Intelligence*, **87**, 343–385, (1996).

[11] S. Mittal and B. Falkenhainer, 'Dynamic constraint satisfaction problems', in *Proceedings of the 8th National Conference on Artificial Intelligence*, pp. 25–32, Boston, MA, (August 1990). AAAI Press.

[12] U. Montanari, 'Fundamental properties and applications to picture processing', *Information Sciences*, **7**, 95–132, (1974).

[13] M. Mouhoub, 'Reasoning with numeric and symbolic time information', *Artificial Intelligence Review*, **21**, 25–56, (2004).

[14] M. Mouhoub, F. Charpillet, and J.P. Haton, 'Experimental Analysis of Numeric and Symbolic Constraint Satisfaction Techniques for Temporal Reasoning.', *Constraints: An International Journal*, **2**, 151–164, Kluwer Academic Publishers, (1998).

[15] D. Sabin and E. C. Freuder, 'Configuration as composite constraint satisfaction', in *Proceedings of the (1st) Artificial Intelligence and Manufacturing Research Planning Workshop*, ed., George F. Luger, pp. 153–161. AAAI Press, 1996, (1996).

[16] P. van Beek, 'Reasoning about qualitative temporal information', *Artificial Intelligence*, **58**, 297–326, (1992).

[17] P. van Beek and D. W. Manchak, 'The design and experimental analysis of algorithms for temporal reasoning', *Journal of Artificial Intelligence Research*, **4**, 1–18, (1996).

[18] M. Vilain and H. Kautz, 'Constraint propagation algorithms for temporal reasoning', in *AAAI'86*, pp. 377–382, Philadelphia, PA, (1986).

[19] Y. Zhang and R. H. C. Yap, 'Making ac-3 an optimal algorithm', in *Seventeenth International Joint Conference on Artificial Intelligence (IJCAI'01)*, pp. 316–321, Seattle, WA, (2001).

Planning, Scheduling and Constraint Satisfaction: From Theory to Practice
L. Castillo et al. (Eds.)
IOS Press, 2005

Integration of fuzzy scheduling into a planning framework

Luis Castillo, Juan Fdez-Olivares, Antonio González*
Dpt. of Computer Science and AI, ETSI Informatica
Universidad de Granada, Spain
email: {L.Castillo,Faro,A.Gonzalez}@decsai.ugr.es

Abstract. This paper presents an approach for the representation and handling of soft temporal constraints in a planning framework. It is achieved in two steps. The first one is the representation of soft temporal constraints by means of fuzzy subsets of a real timeline. And the second one is the successful integration of the temporal reasoning capabilities of a scheduler able to handle these constraints into a planning framework. Then, the result is a temporal planner able to handle ill defined temporal knowledge and to obtain flexible temporal plans, that is, plans whose branches may be safely rescheduled to react to unforeseen delays during their execution.

1 Motivation

The use of AI planning techniques in real world problems requires a number of additional techniques to be integrated to successfully solve a problem. Most of them focus on the dynamism of real world and try to break the usual rigidity of planning systems and obtain flexible planning approaches in any of the forms that flexibility might be interpreted, let say, actions with unpredictable outcomes, plans with conditional branches, planning frameworks able to react to execution failures or to acquire missing knowledge. We present two of these techniques that have been integrated in our planner named MACHINE^{TF}. On the one hand, MACHINE^{TF} allows for the representation and handling of soft temporal constraints as temporal knowledge like deadlines or durations that may not be precisely defined or that represents a soft preference over the timeline. This issue is very important in many real world applications, where the temporal bounds of activities is implicitly considered as flexible bounds at some extent.

On the other hand, the planner is extended with constraint processing capabilities in order to successfully handle these soft constraints. This is achieved by drawing plans (a partially ordered sequence of actions) on top a Fuzzy Simple Temporal Constraint Network [9] (FTCN), a type of temporal constraints network that generalizes the classical Simple Temporal Network [2]. This is a very subtle integration since many of the skills needed to handle temporal constraints are part of scheduling systems. However, MACHINE^{TF} integrates these constraint handling techniques into its planning architecture as intimate parts of the main loop of the planning algorithm. This implies, for example, that an inconsistency of the constraints makes the planner to backtrack immediately or that the consistency of the constraints is included in the heuristic evaluation function that drives the heuristic search of the planning algorithm.

*This work has been partially supported by Spanish MCyT under project TIC2002-04146-C05-02.

2 Extending the knowledge representation

The starting point to be addressed when extending a planning model to account for new knowledge is its model of actions, that is, the way the planning framework represent changes in the world. Other issues to be defined are the definition of problems and the definition of plans. In this case, we have extended the basic model of action of our planner MACHINE [1], a partial order causal link based planner [12], to allow the representation of fuzzy temporal constraints.

2.1 Why and how fuzzy temporal constraints

Planning for real problems is nothing without a valid execution of the plan, and this often implies the need to deal with temporal constraints if one wants to obtain a realistic solution. Some examples of these constraints are the statement of a makespan, the duration of actions, the temporal distance between pair of actions or deadlines goals. There are several examples in the literature that have defined approaches to deal with these constraints [3, 5, 11], however, in many real problems, some (or many) of these constraints are not rigidly defined. This lack of rigidity appears in several different ways. For example, once the user defines a makespan or a deadline goal for a problem that is too strict and no solution may be found, usually he/she tries to relax the constraints so that a consistent solution may be found.

Let us consider that we have designed a plan to carry a package from one location to another including loading, transportation and unloading actions. Let us suppose that the maximum duration for the unloading operation is 60 time units and the whole makespan is 240 time units maximum. A rigid interpretation of temporal constraints would imply a chain of execution failures if the unloading operation takes 61 time units and the makespan finally grows up to 243 time units, and also, in the case of more complex plans, it will surely raise important questions about the causal correctness of the remaining plan. In real life, and depending on acceptability criteria, this relative delay could be acceptable if nothing else can be done and the goal is finally achieved. Perhaps an interval based representation could be appropriate and we could accept that the duration of the unloading could be represented like $[60 - \delta_1, 60 + \delta_1]$ and the makespan like $[0, 240 + \delta_2]$ where δ_1, δ_2 depend on acceptability criteria. This interval based representation has been used in the literature as a valid means to deal with temporal imprecision or temporal preference in planning systems [10, 6], however it presents some drawbacks that need to be clarified. Let us suppose in the previous example that $\delta_1 = 2$ and $\delta_2 = 4$. This would make the execution of the previous plan acceptable, but it would also allow the planner to accept a longer plan with a makespan of say 244.

However, this does not reflect exactly the desires of the user when he relaxed the restrictions. A relaxation of the temporal constraints is not only a widening of the bounds of the constraint, but also a distribution of his preference. In the example, he accepts a makespan between 240 and 244 but, and this is the most important, not all of them are equally preferred, the planner should give priority to plans whose makespan is closer or under 240 time units. At this point it is clear that an interval based representation is not able to represent this information and, therefore, it does not seem expressive enough to represent appropriately the semantics of a relaxation of the constraints in a temporal planning framework.

In order to solve this representation problem, we propose the use of fuzzy intervals to model the concept of soft temporal constraints in temporal planning frameworks as a more

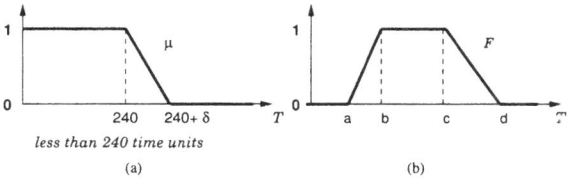

Figure 1: Two fuzzy temporal intervals

expressive formalism able to represent the preferences of the user when he relaxes a temporal constraint, so that the strict constraint represents what the user *desires*, with the highest
priority, and the relaxed constraint represents what the user *would admit* in the case that his
desires cannot be satisfied and giving priority to the values closer to the strict satisfiability. A
fuzzy interval, like that shown in Figure 1.a, is able to represent this information by means
of its membership function μ, i.e., the degree of satisfaction of a temporal constraint over the
timeline [4]. Strict satisfiability is represented as the set of values t such that $\mu(t) = 1$, that
is, the strict desires of the user. The soft constraint is represented as the set of values t such
that $0 < \mu(t) < 1$, i.e., those values that are admissible and that are ordered in preference to
the strict satisfiability, and finally, those values t such that $\mu(t) = 0$ are not admissible at all.
Therefore, the preference of the user regarding a relaxed temporal constraint C are perfectly
modeled as the following membership function

$$\forall t \in T, \mu_C(t) = \alpha$$

where $\alpha \in [0, 1]$ represents the degree of satisfaction of the constraint C. This idea of constraint relaxation, very well known in many CSP approaches [7] indeed, is the main motivation of this paper for dealing with fuzzy sets like the one shown in Figure 1.b that will be
noted as a tuple with their respective points $F = (a, b, c, d)$[1]. In particular, the different types
of fuzzy temporal constraints that will be used are shown in Figure 2.

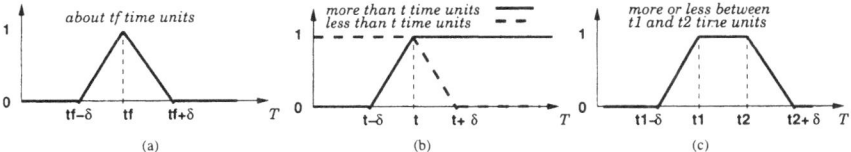

Figure 2: Three different types of fuzzy temporal constraints. The value δ encodes the admissibility limits for
each constraint.

2.2 Actions, preconditions and effects

An action a in MACHINE^{TF} is represented by means of two time points, namely $start(a)$
and $end(a)$, and it has has some effects, that is, some changes in its environment and every
effect is not immediate but takes some time to be achieved. This time may not be precisely
known, so it is represented as the fuzzy temporal constraint "about t_f time units" (Figure 2.a)
that must be between $start(a)$ and $end(a)$. If the delay is perfectly known then $\delta = 0$.

---

[1]Note that this fuzzy notation may also represent a strict interval $[b, c]$ as the tuple (b, b, c, c).

An action also has preconditions, that is, conditions that have to be made true by the effect of another action prior to its execution. Since effects take some time to be achieved this is one of the main source of (soft) temporal constraint posting between actions. Let us consider that the condition f of action a is satisfied by the effect f of action b that takes "about tf time units" to be achieved. Then there must be a (soft) temporal constraint that enforces $start(a)$ to be "more than t_f time units" after $start(b)$ (Figure 2.b).

Finally, actions have a duration that may be either unbounded (not restricted a priori) or bounded. Bounded actions may have a maximum duration ($maxbound$) allowed specified in terms of "less than $maxbound$ time units" (Figure 2.b). All the actions have an minimum duration, that is, the duration required to obtain all its effects.

Then, the *domain* of a planning problem is the set of actions available to solve that problem. In the following we will use examples from a well known planning domain named Zeno [8]. In this domain, there may be planes, cities and persons. Persons may board or debark the plane, the plane may flight at different speeds (different flight times) between cities and may also refuel and the goal is to obtain several traveling plans.

2.3 Problems

Problems are stated like a conjunction of subproblems (literals) that must be solved, so the planner must design a sequence of actions from the domain that achieve these subproblems. In the domain of Zeno a possible goal would be (at scott city-c) to find a plan for a trip for Scott to travel from city-a to city-c. However, a problem may also include soft temporal constraints. like deadlines or makespans. In the case of deadlines, some of the literals have to be achieved at a given time. Deadlines are expressed as a soft constraint in any of the forms shown in Figure 2. For example the deadline goal (at scott city-c) AT (11pm-δ, 11pm, 11pm, 11pm+δ) might be used to require Scott to arrive in city-c "more or less at 11 pm". Makespans involving the total length of the plan may also be described by means of a soft temporal constraint like any of the ones shown in Figure 2.

On the other hand, plans are a partially ordered sequence of action deployed over a FTCN.

Definition 1. *A Fuzzy Simple Temporal Constraint Network* $\mathcal{N} = \langle \mathcal{X}, \mathcal{C} \rangle$ *is composed of a set of variables* $\mathcal{X} = \{X_0, X_1, \ldots, X_{n+1}\}$ *and a set of fuzzy binary temporal constraints defined between them* $\mathcal{C} = \{C_{ij} | 0 \leq i, j \leq n + 1\}$ *[9].*

Every variable X_i is a crisp variable whose domain is the real time scale T. Variables X_0 and X_{n+1} are two dummy variables used to represent the beginning and the end of the network. Every fuzzy binary constraint C_{ij} restricts the possible relative values of X_i and X_j, i.e., $X_j - X_i \leq C_{ij}$. Every constraint C_{ij} is defined as any of the types shown in Figure 2 and it is represented by a possibility distribution π_{ij} over the continuous time scale T. In the framework of MACHINE^{TF}, a FTCN is used to represent a fuzzy temporal plan where every variable represents the execution time of one of the actions of the plan and every fuzzy binary temporal constraint is posted during the resolution process every time that an action solves a subgoal or when actions are reordered to avoid interferences between them, as will be explained later. Figure 3 shows a soft temporal plan where the annotations under each action a represent the soft constraint defined for $start(a)$, i.e., $C_{start(a),0}$ in the FTCN.

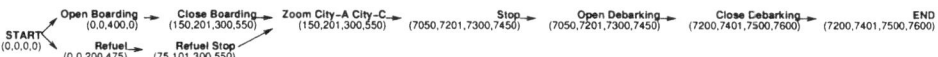

Figure 3: A soft temporal plan for the zeno problem under the makespan constraint (0,0,7500,7600)

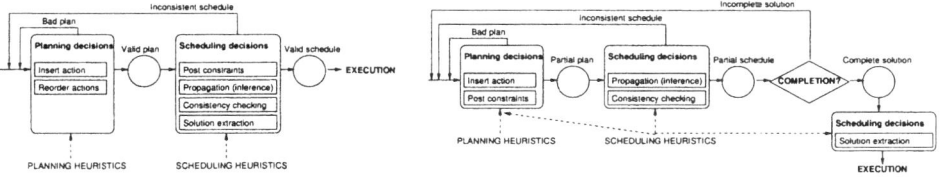

Figure 4: Two different models for the integration of planning and scheduling

3 Integration of planning and fuzzy scheduling

Obviously, in order to successfully handle all these soft temporal constraints, the planning algorithm should be extended to cope with some temporal reasoning capabilities that traditionally belong to scheduling systems like constraint posting and propagation, consistency checking or solution extraction. In the literature, there are mainly two families of architectures for the integration of planning and scheduling. On the one hand (left hand side of Figure 4) a planner and a scheduler execute one after the other in a waterfall model. This model is easier to implement but has many drawbacks mainly related to backtracking points between both isolated systems. Instead, we have followed an interleaved integration (right hand side of Figure 4) where part of the decisions of the scheduler have been introduced intimately into the planning engine. This is easily done by introducing constraint handling procedures of FTCN at every step of the planning process and leaving some of these capabilities until the end of the planning stage. This integration overcomes the backtracking problems of the former approach so that, for example, an inconsistency of the soft constraints makes the planner to backtrack immediately and the consistency of the constraints is included in the heuristic evaluation function that drives the heuristic search of the planning algorithm.

A very interesting issue of this integration is that a soft temporal plan, like the one shown in Figure 3, does not represent a unique solution but a set of solutions such that all of them have the same actions, but they might be scheduled for execution in different orders, all of them consistent with the FTCN of the temporal plan. This is very important since during the design of the plan, MACHINE^{TF} does not commit to assign a precise execution time for every action like most temporal planners [3, 5, 11]. This excess of commitment would make the planner to increase the number of backtracks. Instead, MACHINE^{TF} maintains only the consistency of the soft temporal plan without commit to a crisp solution. Only at the end of the planning process, a ground solution is found and scheduled for execution.

In other words. A crisp solution to a FTCN is a tuple of crisp values $s = (x_0, \ldots, x_{n+1})$ which represents an assignment of the form $X_i = x_i, x_i \in T$. In the framework of MACHINE^{TF}, a solution is an schedule of its actions, that is, an assignment of a crisp execution time for every action of the plan that may be used to execute the plan in practice. The set of solutions of a FTCN may be easily obtained by a solution extraction procedure (Figure 5) and every solution has a degree of consistency which quantifies how accurate the solution is with respect to the constraints of the FTCN.

Definition 2. *A σ-possible solution of a FTCN $\mathcal{N}$ is a tuple $s = (x_0, x_1, \ldots, x_{n+1})$ that*

verifies that $\pi_S(s) = \sigma$ and

$$\pi_S(s) = \min_{0 \leq i,j \leq n+1} \pi_{ij}(x_j - x_i) \tag{1}$$

Additionally, the most accurate solution that could be obtained from the set of solutions to a FTCN is given by the following value α, that may be used as a measure of the "goodness" of the FTCN (the fuzzy temporal plan).

Definition 3. *A FTCN is α-consistent if the set of possible solutions $S \subseteq \mathcal{R}^{n+2}$ verifies*

$$\sup_{s \in S} \pi_S(s) = \alpha \tag{2}$$

In the framework of MACHINE^{TF}, the meaning of the value α is a generalization of the motivation for using fuzzy sets and it needs a further explanation. MACHINE^{TF} is deterministic, that is, all the plans found are valid to solve the problem, so the main difference between all possible valid plans is the degree of satisfaction of the soft temporal constraints α. Those valid plans with the highest value, $\alpha = 1$, are those plans such that there is at least a solution (schedule) that satisfy completely the desires of the user. On the contrary, those plans such that $0 < \alpha < 1$ are admissible plans, that is, plans that contain only admissible solutions (schedules) that do not satisfy the desires of the user but they still satisfy the constraints at some degree greater than 0. A question that immediately arises from this integration is, given that MACHINE^{TF} only commits to a solution at the end of the planning process how does it know which is the best plan, that is, that with a higher value α and therefore the most promising plan?

3.1   Heuristic featuring of fuzzy temporal constraint networks

The answer to the question above may seem easy but it poses a difficult question. Given Equation 2, the value of the maximum degree of consistency α of a FTCN might be a very good source of information for decision making, but up to now, it cannot be obtained analytically. When all of the fuzzy temporal constraints in a FTCN are normalized, i.e., $hgt(\pi_{ij}) = 1$[2]. the degree of consistency α is equal to 1, that is, there is at least one solution that completely meets the constraints [9], otherwise $0 \leq \alpha < 1$. In these cases some search algorithm like simulated annealing or genetic algorithms could be used to find that value, but this will degrade severely the performance of MACHINE^{TF} since this process should be launched to evaluate every possible plan being built.

In the framework of MACHINE^{TF}, although the value of α is not known, it may be bounded and used to guide the search of the planning process. On one hand, a greedy algorithm that encapsulates the solution extraction procedure (Figure 5) is used several times to non deterministically generate a set of candidate solutions following Equation 2. Infeasible solutions ($\sigma = 0$) are rejected and the remaining ones are evaluated following Equation 1 such that the best degree of possibility of these candidates is kept[3] $\delta_l = \max_i \pi_S(sol_i)\ i = 1, \ldots, k$.
Clearly, $\delta_l \leq \alpha$.

---

[2]$hgt(\pi) = \max_{t \in T} \pi(t)$.

[3]The number or runs, k, is fixed previously to the planning process and the greedy algorithm stops when it achieves $\delta_l = 1$ or after k runs.

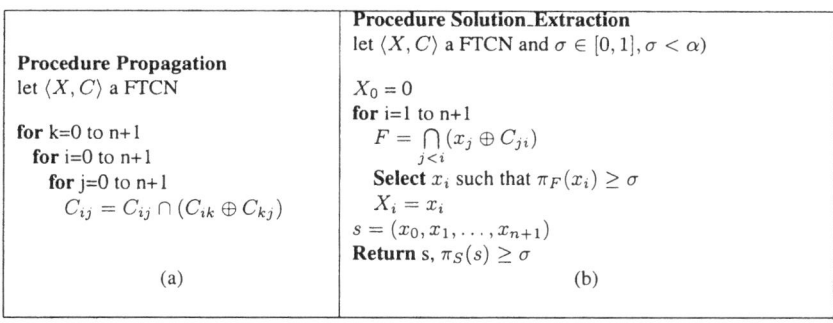

| **Procedure Propagation**
let $\langle X, C \rangle$ a FTCN

for k=0 to n+1
  for i=0 to n+1
    for j=0 to n+1
      $C_{ij} = C_{ij} \cap (C_{ik} \oplus C_{kj})$

(a) | **Procedure Solution_Extraction**
let $\langle X, C \rangle$ a FTCN and $\sigma \in [0,1], \sigma < \alpha$)

$X_0 = 0$
for i=1 to n+1
  $F = \bigcap_{j < i} (x_j \oplus C_{ji})$
  Select x_i such that $\pi_F(x_i) \geq \sigma$
  $X_i = x_i$
$s = (x_0, x_1, \ldots, x_{n+1})$
Return s, $\pi_S(s) \geq \sigma$

(b) |

Figure 5: Some algorithms to handle soft temporal constraints inside the planning algorithm (see right hand side of Figure 4). (a) constraint propagation and (b) solution extraction. $\oplus$ and $\ominus$ are the sum and subtraction operations defined for fuzzy numbers [4, 9]

On the other hand, let us consider the following value $\delta_u = \min_i hgt(\pi_{0i})$ for a FTCN. Given equation 2, it is easy to prove that $\alpha \leq \delta_u$. This is a rather good estimation since it has been obtained from a simplified model: in the case of absolute FTCNs, that is, FTCNs where only absolute constraints of the form C_{0i} are posted and every relative constraint $C_{ij}, i, j \neq 0$ is a transitive constraint, it may be proven that $\alpha = \delta_u$.

Then, both values δ_l and δ_u bounds the unknown value of α

$$\alpha \in [\delta_l, \delta_u]$$

Since the exact value of α is unknown, the centroid of this interval is used to estimate it. This value is then used by MACHINE^{TF} as a secondary ranking criterion during the search process, where the primary ranking criterion is the heuristic evaluation function of MACHINE, that has proven to be very useful in several domains [1]. This implies a deeper integration of planning and scheduling techniques since now the heuristic evaluation that guides the steps of the planner also takes into account the degree of temporal consistency in such a way that, given two plans with the same solving power, MACHINE^{TF} will choose that with the higher temporal consistency. Now, let see how the planner handles all the soft temporal constraints.

3.2 Handling soft temporal constraints during planning

The main loop of the planning algorithm is a best first search guided by a ranking function that takes into account the usefulness of the plan being constructed [1] and the soft consistency of temporal constraints, as explained before. At every step, a pending subgoal is selected for its resolution so that either a new action or a existing one are used to solve it. In both cases new soft temporal constraints are posted to ensure a correct ordering of actions, propagated by means of an all-pairs polynomial algorithm (Figure 5.a), and the soft temporal consistency of the resulting plan is evaluated and taken into account for its ranking. Eventually, if some interferences between concurrent actions is detected, this is corrected by adding new soft temporal constraints to produce a reordering of the actions that avoids the interference.

Goal Satisfaction Let us suppose that an action a with an effect f that takes "about t_f time units", solves a precondition of an action b. Then the following soft temporal constraint

$$start(b) \geq start(a) \oplus (t_f - \delta, t_f, t_f, t_f + \delta)$$

is posted and propagated (Figure 5). The satisfaction of a subgoal is recorded in a structure called causal link in order to avoid that no action that deletes f could overlap in the interval between $start(a)$ and $start(b)$.

Duration of actions For all actions, either with maximum duration $maxbound$ or not, post and propagate

$$dur^{min}(a) = \max_{f' \, in \, effects(a)} (t_{f'} - \delta, t_{f'}, t_{f'}, t_{f'} + \delta)$$

$$dur^{max}(a) = \begin{cases} (-\infty, -\infty, +\infty, +\infty) \text{ (unspecified)} \\ (maxbound - \delta, maxbound, maxbound, maxbound + \delta) \text{ (bounded)} \end{cases}$$

$$start(a) \oplus dur^{max}(a) \geq end(a) \geq start(a) \oplus dur^{min}(a)$$

Deadline goals For every deadline goal g, with deadline $(t_{min} - \delta, t_{min}, t_{max}, t_{max} + \delta)$, meaning that goal g must be achieved "more or less between times t_{min} and t_{max}", which has been solved by an action a with its effect f that takes "about t_f time units", the following soft constraint is posted and propagated.

$$start(a) = (t_{min} - \delta, t_{min}, t_{max}, t_{max} + \delta) \ominus (t_f - \delta, t_f, t_f, t_f + \delta)$$

Concurrent actions and threats Say that action c with the effect $(not \, f)$ that takes "about t_f time units" overlaps with a casual link from actions a to b with respect to the effect f. Then, the overlapping must be avoided by reordering the threatening action c by promotion (putting c after all the effects of b)

$$start(c) \geq start(b) \oplus dur^{min}(b)$$

or demotion (putting a after the negative effect of c)

$$start(a) \geq start(c) \oplus (t_{not(f)} - \delta, t_{not(f)}, t_{not(f)}, t_{not(f)} + \delta)$$

With these new capabilities for handling soft temporal constraints, MACHINE^{TF} is able to obtain soft temporal plans like that shown in Figure 3 by means of the solution extraction procedure shown in Figure 5 and execute the plan. However, there are some additional features that must be mentioned.

4 Monitoring and rescheduling

One of the advantages of MACHINE^{TF} is that the underlying FTCN in a fuzzy temporal plan may be used to monitor its execution and to reschedule part of the plan in the case that a delay has occurred during its execution but maintaining the causal structure of the plan. The algorithm to monitor the execution of fuzzy temporal plans is shown in Figure 6.

It uses the set of actions of the plan still to be executed Π, a set of already executed actions C and a queue of delayed actions Q, that is, actions that should have executed before but they

1. Initialization
   - Given $\Pi = \{a_0, a_1, \ldots, a_{n+1}\}$ a fuzzy temporal plan
   - $C = \emptyset$ and $Q = \emptyset$
   - Initialize $TIME$
2. Design a possible timeline T
   - Fix the execution time for every action in C and consider $TIME$ to be the execution time for every action in Q
   - Use the solution extraction procedure to obtain a timeline $s = \{x_i | a_i \in \Pi \cup Q\}$ with a degree of consistency $\sigma = \pi_S(s)$ given by equation 1 so that action a_i is scheduled to be executed at time x_i.
3. Monitoring the execution
   - (a) If Π and Q are empty then **SUCCESS**
   - (b) For every action $a_j \in \Pi$ such that $x_j = TIME$
     - Extract a_j from Π
     - If $preconds(a_j)$ are true in the environment, then execute a_j ($C = C \cup \{a_j\}$)
     - Otherwise delay a_j ($Q = Q \cup \{a_j\}$)
   - (c) Advance $TIME$ in $\Delta TIME$
4. If $Q \neq \emptyset$ then monitor the queue.
   - (a) For every action $a_j \in Q$
     - If $\pi_{0j}(TIME) = 0$ then **ERROR: TIME OUT**
     - If $preconds(a_j)$ are true in the environment, then extract a_j from Q and execute a_j ($C = C \cup \{a_j\}$)
   - (b) Go to Step 2
5. Go to Step 3

Figure 6: Monitoring algorithm for fuzzy temporal plans

are not able to execute because, for some reason, some of its preconditions have not been achieved yet by their producing actions. The variable $TIME$ is used to track the evolution of the schedule. It works as follows. The monitoring procedure defines a tentative schedule by obtaining a solution with maximal consistency. If nothing goes wrong ($Q = \emptyset$), every action whose execution time equals to $TIME$ and whose preconditions have already been satisfied, is executed and the variable $TIME$ is increased to the earliest execution time of the remaining actions in Π.

However a delay (either with local scope or global scope) might occur at time $TIME$, that is, some of the effects of an action might take longer than expected producing the delay of all of the actions that had been scheduled to time $TIME$ but that have that missing effect in their preconditions. In this case, delayed actions are included in the queue Q and variable $TIME$ is continuously increased by a minimum $\Delta TIME$ producing, in every iteration, a re-computation of the schedule for actions either in Q or Π. This reschedule of the remaining actions in the plan is needed to propagate the delay of the actions in Q to any future action that could have any temporal constraint relative to them. This procedure allows to readapt the schedule to the detected delay. It must be said that, in the case of delays, since new schedules are being continuously obtained to fit the delay, the consistency σ of the schedules may decrease due to the violation of any fuzzy temporal constraint but it will still be acceptable whenever $\sigma > 0$. The extreme case is when the accumulated delay is completely unacceptable and the consistency of the schedule is 0. This is detected in step 4 when the variable $TIME$ takes an infeasible value for some action a_j such that $\pi_{0j}(TIME) = 0$.

This capability for monitoring fuzzy temporal plans is very useful in realistic domains. One could have argued that this could have also been achieved by obtaining a rigid temporal plan and executing it in a flexible manner, however this would pose severe questions on the consistency of the explicit delay of an action since it might produce unsolvable flaws with respect to future actions causally dependent of the delayed action or produce any unexpected interference with the effects of other concurrent actions. In the case of MACHINE^{TF}, the delay of actions in order to flexibly modify a previous schedule is a safe process since it is based on the fuzzy temporal constraints explicitly included in the plan, which have been obtained taking into account the existence of threats and causal relations between actions, as explained in the previous section. Hence, no feasible delay nor reschedule obtained on the basis of the FTCN of the plan could produce an unexpected interference between parallel actions, either on local delays or global delays.

5 Final remarks

In summary, this paper has presented MACHINE^{TF} a planner able to handle successfully soft temporal constraints by using fuzzy sets. The result is a temporal planner able to handle ill defined temporal knowledge and to obtain flexible temporal plans, that is, plans whose branches may be safely rescheduled to react to unforeseen delays during their execution.

References

[1] L. Castillo, J. Fdez-Olivares, and A. González. Mixing expresiveness and efficiency in a manufacturing planner. *Journal of Experimental and Theoretical Artificial Intelligence*, 13:141–162, 2001.

[2] R. Dechter, I. Meiri, and J. Pearl. Temporal constraint networks. *Artificial Intelligence*, 49:61–95, 1991.

[3] M. Do and S. Kambhampati. SAPA: a domain-independent heuristic metric temporal planner. In *European Conference on Planning*, pages 109–120, 2001.

[4] Didier Dubois, Hélène Fargier, and Henri Prade. The use of fuzzy constraints in job-shop scheduling. In *Proc. of IJCAI-93/SIGMAN Workshop on Knowledge-based Production Planning, Scheduling and Control*, Chambery, France, August 1993.

[5] P. Haslum and H. Geffner. Heuristic planning with time and resources. In *European Conference on Planning*, pages 121–132, 2001.

[6] P. Laborie and M. Ghallab. Planning with sharable resource constraints. In *IJCAI'95*, pages 1643–1649, 1995.

[7] J. Larrosa and P.Meseguer. Restricciones blandas: modelos y algoritmos. *Inteligencia Artificial*, 20, 2003. (In spanish).

[8] D. Long and M. Fox. The 3rd international planning competition: Results and analysis. *Journal of Artificial Intelligence Research*, 20:1–59, 2003.

[9] R. Marín, M.A. Cárdenas, M. Balsa, and J.L. Sánchez. Obtaining solutions in fuzzy constraint networks. *International Journal of Approximate Reasoning*, 16:261–288, 1997.

[10] N. Muscettola. HSTS: integrating planning and scheduling. In M. Zweben and M. Fox, editors, *Intelligent scheduling*, pages 169–212. Morgan Kaufmann, 1994.

[11] D.E. Smith and D.S. Weld. Temporal planning with mutual exclusion reasoning. In *IJCAI'99*, pages 326–337, 1999.

[12] D. Weld. An introduction to least commitment planning. *AI Magazine*, 15(4):27–61, 1994.

Planning, Scheduling and Constraint Satisfaction: From Theory to Practice
L. Castillo et al. (Eds.)
IOS Press, 2005

79

A Constraint-Based Algorithm for Planning the Substitution of Faulty Parts

Antonio MÁRQUEZ[1], Carmelo DEL VALLE[2], Rafael M. GASCA[2], Miguel TORO[2]

[1] *Dept. Ingeniería Electrónica, Sistemas Informáticos y Automática, Univ. Huelva,*
Campus de La Rábida. Ctra. Huelva-Palos de la Frontera, 21071 Palos Fra. – Huelva
amarquez@uhu.es
[2] *Dept. Lenguajes y Sistemas Informáticos, Univ. Sevilla,*
Avda. Reina Mercedes s/n, 41012 Sevilla, Spain
{carmelo, gasca, mtoro}@lsi.us.es

Abstract. This work presents a CSP (Constraint Satisfaction Problem) model and proposes the use of Constraint Programming for the optimal sequencing of disassembly and assembly tasks when repairing or substituting faulty parts. The goal of the plan is the minimization of the total repairing time, taking into account the execution of tasks in a system with multiple workstations. The model also considers, apart from the durations and resources used for the assembly and disassembly tasks, the necessary delays due to the change of configuration in the machines, and those due to the movement of intermediate subassemblies between different machines. The set of all feasible assembly and disassembly plans are represented by an extended *And/Or* graph. In this work we propose a branch-and-bound algorithm, which selects the tasks through an exploration of the *And/Or* graph. This algorithm is based on Constraint Programming, a powerful programming paradigm that is increasingly used to model and solve many hard real-life problems. In order to improve the efficiency of the algorithm, we propose the use of a heuristic function based on the minimal time needed for the execution of each task and its successor ones.

1. Introduction

This work presents a CSP (Constraint Satisfaction Problem) model and proposes the use of Constraint Programming [1] [2] in *branch and bound* algorithms for solving a planning problem corresponding to the optimal sequencing of disassembly and assembly tasks for repairing or substituting faulty parts.

Assembly planning is a very important problem in the manufacturing of products. It involves the identification, selection and sequencing of assembly operations, specified by their effects on the parts. The identification of assembly operations is usually tackled by analyzing the product structure and the feasibility of each possible assembly task [3] [4]. The identification of these operations usually leads to the set of all feasible plans. An optimum assembly plan is now sought, selected from the set of all feasible plans. Most approaches used for choosing an optimal one employ different kind of rules in order to eliminate assembly plans including difficult tasks or awkward intermediate subassemblies [5][6].

On the other hand, disassembly planning has been object of different studies, varying from maintenance or repairing purposes to recycling or recovering of useful materials [7] [8] [9].

This work supposes that the diagnosis task in a system [10] [11] detects a simple fault, so that a single part must be repaired. The work is focused on the selection of assembly and disassembly tasks and their optimal ordering. The objective is the minimization of the total reparation time, taking into account their execution in a generic multi-robot system, so that all factors that can have an influence on it are taken into account. For this reason, our model also consider, apart from the durations and resources used for the assembly and disassembly tasks (machines and configurations), an estimation of the time needed for doing auxiliary operations between the execution of two tasks, such as the transportations of intermediate subassemblies between different machines, and the change of configurations in machines, that may be of the same order than assembly and disassembly tasks and should not be underestimated.

The planner must obtain the optimal sequence of disassembly operations (in order to extract the faulty part), the substituting or repairing task, and the re-assembly tasks. There is little work tackling the problem of scheduling alternative tasks, so that the development of constraint-based techniques considering it is an especially interesting issue [12].

The rest of the paper is organised as follows: Section 2 details the planning model proposed, and Section 3 states the CSP model for the planning problem corresponding to the substitution or reparation of a faulty part. Section 4 shows the proposed algorithm that solves the problem, and Section 5 presents the heuristic used in the branch and bound schemes in order to improve its efficiency, both for bounding solutions and for selecting the exploration order. Section 6 presents some of the results obtained, and finally, some remarks are made in the concluding section, as well as future work to be developed starting from the model proposed is outlined.

2. The Planning Model

An usual way of describing and representing the set of all feasible assembly and disassembly plans is through *And/Or* graphs [13]. In these graphs, each assembly plan is associated to an assembly tree, an *And/Or* path starting at the root node and ending at the leaf nodes, which contain a set of tasks enough for the assembly of the complete product, and showing the precedence constraints among the tasks contained in the assembly plan. In this representation, the *Or* nodes correspond to sub-assemblies, the top node corresponds to the complete assembly, and the leaf nodes correspond to the individual parts. Each *And* node corresponds to the assembly task joining the sub-assemblies of its two *Or* nodes below it producing the sub-assembly corresponding to the *Or* node above it. The *And* nodes immediately below an *Or* node correspond to the alternative assembly tasks that might be selected in order to obtain the subassembly corresponding to the *Or* node. Furthermore, each *And* node corresponds to the disassembly task, opposite to the assembly task, that decomposes the same sub-assemblies. Figure 1 shows an example of this representation.

This representation shows both precedence constraints and those related to the correct construction of a disassembly and assembly plan. An extension of this representation can be defined so that it includes all constraints involved in the problem, adding those constraints due to the use of resources by the tasks, and taking into account the delays due to the transportation of intermediate subassemblies and to the change of configurations in the machines. $\Delta_{cht}(M, C, C')$ will denote the time needed for changing the configuration (for instance, change of tools) of the machine M from C to C'. $\Delta_{mov}(SA, M, M')$ will denote the time needed for transporting the subassembly SA from machine M to machine M'.

This representation allows a direct mapping from the planning problem to a Constraint Satisfaction Problem (CSP), in order to be solved using Constraint Programming.

The resulting planning problem has the following tasks:

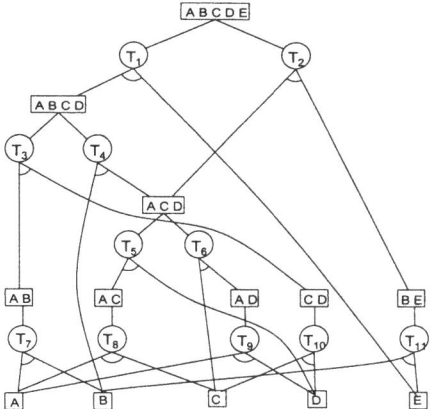

Figure 1. The And/Or graph for the product ABCDE

- assemble(sub1,sub2,result): assembles sub-assemblies sub1 and sub2 and obtains sub-assembly result.
- disassemble(result,sub1,sub2): disassembles result in two sub-assemblies, sub1 and sub2.
- move-subassembly(sub,mach1,mach2): moves the sub-assembly sub from machine mach1 to machine mach2.
- change-configuration(mach,conf1,conf2): changes the configuration of the machine mach from conf1 to conf2.
- repair-part(p): repairs or substitutes the part p.

To describe our work, some previous concepts must be defined:

Definition 1. A *reparation graph* is an *And/Or* graph which only contains assembly and disassembly tasks that handle subassemblies that contain the faulty part.

Definition 2. An assembly (disassembly) task T is *reversible* if its corresponding disassembly (assembly) task T' exists, i.e., if both tasks handle the same subassemblies, but in an opposite way.

Definition 3. A *reversible plan* is a tree of the reparation graph that only contains reversible tasks.

In the current work we suppose that all feasible plans are reversible and that each assembly task is executed in the same machine that its corresponding disassembly task, so that the subassemblies corresponding to *Or* leaf nodes remain in the same machine (or its environment) until it will be reused by the assembly task, i.e. all subassemblies which not contain the faulty part will maintain complete.

Consequently, in the *And/Or* graph shown in the figures, the *And* nodes represent reversible (assembly and disassembly) tasks.

3. The CSP Model

In order to obtain the solution we can simplify the *And/Or* graph, eliminating those And nodes bellow the *Or* nodes corresponding to subassemblies which do not contain the faulty part. This can be done through a depth-first traversal of the *And/Or* graph. Now, the leaf nodes are the individual parts and the subassemblies which do not contain the faulty part.

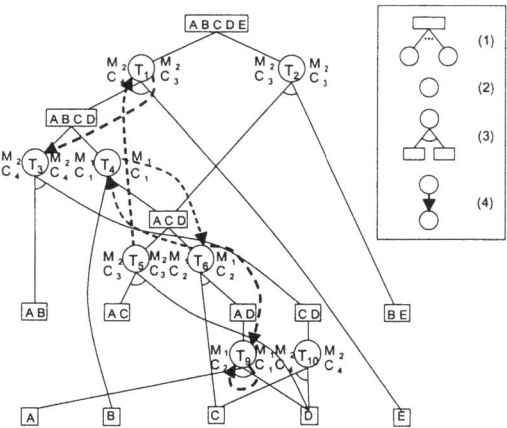

Figure 2. The extended and simplified And/Or graph for the
substitution of the D part in the product ABCDE

All these nodes will have the same processing, except for the faulty part. Figure 2 shows
the extended and simplified *And/Or* graph resulting for the product *ABCDE* when substituting the part *D*.

Each node of the *And/Or* graph is associated to a set of variables: for each (assembly or disassembly) task *T* (*And* node), its duration $dur(T)$, the machine used $M(T)$, and the
necessary configuration on it, $C(T)$, as well as its starting time, $t_i(T)$, and ending time, $t_f(T)$.
For each subassembly *SA* (*Or* node), the machine used for its assembly $m(SA)$, the machine
where it is obtained after the corresponding disassembly task $m'(SA)$, the times when it is
obtained after assembly $t_{OR}(SA)$, and disassembly $t'_{OR}(SA)$, and the delays related to the
transportation between each two machines.

On the other hand, each task may not be present in the final solution. In order to
build a correct solution, all the tasks selected must belong to one of the possible trees of the
And/Or graph. Moreover, depending on the execution of some tasks or others, some intermediate sub-assemblies will be formed and not another ones. So, an additional boolean
variable is defined for each node in the *And/Or* graph, indicating if the node is selected for
the solution. These boolean variables, which are related to the selection of alternative plans,
are denoted as $s(T)$ and $s(SA)$, and indicate, respectively, that the solution contain the assembly task *T* (and its corresponding disassembly task *T'*), and that the subassembly *SA* is
present in the solution.

A last factor in the problem is the delay related to the reparation or substitution of
the faulty part, denoted as $\Delta_{sust}(P)$, *P* being the part to be repaired. In this work, we will
suppose that $\Delta_{sust}(P)$ does not depend on the machine where *P* is repaired or substituted.

Table 1 shows some indicative examples of the different types of constraints between
the variables, corresponding to the extended and simplified *And/Or* graph of Figure 2.

Constraints of type (1) relate on one hand the selection of tasks *T* (and its equivalent
T') with that of sub-assemblies, expressed through the XOR operator, since one and only
one alternative task can be selected to build a sub-assembly, if that sub-assembly takes part
in the solution. On the other hand, these constraints establish the relations between t'_{OR} and
the starting time of *T'*, and considering the possible transportation of the subassembly if the
two consecutive disassembly tasks involving it use different machines. Moreover, they define the constraints associated to the machine and the assembly times of *Or* nodes, related
to the tasks that can be selected. A special case is for the complete product and for the

Table 1. Set of constraints for the And/Or graph from Figure 2.

Type	Constraints
(1)	$s(ABCDE) = s(D) = true \quad \wedge \quad t'_{OR}(ABCDE) = 0$
	$s(ABCDE) \Rightarrow \left(s(T_1) \; XOR \; s(T_2) \right)$
	$s(T_1) \Rightarrow \left(m(ABCDE) = M_2 \wedge t_{OR}(ABCDE) = ft(T_1) \wedge st(T_1') \geq t'_{OR}(ABCDE) \right)$
	$s(T_2) \Rightarrow \left(m(ABCDE) = M_2 \wedge t_{OR}(ABCDE) = ft(T_2) \wedge st(T_2') \geq t'_{OR}(ABCDE) \right)$
	$s(ABCD) \Rightarrow \left(s(T_3) XOR \; s(T_4) \right) \quad \wedge \neg s(ABCD) \Rightarrow \left(\neg s(T_3) \wedge \neg s(T_4) \right)$
	$s(T_3) \Rightarrow \left(m(ABCD) = M_2 \wedge t_{OR}(ABCD) = ft(T_3) \wedge st(T_3') \geq t'_{OR}(ABCD) + \Delta_{mov}\left(ABCD, m'(ABCD), M_2 \right) \right)$
	$\vdots$
	$s(SA) \Rightarrow \left(m(SA) = m'(SA) \wedge t_{OR}(SA) = t'_{OR}(SA) \right), SA \in \left\{ AB, AC, BE, A, B, C, E \right\}$
	$s(D) \Rightarrow \left(m(D) = m'(D) \wedge t_{OR}(D) = t'_{OR}(D) + \Delta_{sust}(D) \right)$
(2)	$s(T_1) \Rightarrow \left(ft(T_1) = st(T_1) + dur(T_1) \wedge ft(T_1') = st(T_1') + dur(T_1') \right)$
	$\vdots$
	$s(T_{10}) \Rightarrow \left(ft(T_{10}) = st(T_{10}) + dur(T_{10}) \wedge ft(T_{10}') = st(T_{10}') + dur(T_{10}') \right)$
(3)	$s(T_1) \Rightarrow \left(s(ABCD) \wedge m'(ABCD) = M_2 \wedge t'_{OR}(ABCD) = ft(T_1') \wedge st(T_1) \geq t_{OR}(ABCD) + \Delta_{mov}\left(ABCD, m(ABCD), M_2 \right) \right)$
	$s(T_1) \Rightarrow \left(s(E) \wedge m'(E) = M_2 \wedge t'_{OR}(E) = ft(T_1') \wedge st(T_1) \geq t_{OR}(E) \right)$
	$\vdots$
	$s(T_{10}) \Rightarrow \left(s(C) \wedge m'(C) = M_2 \wedge t'_{OR}(C) = ft(T_{10}') \wedge st(T_{10}) \geq t_{OR}(C) \right)$
	$s(T_{10}) \Rightarrow \left(s(D) \wedge m'(D) = M_2 \wedge t'_{OR}(D) = ft(T_{10}') \wedge st(T_{10}) \geq t_{OR}(D) \right)$
(4)	$\left(s(T_5) \wedge s(T_1) \right) \Rightarrow \left(st(T_5') \geq ft(T_1') \wedge st(T_1) \geq ft(T_5) + \Delta_{cht}(M_2, C_3, C_4) \right)$
	$\vdots$
	$s(T_9) \Rightarrow \left(st(T_9) \geq ft(T_9') + \Delta_{cht}(M_1, C_1, C_2) \right)$
	minimize $t_{OR}(ABCDE)$

faulty part, which always will be part of the solution, so that the corresponding boolean variables s are *true*. Moreover, for the *Or* leaf nodes, t'_{OR} and t_{OR} are equals, except for the faulty part, in which the delay corresponding to the reparation is considered. The origin of times is set to the t'_{OR} variable of the complete product, and the goal is the minimization of the t_{OR} variable of the complete product.

The constraints of type (2) consider the durations of tasks and correspond to the relationships between the starting and ending times of the assembly and disassembly tasks.

The constraints of type (3) include the precedence between the start times of *And* nodes and the assembly times of *Or* nodes, and the possible delays due to the transportation of sub-assemblies between different machines. Moreover, they relate the selection of sub-assemblies to that of the tasks using them to build another bigger one. They also include the relationships between t'_{OR} and the ending time of the disassembly task, and allow to obtain the corresponding variable m' (machine) through the disassembly task.

The constraints of type (4) are due to the delay needed for a change of configuration in a machine between the executions of tasks using the same machine with precedence constraints among them. Notice that it is only needed relating each task to its closest predecessor one in the *And/Or* graph that uses the same machine. Furthermore, when both tasks use the same configuration, the resulting constraint is superfluous and can be eliminated. A new type of link between *And* nodes has been added in order to represent this kind of constraints in the extended *And/Or* graph of Figure 2.

4. Algorithm Description

In order to solve the problem described, and taking into account all those factors, we propose a constraint-based algorithm that uses a backtracking scheme. Its behavior is based in extracting the different disassembly trees from the *And/Or* graph, deleting those alternatives which lead to trees that can not improve the solutions obtained. In order to make this pruning, the algorithm applies *branch and bound* with a heuristic criterion, described below, when extracting the different trees of tasks.

Figure 3 shows the details of the algorithm that we propose to solve the problem. The algorithm undertakes the construction of the different trees existing in the *And/Or* graph, and for each one it calculates its optimal solution. In order to fulfil this, the algorithm maintains a set of tasks, all belonging to the same tree of the *And/Or* graph, the constraints related to these tasks, and the next *Or* node to be expand, denoted *OrNext*, which is a term *<SA, TFather>* that represents the subassembly (*Or* node) and the disassembly task above it (which decompose it from another larger subassembly), respectively. At first, the *OrNext* node corresponds to the root of the *And/Or* graph.

In each recursive call, the algorithm extracts the *OrNext* node and selects one of its child tasks in order to construct the reparation tree (plan). Once a task has been introduced, the constraints related to it are added and propagated. If after propagating the constraints we detect that this path does not lead to a better solution than the best solution found so far, the new task could be discarded and all the sub-trees below it will be pruned. Otherwise, the *OrNext* node to be explored is updated with the addition of the *Or* node below the task, which correspond to a non-leaf sub-assemblies (i.e. the subassembly that contain the faulty part), if it corresponds to a non-trivial faulty part. Then, a new recursive call is done with the new *OrNext*.

The expansion step that the algorithm makes when exploring the *And/Or* graph, determines the order of generation of trees. The expansion of an *Or* node consists on selecting one of the alternative disassembly tasks immediately below the *Or* node in the *And/Or* graph, in order to build a specific reparation tree. Once the disassembly task is selected from the *And/Or* graph, an instance of it is created for the CSP and its constraints added (and deleted when backtracking) dynamically.

```
algorithm solve(OrNext)
 if isNull(OrNext)
  <ok,solution>=findSolution()
  if ok    //solution<optimum
   optimum=solution
   addConstraint(makespan<optimum)
  endif
 else
  [<SA,TFather>]=OrNext
  rankTasks(SA, heuristic)
  for i = 1 to nAnd(SA)
   createConstrainsTask(T_i(SA),SA,TFather)
   continue = propagateConstraints()
   if continue // else, prune tree
    if not isLeaf SA_1
     OrNext = [<SA_1,T_i(SA)>]
    else if not isLeaf SA_2
     OrNext = [<SA_2,T_i(SA)>]
    else
     OrNext = NULL
    endif
    solve(OrNext)
   endif
   removeConstraintsTask(T_i(SA))
  endfor
 endif
end
```

Figure 3. *The Backtracking Algorithm*

When the algorithm arrives to the faulty part (an *OrNext* node does not exist), it completes the solution after solving the CSP associated to the set of disassembly and assembly tasks (temporal variables and constraints) of the plan. If it is better than the best solution found so far, it updates the optimal solution and constrains the upper bound for the *makespan* with the new value obtained, so that those trees that remain to be explored can be discarded if, according to the constraints considered by the algorithm, they do not lead to a better solution.

This way, the algorithm constructs the promising reparation trees from the *And/Or* graph and then calculates their optimal solution, or fails if they cannot improve the best solution obtained so far. In order to prune and discard the non-promising trees, the algorithm, when adding a new disassembly task, propagates its corresponding constraints, so that, if the optimum can not be improved, the disassembly task is discarded, and consequently also all the trees derived from it, avoiding their exploration.

5. A Heuristic to Improve the Algorithm

In this work a *heuristic function* is used, carrying out optimistic estimations of the solutions. It is based on separating what can be pre-calculated *offline* from those calculations that must wait until the execution of the *branch and bound* algorithm, in order to minimize the computational cost.

This heuristic takes into account the minimum time needed to execute each disassembly and assembly tasks and its successors in the *And/Or* graph, without considering the possible delays due to the changes of configuration in the machines and to the transportation of subassemblies between machines.

This way, the minimum time to execute a disassembly task T' and its successors is estimated by the expression:

$$h(T', P) = dur(T') + dur(T) + \min_{T_i' \in Or(P)} (h(T_i', P)) \tag{1}$$

where T'_i refer to the tasks associated to the *Or* node connected by T' which contains the part P. The minimum operation refers to the selection of the most favourable task in the *Or* node (only one is executed).

When P is directly obtained from the task T':

$$h(T', P) = dur(T') + dur(T) + \Delta_{sust}(P) \tag{2}$$

Notice that these calculations can be done off-line, i.e., before the algorithm starts the search for solutions.

If task T' was added to a partial solution, a lower estimation of the total assembly time (*eft*) would be:

$$eft = est(T') + h(T', P) \tag{3}$$

est(T') being the earliest start time of task T' and *h(T',P)* the estimation for the minimum time needed for executing T' and all tasks below it from any subtree.

The previous calculations will allow excluding those tasks (and deleting its associated subtrees) that have an estimation of the accumulated time *eft* not less than the value of the current best solution. In addition, if all the tasks corresponding to one branch have been eliminated, the partial solution should be discarded and the algorithm must backtrack to the closest choice point. These estimations are taken into account in the algorithm, in order to obtain a more bounded domain for the variables $st(T')$ and $ft(T')$.

On the other hand, this heuristic function is used in order to select the order of exploration in the search tree. According to this, we can use the heuristic function h defined for bounding solutions in order to rank the *And* nodes. Therefore, the selector function *rankTasks* would select the tasks with lower values of h. In order to evaluate their influence in the computational efficiency of the algorithm, for the selection of tasks in the function *rankTasks*, we have tested two different strategies: selecting the tasks in increasing order according to the heuristic *h* considered and using the order used in the *And/Or* graph (referred as none strategy). Finally, we have used two different constraints in the function *createConstraintsTask*, corresponding to the use of *h* or none, so that the domains of variables could be reduced and so that it could affect the search.

6. Results

The algorithm has been implemented using ILOG Solver and Scheduler [14], a C++ library for Constraint Programming and scheduling problems. The algorithm has been tested in a variety of situations, considering different product structures (number of parts, number of connections between parts), different types of *And/Or* graphs (number of sub-assemblies, number of assembly and disassembly tasks for each sub-assembly), and different assembly resources (number of machines and configurations) and different durations for the tasks.

Table 2 shows the average number of *And* and *Or* nodes in the *And/Or* and simplified *And/Or* graphs for each set of hypothetical products of 30, 40, 50 and 60 parts, respectively.

The results in Tables 3-6 correspond to the products of Table 2. The tables show the effect of having more or less resources for assembling the product in the performance of the algorithm. The results refer to 110 (5 *And/Or* graphs x 2 faulty parts x 11) different problems generated randomly (each one of the 11 problems for one *And/Or* graph and one faulty part has a different combination of durations and resources for the tasks in the *And/Or* graph) in a system with 2 and 4 different machines and 2 and 4 different configurations for each machine. The values in the tables correspond to the execution time, in milliseconds, using a Pentium IV (1.91 GHz).

The problems were tested without using a specific method for selecting the next *And* nodes from the alternatives in the algorithm, denoted as "-" heuristic, and using the heuristic *h* described above. The tables show, for each case, the average nodes visited and how many problems (in percentage) the nodes visited were less than in the other case and the average time and how many problems (in percentage) were solved in less time than in the other case.

7. Conclusions and Future Work

This work presents a CSP model and a constraint-based algorithm for the selection of optimal disassembly and assembly sequences in order to repair or substitute a faulty part in a generic multirobot system. The objective of the plan is the minimization of the total assembly time. To meet this objective, the model takes into account, in addition to the times and resources for each assembly and disassembly task, the times needed to change configurations in the machines and to transporting intermediate subassemblies between different machines.

Table 2. Number of And and Or nodes (average) for each problem

Problem	*And/Or* graph		simplified *And/Or* graph	
	#Or	#And	#Or	#And
30	401	820	347	459
40	733	1945	575	823
50	1151	3722	806	1320
60	1755	7188	1535	3077

Table 3. Results for 2 machines and 2 configurations/machine

Problem	Heuristic	*And* nodes visited		Time (ms)	
		Ave	%	Ave	%
30	-	556	9.09%	810	15.45%
	h	317	90.91%	480	84.55%
40	-	1193	3.64%	770	1.82%
	h	460	96.36%	130	98.18%
50	-	1594	0.91%	970	0.91%
	h	716	99.09%	300	99.09%
60	-	4648	0.91%	2760	1.82%
	h	1681	99.09%	1890	98.18%

Table 4. Results for 2 machines and 4 configurations/machine

Problem	Heuristic	*And* nodes visited		Time (ms)	
		Ave	%	Ave	%
30	-	556	8.18%	830	12.73%
	h	319	91.82%	480	87.27%
40	-	1221	4.55%	770	2.73%
	h	481	95.45%	130	97.27%
50	-	1617	0.91%	980	0.00%
	h	751	99.09%	300	100.00%
60	-	4462	1.82%	2720	5.45%
	h	1749	98.18%	1940	94.55%

Table 5. Results for 4 machines and 2 configurations/machine

Problem	Heuristic	*And* nodes visited		Time (ms)	
		Ave	%	Ave	%
30	-	559	4.55%	840	8.18%
	h	309	95.45%	500	91.82%
40	-	1190	5.45%	860	3.64%
	h	455	94.55%	270	96.36%
50	-	1612	1.82%	2080	0.00%
	h	758	98.18%	1420	100.00%
60	-	4807	2.73%	36050	4.55%
	h	1646	97.27%	35170	95.45%

Table 6. Results for 4 machines and 4 configurations/machine

Problem	Heuristic	*And* nodes visited		Time (ms)	
		Ave	%	Ave	%
30	-	576	4.55%	830	7.27%
	h	313	95.45%	430	92.73%
40	-	1238	2.73%	840	1.82%
	h	466	97.27%	270	98.18%
50	-	1615	1.82%	2120	0.91%
	h	728	98.18%	1400	99.09%
60	-	4500	1.82%	36680	1.82%
	h	1607	98.18%	35860	98.18%

The problem is solved by generating the different reparation plans (trees of the *And/Or* graph). A reparation plan is modelled as a CSP, with precedence constraints among the assembly and disassembly tasks defined in the *And/Or* graph, and the corresponding resource constraints.

In order to improve the computational behaviour of the algorithm, a heuristic is proposed, both for bounding solutions and for selecting the exploration order of the algorithm. Some results of the use of this criterion are presented.

As future work, we plan to experiment with new heuristic functions in order to improve the efficiency of the algorithm. In the other hand, we plan to extend our work to more general reparation planning problems.

Acknowledgements

This work has been partially funded by the Spanish Ministerio de Ciencia y Tecnología under grant DPI2003-07146-C02-01, and the European Regional Development Fund (ERDF/FEDER).

References

[1] Y. Caseau and F. Laburthe. Improving Branch and Bound for Jobshop Scheduling with Constraint Propagation. *Proc. 8th Franco-Japanese 4th Franco-Chinese Conference CCS'95.*

[2] P. Esquirol, H. Fargier, P. Lopez, T. Schiex. Constraint programming. *Belgian Journal of Operations Research, Statistics and Computer Sciences*, 1996.

[3] Homem de Mello, L.S., Sanderson, A.C.: A Correct and Complete Algorithm for the Generation of Mechanical Assembly Sequences. *IEEE Transactions Robotic & Automation*, Vol. 7 (2) 228-240, 1991.

[4] Calton, T.L.: Advancing design-for-assembly. The next generation in assembly planning. *Proc. 1999 IEEE ISATP*, 57-62, 1999.

[5] Homem de Mello, L.S., Lee, S. (eds.): Computer-Aided Mechanical Assembly Planning. Kluwer Academic Publishers, 1991.

[6] Goldwasser, M.H., Motwani, R.: Complexity measures for assembly sequences. *Int. Journal of Computational Geometry and Applications*, 9 371-418, 1999.

[7] Li W., C. Zhang, Design for disassembly analysis for environmentally conscious design and manufacturing, *Proc. 1995 ASME Int. Mech. Eng. Congress*, 2 969-976, 1995.

[8] Lambert, A.J.D., Optimal Disassembly of Complex Products, *Int. J. Prod. Res.*, 35 2509-2523, 1997.

[9] Lambert, A.J.D., Optimal Disassembly Sequence Generation for Combined Material Recycling and Part Reuse. *Proc. 1999 IEEE ISATP*, 146-151, 1999.

[10] J. De Kleer and B.C. Williams. Diagnosing multiple faults. *Artificial Intelligence*, 32 (1) 97-130, 1987.

[11] R. Reiter. A theory of diagnosis from first principles. *Artificial Intelligence*, 32 (1) 57-96, 1987.

[12] J. C. Beck and M. S. Fox. Constraint-directed techniques for scheduling alternative activities. *Artificial Intelligence*, 121 (2000) 211-250.

[13] Homem de Mello, L.S., Sanderson, A.C.: And/Or Graph Representation of Assembly Plans. *IEEE Trans. Robotics Automation*. Vol. 6 (2) 188-199, 1990.

[14] ILOG, France, http://www.ilog.fr/.

Planning, Scheduling and Constraint Satisfaction: From Theory to Practice
L. Castillo et al. (Eds.)
IOS Press, 2005

89

Plan Validation and Mixed-Initiative Planning in Space Operations

Richard Howey   Derek Long
Maria Fox

richard.howey, derek.long, maria.fox @cis.strath.ac.uk

Department of Computer and Information Systems
University of Strathclyde, Glasgow, UK

Abstract. This paper describes our experiences in using our plan validation tool, VAL, in the development of a mixed-initiative plan construction tool intended to support space operations planning. VAL was initially developed to support the 3rd International Planning Competition (IPC), but has subsequently been extended in order to exploit its capabilities in plan validation and development. In particular, it has been extended to include advanced features of PDDL2.1 that were untested in the 3rd IPC but which have proved important in its application to mixed-initiative planning in the space operations project. The tool has also been extended to keep abreast of developments in PDDL, providing critical support to participants and organisers of the 4th IPC.

1 Introduction

VAL is a plan validation tool for PDDL. It played an important role in the 3rd IPC [9], allowing reliable validation of the several thousand plans produced by the competitors, as well as providing competitors with support for their development and debugging cycles. We have found the capabilities of VAL to be critical in understanding the structures of large plans, providing visualisation and reporting facilities [4]. VAL continued to play an important part in the 4th IPC [3], which saw seen several minor extensions to PDDL and its semantics.

VAL has also been extended to support features that were included in the definition of PDDL2.1, although not used in the competitions, including the expression of continuous change. In this paper we breifly describe the semantic developments of PDDL required to support continuous change and go on to give a motivating example for the role of this extension, based on a project in space operations planning. VAL has proved to be a valuable resource for this project, supporting the development of a domain description, the validation of plans constructed by humans and, using a new extension to the system, providing advice on the correction of flawed plans. In this paper we describe this recent feature and discuss ways in which the tool can be exploited in plan development in a mixed-initiative mode. We also briefly discuss how this approach might be developed to allow VAL to play a key role in fully automated plan construction.

2   PDDL and its Semantics with Continuous Effects

When Drew McDermott and the first planning competition committee proposed PDDL as a community standard [12] planning domain description language, they initiated an important process of development in which the planning research community has seen incremental extensions and modifications as the language has adapted to various goals. In the first instance, the core of PDDL was a STRIPS language, offering an ADL extension. This language has a semantics that is widely accepted, based on a simple state-transition model, with few areas of potential ambiguity. Perhaps the most significant issue for which alternative resolutions exist is concurrency: classical plans are often considered to be *sequences* of steps, representing state transitions, but partial-order planning [11] and Graphplan [2] both offer alternative models in which some form of parallelism is considered.

McDermott developed a simple plan validation tool for PDDL, intended only for sequential plans. However, the question of interpretation for more complex extensions of PDDL is more difficult. There is no prior widely accepted model, so choices must be made that are not necessarily universally accepted. Since the language plays a central role in communication of domains between researchers, it is important that there be a standard by which a common understanding may be developed for the semantics of domains and plans for those domains. A formal semantics is the first component of this. However, a formal semantics is not sufficient by itself, because a formal semantics is notoriously difficult to read. In practice, many formal semantics are read in detail by few and understood in all details by even fewer. To make the semantics accessible, their implementation as a validation tool is an important step. In this form, it is possible to confirm understanding of the semantics by testing various plans and domains with the tool, confirming the behaviour is as expected. VAL supplies a variety of forms of feedback, making it possible to explore quite precisely what might be wrong with a flawed plan and aiding in the interpretation of the more subtle details of the semantics.

Continuous effects are an important extension to PDDL for accurately modelling change in real world situations, their implementation in VAL is crucial in the mixed initiative application for the Beagle 2. Continuous effects can only affect metric quantities: it is not possible to change a propositional fluent continuously. A metric variable that can be changed by a continuous effect is called a *Primitive Numerical Expression (PNE)*. A durative action that has a continuous effect on a PNE changes it so that the values taken are described by a continuous function of time. We have developed formal semantics for the inclusion of continuous effects in PDDL, so called PDDL2.1 level 4. The semantics can be described by continuous activity on a real time line punctuated with discrete activity; for details see [5, 6]. When defining continuous effects in the domain model the rates of change of the PNEs are defined, it is possible for these rates of change to refer to PNEs that are themselves changing continuously. In this way the continuous effects are defined by a system of differential equations. These differential equations must be solved in VAL, however it is infeasible to solve all possible systems of differential equations, so we restrict ourselves to an interesting subset. Namely solutions that are given by polynomials or certain classes of exponential functions (also some numerical solutions). Apart from solving differential equations it is also a requirement to find the roots of real valued functions on given intervals. This is due to invariant conditions of durative actions which must hold over the application of the durative action. An invariant condition may state that a PNE must be below a certain threshold, for example $f < k$ on $(0, T)$, and if f is changing continuously we need to consider the roots of $f - k$ on $(0, T)$. For details on differential equations and rooting finding techniques in the context of plan validation see [5].

3 Space Operations Planning for the Beagle 2 Lander

On December 25th, 2003, a small lander, travelling with the Mars Express orbiter, was expected to land on Mars surface. Unfortunately, as with a high proportion of Mars landers, the Beagle 2 lander was unsuccessful. Various explanations of its failure have been proposed, including the possibility that the density of the Martian atmosphere is not as high as had been thought and, as a result, the parachute-brake failed to slow the lander sufficiently before impact. Despite this major setback, the design of the lander is considered so innovative and efficient (both in terms of cost and in terms of science-to-mass) that a future repeat attempt is being seriously considered. Funded by the European Space Agency, the authors have explored the possible roles of planning technology in space operations [13]. The project includes examining interactions between human operations planners and automated technology, initially in the context of operations plans for Beagle 2. Considerable expertise was built up around the Beagle 2 systems, including a partial domain model for human planning operations, and this has formed the core of a project to exploit planning technology to support mixed-initiative and partially automated planning for the lander operations.

Beagle 2 is a static lander, equipped with a jointed arm carrying an array of scientific instruments in a "paw" at its end. Included in the paw is a mole capable of drilling into soil around the lander to a distance of more than 2 meters, to retrieve soil samples for gas analysis on board the lander. Beagle 2 is essentially a geological survey system, capable of performing an array of geological and environmental measurements in its immediate surroundings.

Figure 1: Beagle 2

All lander operations are constrained by power availability, provided by solar energy with a battery for storage, and by temperatures. In addition, the lander is equipped with storage buffers for instrument data. These are too small to store all the data generated by the succession of experiments performed by the lander. Data must therefore be uplinked from the lander not only to return it to the scientists, but also to free up space for storage of succeeding measurements. Uplink windows are constrained, both in duration and in bandwidth, so that it is not possible to empty all the buffers in a window. Thus, there is a further problem of scheduling the uplinking of data into the communication windows in order to allow buffers to be emptied in time for experiments to be performed. These constraints make the management of data and communication a critical element of the planning problem, in common with other deep space missions.

Therefore, planning lander operations involves managing constraints on continuously changing quantities (the generated power levels and temperatures), scheduling the use of resources, planning the movement sequences of the arm and use of the instruments. Human operations planners were to have carried out the planning for the lander in a complex process involving scientists, providing mission goals and the operations to achieve them, and lander operations personnel, concerned with lander security and, therefore, the power resources and internal lander monitoring systems. When we became involved in the project we discovered that the existing partial domain description was in a form that closely resembled PDDL2.1 durative action descriptions. It was possible to translate the description into PDDL automatically using a simple automatic translator. The domain encoding began with over 50 actions and this has increased to nearly 70 actions following further domain analysis.

Power is the most important continuous factor in the operations of the lander. The lander operates close to margins and the model of the solar generation and the battery charging profiles are vital in determining when operations can be planned. The management of battery and solar power is sufficiently close to the margins of operational envelopes that it plans must interact with the continuous changes involved in the physical system rather than with abstractions into coarse-grained simple step-function changes. Of course, with sufficiently small time-steps a step-function model can approximate the continuous change adequately, but it is infeasible to attempt to model this level of granularity explicitly in the planning domain description. Therefore, this problem demands that the planner has access to a sufficiently detailed model of the continuous changes that affect the power systems.

4   Mixed-Initiative Planning

Mixed-initiative planning is a well-recognised path by which to introduce automatic planning technology into a context in which planning is currently performed manually. The idea is to allow human and automatic planners to cooperate in producing a plan. There are several aspects to this interaction. It simplifies the problems facing the automatic planning, since difficult choices in plan construction can be passed to a human, while the human can benefit from not having to manage the bulk of easier planning decisions and simple book-keeping tasks. However, the requirement for interaction imposes a more stringent demand on the system developers to ensure that feedback from the planner can be provided in a way that makes sense to the human planner, in terms that the human planner can relate to the planning task with which they are familiar. Furthermore, the automatic planning task changes from that of complete plan construction to one of plan repair and iterative plan improvement. We are not concerned with all the details of the demonstrator we have developed in this paper. Instead, we focus on the role that VAL has played in supporting the problems of feedback and plan repair.

4.1   Using VAL in Mixed-Initiative Planning

When VAL is used in its simplest form, without any parameters, in the case of plan failure it reports only that the plan has failed. An option is available for verbose output in which the system generates a report explaining which action in a plan has failed. However, this is still of limited use since no indication is given of how an action precondition might have failed to be satisfied. The action precondition might be very complex, but only failed due to one literal with the incorrect truth value. For example, a large factory machine may have an action for starting processing with a complicated precondition, but an instance of the action in a plan might fail simply because the machine is not switched on prior to planned execution of the start action. Feedback from the plan validation reporting that the machine needs to be switched on would be invaluable advice on how to fix the plan. In complex plans identifying even simple failures such as this can be difficult due to the obscuring effects of the actions surrounding the failure.

With the intention of supplying more informed feedback we have developed in VAL a detailed advice sub-system indicating how to satisfy unsatisfied preconditions in an invalid plan. The advice can be used in a *mixed-initiative planning* cycle in which the human planner firstly produces a plan either by hand or with the aid of software before VAL simulates execution of the plan giving detailed advice on how to repair the plan for each unsatisfied action precondition (or invariant condition or goal). The advice can then be used by the human planner to produce a new plan to correcting the errors, or at least some of them. The new plan can then be executed using VAL which produces new plan repair advice, and so on.

In general, the advice offered by VAL indicates why a given plan failed and what conditions must be achieved in order to repair it. It does not indicate which actions might be applied to achieve those conditions or explore the interactions they might introduce into the plan if they are added to it. Therefore, the advice from VAL must be seen as the first stage in the repair or reconstruction of a flawed plan: other components are necessary to decide how best to act on the advice if this decision is to be made automatically.

4.2 Structure of Plan Repair Advice

The advice given for a failed precondition is derived from a PDDL precondition expression and stored in a structure called an *advice proposition*.

Definition 4.1. Advice Proposition *For a given PDDL precondition of an action in a plan the* advice proposition *provides instructions on how the state, S, must be altered at this point in the plan in order to satisfy the precondition. An advice proposition (AP) is one of the following:*
- *Instructions to set A to true, for some literal A.*
- *Instructions to set A to false, for some literal A.*
- *Instructions to satisfy a comparison consisting of numerical expressions where each PNE has its current value reported.*
- *A list of APs where all must be followed (conjunction AP).*
- *A list of APs where at least one must be followed (disjunction AP).*
- *No advice (the empty advice case).*

VAL produces advice for each unsatisfied precondition by mapping the precondition and state to an advice proposition.

Definition 4.2. *Let ϕ be the mapping from a PDDL precondition, P, and a state, S, to an advice proposition defined as follows if P is a literal, comparison or connective respectively.*

$$\phi(P, S) := if\ S \models P\ then\ \text{no advice}\ else\ \text{set } P \text{ to true}$$
$$\phi(P, S) := if\ P\ is\ an\ unsatisfied\ comparison\ then\ \text{satisfy } P$$
$$\phi(\wedge_i X_i, S) := \wedge_i \phi(X_i, S),\ for\ each\ unsatisfied\ X_i\ in\ S$$
$$\phi(\vee_i X_i, S) := \vee_i \phi(X_i, S),\ for\ each\ unsatisfied\ X_i\ in\ S$$
$$\phi(X \rightarrow Y, S) := \phi(\neg X \vee Y, S)$$

If P is a negation, $P = \neg Q$, then $\phi(P) = \psi(Q)$ where ψ is defined as below if Q is a predicate, comparison or connective respectively.

$$\psi(Q, S) := if\ Q \not\models S\ then\ \text{no advice}\ else\ \text{set } Q \text{ to false}$$
$$\psi(Q, S) := if\ Q\ is\ an\ unsatisfied\ comparison\ then\ \text{satisfy } Q$$
$$\psi(\wedge_i X_i, S) := \vee_i \phi(\neg X_i, S),\ for\ each\ satisfied\ X_i\ in\ S$$
$$\psi(\vee_i X_i, S) := \wedge_i \phi(\neg X_i, S),\ for\ each\ satisfied\ X_i\ in\ S$$
$$\psi(X \rightarrow Y, S) := \phi(X \wedge \neg Y, S)$$
$$\psi(\neg Q', S) := \phi(Q', S)$$

The map ϕ is well defined since PDDL preconditions and states are finite. Starting from a PDDL precondition that is not satisfied always yields a non-empty advice proposition. The advice takes the form of lists of APs, conjoined or disjoined according to contex. Further advice lists may then be nested. The actual conditions that need to be changed in the state will be the truth value of predicates and the numerical values of PNEs.

4.3   Advice on Invariants depending on Continuous Effects

The introduction of continuous effects into a plan further complicates the validation of an invariant over a given interval. There is a natural extension to the plan repair advice given by ϕ to invariant conditions depending on continuously changing PNEs. An invariant condition must hold for all values on a given interval, this further consideration only changes the advice given by ϕ for comparisons that depend on continuously changing PNEs. Instead of considering just one state the advice for satisfying an invariant must consider: one logical state (for the predicates), and a continuously changing numerical state on the interval in question for comparisons depending on continuous effects. The advice for such a comparison is that it needs to be satisfied on the interval, together with a report of the subset of values of the interval that the comparison is satisfied on.

For a disjunctive advice proposition which states that one of the following must be satisfied the meaning should be interpreted appropriately when referring to invariant conditions. That is, for each time value in the invariant interval one of the advice propositions must be followed. The advice proposition that is followed need not be the same advice proposition for each time value. See [5], section 7.2 for more details on disjunctive invariants.

4.4   Plan Repair Example Using VAL: Beagle 2 Plan

In this section we consider an example of the use of VAL in a mixed-initiative setting for the Beagle 2 planning problem. In this simple scenario, starting shortly after dawn, the Beagle begins with its arm stowed and its battery at a low state of charge (due to overnight operations). The operations planner wishes to construct a plan that will allow examination of a rock that has been named "peanuts". The examination procedure consists of taking a close up image with the stereoscopic camera, then a closer image with the microscope, grinding a core sample, transferring it to the ovens and processing it in the gas analysis system (GAP). We will examine only the first few actions. An initial plan is constructed (through a GUI that is not critical to the work described here):

```
1:      (generate-solar-power) [43200] ;Starts continuous power generation
1:      (PAW-move stowed wind_high_modified) [100]
500:    (PAW-move wind_high_modified closeup_peanuts) [800]
1400:   (SEQ-SCS-CLOSEUP closeup_peanuts) [130]
3550:   (SEQ-MIC-FULL_SET_COMPRESS_EACH peanuts) [17300]
```

VAL is then applied to it, reporting failure with advice as shown below.[1]

```
Only one possible achiever for the condition:
    (MIC_FOCUS_RANGED peanuts_sample)
Adding SEQ-MIC-FIND_FOCUS_RANGE to complete before 3550
Added PAW-move action from peanuts_closeup to peanuts starting at 3349
```

---

[1]For simplicity we show all times in seconds relative to the plan start. In fact, the GUI uses absolute times and reports are given in terms of these.

Examination of the LaTeX report reveals that the reason for this advice is that two invariants for the action (SEQ-MIC-FULL_SET_COMPRESS_EACH peanuts) are violated. One is that the microscope must be properly focussed before attempting to use it to capture images and the second is that the microscope must be in position at "peanuts" in order to be able to capture the images. The first condition is achieved by the addition of a new action (there is only one choice) and the second by a proposed addition on an additional PAW movement action. Note, however, that the new action (SEQ-MIC-FULL_SET_COMPRESS_EACH peanuts) has a precondition that is also unsatisfied. The validation process is, deliberately, not invoked recursively to attempt to repair flaws in the first phase of repairs. This is to ensure that the human has some opportunity to monitor the process of repair and to interact with it by accepting parts of the repair and rejecting or modifying others.

Where advice is generated for PAW movement, the plan repair machinery finds efficient paths between known arm configurations for the path, possibly generating a sequence of PAW-moves in order to traverse a path. There is no geometric planning involved in this — individual moves between specific pairs of locations are preplanned as command sequences for the individual motors in the arm controller. However, the recognition of the path-planning problem that is involved in identifying the sequence of waypoints for the arm to traverse is an important element of the repair process. This machinery depends on the recognition of the underlying behaviour of PAW-move actions as a *mobile generic type* [8].

If, at this point, the human operator simply chooses to reinvoke the replanning system then the following plan is passed to VAL.

```
1:      (generate-solar-power) [43200] ;Starts continuous power generation
1:      (PAW-move stowed wind_high_modified) [100]
500:    (PAW-move wind_high_modified peanuts_closeup) [800]
1400:   (SEQ-SCS-CLOSEUP peanuts_closeup) [130]
1567:   (SEQ-MIC-FIND_FOCUS_RANGE peanuts) [1982]
3550:   (SEQ-MIC-FULL_SET_COMPRESS_EACH peanuts) [17300]
```

The observant reader will notice that this plan does not contain the additional PAW movement action advised above. This is because the interface between the GUI and VAL relies on a plan representation that is convenient to the human operator, abstracting details that seem obvious. In particular, a PAW-move action only includes its destination argument — it is assumed that the starting point for each move is wherever was the last location of the PAW. In the partially repaired plan proposed after the first cycle the inserted PAW-move comes too late to achieve the invariant condition of the (SEQ-MIC-FULL_SET_COMPRESS_EACH peanuts) action, so the system infers that the PAW must actually be moved earlier and that this subsequent move is a redundant attempt to move the PAW from "peanuts" to itself. This is reported as a flawed action and deleted from the plan, which is why it does not appear in the plan listed above. The repair advice is therefore:

```
Error in finding duration for: (PAW-move peanuts peanuts)
Action instance does not exist!
Plan failed to execute
Report in report.ps
Added PAW-move action from peanuts_closeup to peanuts starting at 1366
```

The plan now becomes:

```
1:      (generate-solar-power) [43200] ;Starts continuous power generation
1:      (PAW-move stowed wind_high_modified) [100]
500:    (PAW-move wind_high_modified peanuts_closeup) [800]
1366:   (PAW-move peanuts_closeup peanuts) [200]
1400:   (SEQ-SCS-CLOSEUP peanuts_closeup) [130]
1567:   (SEQ-MIC-FIND_FOCUS_RANGE peanuts) [1982]
3550:   (SEQ-MIC-FULL_SET_COMPRESS_EACH peanuts) [17300]
```

and it still contains an important flaw. The new attempt to position the necessary PAW-move action has created a different conflict, this time with the action (SEQ-SCS-CLOSEUP peanuts_closeup), which requires that the PAW stays immobile during the image capture. Repairing this flaw is a more difficult problem. The plan repair system observes that the profile for the behaviour of the required condition is that it is true in the interval following the second PAW-move up to the third PAW-move. It proposes to exploit this by moving the action (SEQ-SCS-CLOSEUP peanuts_closeup) earlier, but there is not sufficient time between the two PAW-moves to allow the stereo-camera image to be captured. Therefore, the third PAW-move is moved later to make space and all of the actions dependent on the third PAW-move are delayed by the same amount of time. This repair is explained in the following output from the system:

```
Propose to delay (PAW-move peanuts_closeup peanuts) by 66 seconds
Propose to delay (SEQ-MIC-FIND_FOCUS_RANGE peanuts) by 66 seconds
Propose to delay (SEQ-MIC-FULL_SET_COMPRESS_EACH peanuts) by 66 seconds
Propose to bring forward (SEQ-SCS-CLOSEUP peanuts_closeup) by 99 seconds
```

The final plan is:

```
1:      (generate-solar-power) [43200] ;Starts continuous power generation
1:      (PAW-move stowed wind_high_modified) [100]
500:    (PAW-move wind_high_modified peanuts_closeup) [800]
1301:   (SEQ-SCS-CLOSEUP peanuts_closeup) [130]
1432:   (PAW-move peanuts_closeup peanuts) [200]
1633:   (SEQ-MIC-FIND_FOCUS_RANGE peanuts) [1982]
3616:   (SEQ-MIC-FULL_SET_COMPRESS_EACH peanuts) [17300]
```

If the final plan is validated one last time, VAL reports success and generates a report complete with graphs illustrating the power levels during execution. If this same plan is executed from a state in which the battery state of charge is close to its critical minimum level then a different outcome can be generated:

```
Problem found without any repairs:
Condition unsatisfied for:
    (generate-solar-power) at time 1
```

This is due to the fact that the initial powerdraw due to the use of the instruments occurs too early in the recharging cycle and the power level dips below the minimum level. This is seen in the report generated by VAL, which explains that the invariant (that the charge remain above the critical level) is unsatisfied over particular intervals and in the graph of charge produced by VAL for the report (figure 2). The curve shows that the charge dips low in the early stages of the plan, when powerdraw exceeds solar-power generation. The shape is complex due to the changing demands of the different activities across the interval. The repair for this is to slide all the activity later in the day when power has been generated by solar generation, but our machinery is not yet capable of generating this repair automatically. (It can handle simpler cases in which single actions must be slipped to account for violation of invariants by continuously changing PNEs).

The process of repair depends on a rich plan representation, capturing the dependency structure between the actions and possible external events. This temporal aspect of the structure is an important additional element, along with the effect of continuous change, that is not considered in the otherwise closely related work of Lemai and Ingrand [7] on plan repair. In their work they consider plans as partial order structures and build repairs using traditional partial-order planning flaw repair strategies. This is a valuable approach to handling plan flaws and can be generalised to handle metric conditions to some extent. However, they do not consider continuous change or its impact on invariants and this is an important aspect of the current work. In the context of the space operations project, management of continuously

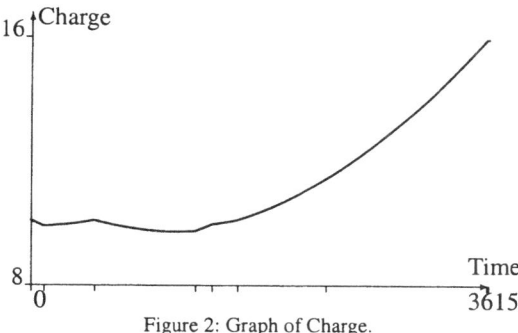

Figure 2: Graph of Charge.

changing power supplies is a vital part of the planning problem, as has also been observed in the development of MAPGEN [1], the NASA tool used for mixed-initiative planning for the Mars Exploratory Rovers mission. MAPGEN does not attempt to model the power management directly, relying instead on a separate purpose-built model. This has the advantage of being highly accurate, but the important disadvantage of being opaque to the planning and validation process. This means that it is difficult to make predictions about the right way to repair plans that violate the power envelope.

5   Further Work and Concluding Remarks

Polynomials were the first continuous effects to be handled by VAL [5]. The approach can be extended to continuous effects described by more complex functions, by using polynomials to approximate the functions. This approach has been implemented for exponential functions in VAL. This extension has been an important step in the exploitation of VAL in the context of the Beagle 2 operations, since the power models are sufficiently complex that they cannot easily be modelled using simple polynomials alone. In fact, to model them it has been necessary to numerically solve certain classes of differential equations: we have used the Runge-Kutta-Fehlberg [10] method with very encouraging results.

We are investigating ways to improve the advice given for repairing a plan, for example which actions should be added, removed or moved within the plan. In particular how a durative action with an invariant condition which depends on continuous activity, may be moved within the plan to satisfy the invariant. We are aiming for the least human input in the mixed-initiative planning process, so that most plan repair activity can be automated by VAL. Ultimately, VAL should support a complete plan repair strategy.

This work is part of a larger project exploring the transfer of planning technology into space operations planning in European space missions. This is in the context of world-wide efforts in space exploration and the NASA mobile robots missions currently being pursued on Mars. These missions also make extensive use of mixed-initiative planning aids, including the MAPGEN[1] tool, used successfully in the Mars Exploratory Rover missions.

Applying planning technology to real problems highlights the need to provide solutions to problems that are often not considered in the pure planning research community. Mixed-initiative planning has long been considered an important bridging technology to help human planners to become familiar with and more trusting of automatic planning technologies, while also solving some of the difficulties faced by planners in complex and realistic domains.

In this paper we have discussed the use of VAL, our plan validation technology, as a tool in mixed-initiative planning for space operations. An important aspect of this tool is that it is directly linked to our development of the semantics of PDDL and therefore provides a basis for formal validation of the domain descriptions we are constructing. The importance of continuous change in this domain is an added complication. We have advocated the role of continuous change in planning domain models for some time and this domain is an illustration that it is of key importance in real domain problems.

In the context of the space operations planning we have integrated VAL into the tool intended for Beagle 2 operations planning. We anticipate that this bridge between theory and practice will continue to inspire and motivate further developments in our planning technology.

References

[1] M. Ai-Change, J. Bresina, L. Charest, J. Hsu, A.K. Jónsson, R. Kanefsy, P. Maldegue, P. Morris, K. Rajan, and J. Yglesias. MAPGEN: Mixed intitive activity planning for the Mars Exploratory Rover mission. In *Proceedings of Demonstration Systems Track, ICAPS'03*, 2003.

[2] A. Blum and M. Furst. Fast Planning through Plan-graph Analysis. In *Proceedings of IJCAI*, 1995.

[3] S. Edelkamp, J. Hoffmann, and committee. The 4th International Planning Competition 2004, www.informatik.uni-freiburg.de/~hoffmann/ipc-4/.

[4] R. Howey and D. Long. VAL's progress: The automatic validation tool for PDDL2.1 used in the international planning competition. In *Proc. of ICAPS Workshop on the IPC*, 2003.

[5] R. Howey and D. Long. Validating plans with continuous effects. In *Proceedings of the 22nd Workshop of the UK Planning and Scheduling Special Interest Group*, pages 115–124, December 2003.

[6] R. Howey and D. Long. VAL: Automatic plan validation, continuous effects and mixed initiative planning using PDDL. In *Proc. of The 16th IEEE International Conference on Tools with Artificial Intelligence*, Florida, USA, 2004.

[7] S. Lemai and F. Ingrand. Interleaving temporal planning and execution in robotics domains. In *Proceedings of AAAI'04*, 2004.

[8] D. Long and M. Fox. Recognizing and exploiting generic types in planning domains. In *International AI Planning Systems conference, AIPS 2000, Breckenridge, Colorado, USA.*, 2000.

[9] D. Long and M. Fox. The 3rd International Planning Competition: Results and analysis. *Journal of AI Research*, 20, 2003.

[10] J. H. Mathews and K. K. Fink. *Numerical Methods Using Matlab*. Prentice-Hall Inc., New Jersey, USA, 4th edition, 2004.

[11] D. McAllester and D. Rosenblitt. Systematic nonlinear planning. In *Proceedings of the Ninth National Conference on Artificial Intelligence (AAAI-91)*, volume 2, pages 634–639, Anaheim, California, USA, 1991. AAAI Press/MIT Press.

[12] D. McDermott and AIPS'98 IPC Committee. PDDL–the planning domain definition language. Technical report, Available at: www.cs.yale.edu/homes/dvm, 1998.

[13] M.J. Woods, R.S. Aylett, D. Long, M. Fox, and R. Ward. Assessing planning and scheduling technologies for deep space exploration. In *Proceedings of 4th British Conference on (Mobile) Robotics: Towards Intelligent Mobile Robots*, 2003.

Planning, Scheduling and Constraint Satisfaction: From Theory to Practice
L. Castillo et al. (Eds.)
IOS Press, 2005

Combining Heuristics in Assembly Sequence Planning

Carmelo DEL VALLE[1], Miguel TORO[1], Eduardo F. CAMACHO[2], Rafael M. GASCA[1]

[1]*Dept. Lenguajes y Sistemas Informáticos, Univ. Sevilla, Spain*
[2]*Dept. Ingeniería de Sistemas y Automática, Univ. Sevilla, Spain*

Abstract. Assembly Sequence Planning is tackled by modelling and solving a planning problem that considers the execution of the plan in a system with multiple assembly machines. The objective of the plan is the minimization of the total assembly time (makespan). To meet this objective, the model takes into account the durations and resources for the assembly tasks, the change of configuration in the machines, and the transportation of intermediate subassemblies between different workstations. In order to solve the problem, different heuristics has been defined from two relaxed model of it, one considering only the precedence constraints among tasks, and the other one considering only the use of shared resources. From these basic heuristics, other ones have been defined, combining both types of information from the problem, so that the refinement produces substantial improvements over the initial heuristics.

1. Introduction

Assembly planning is a very important problem in the manufacturing of products. It involves the identification, selection and sequencing of assembly operations, stated as their effects on the parts. The identification of assembly operations is done through the analysis of the product structure, using interactive planners [1] [2], or automatically from a geometric and relational model of the assembly [3] and from a CAD model and other non-geometric information [4] [5]. The identification of assembly operations usually leads to the set of all feasible assembly plans. The number of them grows exponentially with the number of parts, and depends on other factors, such as how the single parts are interconnected in the whole assembly, represented in the graph of connections. In fact, this problem has been proved to be NP-complete [6].

The representation of assembly plans is an important issue within this scope. The use of *And/Or* graphs for this purpose [7] has became one of the most standard ways of representing all possible assembly plans. The result is a representation which is adequate for a goal-directed approach. Moreover, this structure is more efficient in most cases than other enumerative ones [7] [8].

Two kinds of approaches have been used for searching the optimal assembly plan. One, the more qualitative, uses rules in order to eliminate assembly plans that include difficult tasks or awkward intermediate subassemblies. A more quantitative approach uses an evaluation function that computes the merit of assembly plans. Several of these proposals can be found in [9] and [10].

The criterion followed in this work is the minimization of the total assembly time (makespan) of the plan executed in a system with multiple machines [11]. To meet this objective, a scheduling-based model is used [12], which takes into account all factors having an effect on the makespan: an estimation of the duration of tasks; the resources used for them (machines and configurations); the times needed for changing tools in the robots; and the delays due to the transportation of intermediate subassemblies between different workstations.

The rest of the paper is organized as follows: Section 2 describes the assembly sequence planning problem and the model proposed. The details of the A* algorithm are described in Section 3. Section 4 presents the basic heuristics taken from two relaxed models of the problem, and Section 5 shows how these heuristics are combined in order to improve their estimations. Some comparative results when using the different heuristics are shown in Section 6, and some final remarks are made in the concluding section.

2. Assembly Sequence Planning

The process of joining parts together to form a unit is known as assembly. An assembly plan is a set of assembly tasks with ordering amongst its elements. Each task consists of joining a set of sub-assemblies to give rise to an ever larger sub-assembly. A sub-assembly is a group of parts that can be assembled independently of other parts of the product. This works supposes that in an assembly task there are two initial sub-assemblies to form a final one. An assembly sequence is an ordered sequence of the assembly tasks satisfying all the ordering constraints. Each assembly plan corresponds to one or more assembly sequences.

An *And/Or* graph [7] is a representation of the set of all assembly plans for a product. The *Or* nodes correspond to sub-assemblies, the top node corresponding to the whole assembly, and the leaf nodes to the individual parts. Each *And* node corresponds to the assembly task joining the sub-assemblies of its two Or nodes below it producing the sub-assembly of the Or node above it. An And/Or graph consists on several trees whose top nodes are the top node of the And/Or graph and whose leaf nodes are the leaf nodes of the And/Or graph. Each tree is associated to an assembly plan, and is referred to as an assembly tree. An important advantage of this representation, used in this work, is that the And/Or graph shows how different assembly tasks can be executed in parallel. Figure 1 shows an example of this representation, where Or nodes are represented as rectangles, and And nodes are represented as hyperarcs.

This work is about the selection of the best assembly plan, that is, one of the And/Or

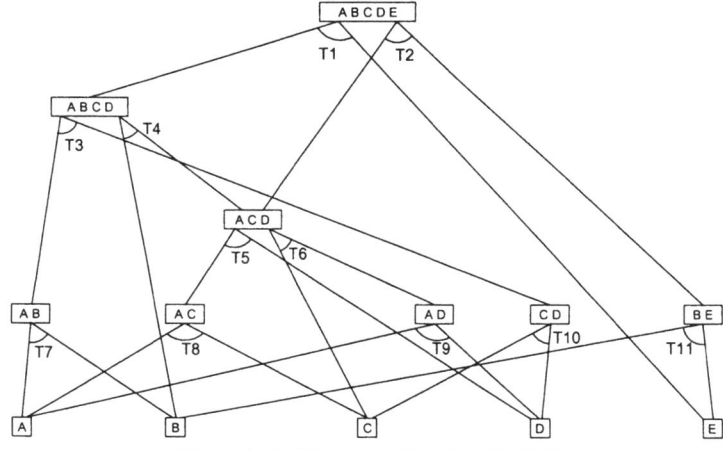

Figure 1. And/Or graph of product ABCDE

trees of the And/Or graph. Most of approaches used up to now make this selection in a planning phase in which neither the assembly system, nor how the assembly tasks within it will be materialized, is taken into account.

This work takes into account the physical realization of the assembly. It is assumed that the assembly tasks corresponding to the And/Or graph have been evaluated separately, in order to estimate the resources necessary for their realization (robots, tools, fixtures...) as well as their approximate duration times. For an And/Or graph with a large number of nodes this is not an easy task, and the help of a computer-aided system is necessary. The nodes corresponding to tasks which are not realizable are eliminated from the And/Or graph, as the sub-assemblies which cannot be part of a solution.

An assembly plan can be defined by means of the assembly tasks that form the successive sub-assemblies until the final product is made. An assembly task is defined from the initial and final sub-assemblies involved. An assembly task is defined to be performed in an assembly machine with a determined configuration, and has an estimated duration. If there are different ways (machine-configuration-duration) of joining two sub-assemblies to form another larger sub-assembly, we refer to those as different assembly tasks, which would correspond to additional And nodes in the And/Or graph.

The selection of the assembly plan is made through evaluating the optimal sequencing of their tasks, so that we would be solving at the same time a planning and scheduling problem. In order to evaluate more precisely the cost of the solutions, i.e. the total assembly time, other factors have been taken into account: the change of configurations in the machines and the transportation of subassemblies between different machines. The corresponding tasks (actions) are easily generated and sequenced from the set of assembly tasks defined by the sub-assemblies involved in them: for each two successive assembly tasks executed in a machine using different configurations there will be an adequate *change of configuration task* on the machine between them; if a sub-assembly is generated by an assembly task in a machine and it is required to be used as an initial sub-assembly by another assembly task in another machine, there will be a *transportation task* of this sub-assembly from one machine to the other one between the execution of the two assembly tasks.

Since assembly plans and assembly sequences are defined using only the assembly tasks, some delays are used for modelling both auxiliary tasks: $\Delta_{cht}(M, C, C')$ denotes the time needed for changing the configuration of the machine M from C to C'; and, on the other hand, $\Delta_{mov}(SA, M, M')$ denotes the time needed for transporting the subassembly SA from machine M to machine M'.

The model proposed supposes a well-dimensioned system, with a perfect planning when executing the assembly plan, so that, when a part would be required in a machine for executing an assembly task, it will be present there. The same cannot be guaranteed for an intermediate sub-assembly, because it could be built in a machine and required immediately in another one to form another subassembly.

In order to an easier reasoning, we will suppose in the rest of the paper that the precedence constraints are in the opposite direction, so that we will refer to a task preceding another one if the first one appears higher in the And/Or graph. This is as if we think about the opposite problem, that of the disassembly. To get the correct solution of the problem, we must only reverse the sequence given by the algorithm.

As mentioned above, with this model, the choice is not limited to the assembly plan, but also it can be specified when each assembly task is to be carried out in order to minimize the makespan (some assembly tasks which could potentially be carried out in parallel have to be delayed because they need common resources).

The results derived from this model can be used in different stages of the whole planning process, from the design of the product and of the manufacturing system, to the final execution of the assembly plan.

3. The A* Algorithm

An algorithm, based on the A* search [13], has been developed to solve the problem stated in the previous section. The algorithm has two well-differentiated parts: one of them considers the sequential execution of assembly tasks imposed by the precedence constraints defined in the And/Or graph, i.e. in the high part of the And/Or graph. The other solves the parallel execution of assembly tasks (the representation through the And/Or graph allows a natural study of this stage). This is actually the most complex section, because the execution of tasks on one side of the global assembly is not independent of the rest, and can influence the execution of tasks in the other part of assembly.

The algorithm starts from the root of the And/Or graph. The sequential part of the algorithm is used while the tasks considered involves only one non-trivial sub-assembly below the corresponding And node. It is the case of tasks T1 and T4 in Figure 1. When an assembly task takes two non-trivial sub-assemblies (for example, task T2 in Figure 1), the parallel part of the algorithm is used for obtaining the solution from the node in the search tree. In that moment, the algorithm generates all the assembly trees below that And node. Each of them is used for obtaining an optimal order for the tasks included in them, through a separate A* algorithm. The global algorithm orders previously all these trees using an estimation of the time needed for the execution of its tasks, so that not all the trees must been completely solved, because of the pruning of the search.

In the search tree of the algorithm, a node represents a state corresponding to the execution of the set of assembly tasks that have been included into the solution in the previous steps (with the corresponding auxiliary tasks –see Section 2). The order of including assembly tasks specifies the order of execution of them. So, an assembly task will not be included until all its predecessor assembly tasks in the And/Or graph have been included. This strategy allows verifying the precedence constraints of the problem. The state of a node n can be obtained also through the set of assembly tasks $cand(n)$ that can be included in the next expansion step, denoted *candidates*. For each candidate assembly task T we take the earliest start time, $est(T)$, if it were introduced in the next step. The description of the state of n is completed with the time corresponding to the last used of each machine M due to the tasks that have been included, $lastTime(n, M)$, and the last configuration used in each machine, $lastConf(n, M)$. An expansion step of the algorithm corresponds to selecting a candidate assembly task T, and including it in the partial solution as it is executed starting at $est(T)$, recalculating the state for the successor node and including in the set of candidate tasks the successor assembly tasks of T.

The objective function, $f(n)$, is given by the time needed for the execution of the tasks included in n, $g(n)$, plus an estimation of the time needed to complete a solution, $h(n)$. Function $g(n)$ can be defined as:

$$g(n) = \max\left(\max_{T_i \in cand(n)} \left(est(n, T_i)\right), \max_{M_i \in machines} \left(lastTime(n, M_i)\right) \right) \qquad (1)$$

Some different heuristic functions can be defined for $h(n)$. In order to maintain the admissibility of the A* algorithm, $h(n)$ must be an optimistic estimation of the remaining time for an optimal solution from n. In order to calculate properly the objective function f from g and h, two different types of slack have been defined, one for the candidate tasks, $e(n, T) = g(n) - est(n, T)$, and another one for the machines, $e(n, M) = g(n) - lastTime(n, M)$.

4. Basic Heuristic Functions

For the sequential part of the algorithm, $h(n)$ can be defined as:

$$h(n) = \min_{T_i \in ntOr(n)} \left(hs(T_i) \right) \tag{2}$$

$ntOr(n)$ denoting the non trivial Or nodes below the last task introduced in n, and

$$hs(T) = dur(T) + \max\left(\min_{T_i \in Or_1(T)} \left(hs(T_i) \right), \min_{T_i \in Or_2(T)} \left(hs(T_i) \right) \right) \tag{3}$$

where $dur(T)$ is the duration of task T and $Or_1(T)$ and $Or_2(T)$ are the Or nodes corresponding to the initial sub-assemblies involved in task T. In these expressions, $T \in Or$ represents the tasks T immediately below the Or node in the And/Or graph.
   Notice that only the precedence constraints have been used in the definition of $h(n)$ for the sequential part of the algorithm. For the parallel part, the constraints due to the use of resources can be taken into account. Because of the separation of the assembly trees, for each sub-problem all tasks are defined, i.e. there are not alternative tasks, and then the amount of usages for the different resources are known.
   Two basic heuristic functions can be defined for the parallel part of the A* algorithm, considering separately the two types of constraints: the precedence of tasks, and the use of resources.

4.1 The heuristic function h_1: precedence of tasks

It corresponds to an estimation of the time remaining if the interdependencies between different branches in the tree are not taken into account. It is looked at only in depth. It can be defined with following equations:

$$h_1(n) = \max\left(0, \max_{T_i \in cand(n)} \left(h_1(T_i) - e(n, T_i) \right) \right) \tag{4}$$

$$h_1(T) = dur(T) + \max_{T_i \in suc(T)} \left(h_1(T_i) + \tau_{mov}\left(T_i, T \right) \right) \tag{5}$$

$$\tau_{mov}\left(T_i, T \right) = \max\left(\tau\left(T_i, M(T), C(T) \right), \Delta_{mov}\left(sa(T_i), M(T_i), M(T) \right) \right) \tag{6}$$

$$\tau(T, M, C) = \max\left(0, \max_{T_i \in suc(T)} \left(h_1(T_i) + \tau\left(T_i, M(T), C(T) \right) - h_1(T) \right) \right) \tag{7}$$

In the above expressions, $M(T)$ and $C(T)$ are the machine and configuration necessary for the execution of the assembly task T. $\tau(T, M, C)$ is the added delay, due to the fact that the configuration C is being used by machine M in task T and successors, because of the necessary changes in configuration. The equation (7) defines $\tau(T, M, C)$ when $M \neq M(T)$. In the case $M=M(T)$, $\tau(T, M, C)$ is defined as $\Delta_{cht}(M, C(T), C)$ (that could be zero if $C=C(T)$). Finally, $\tau_{mov}(T, T')$ is the delay considering the possible transportation of the intermediate subassembly generated between the execution of T and T', and that of the possible change of configurations.
   Notice that $h_1(T)$ does not depend on the expansion nodes, so that it can be calculated for each task prior to using the A* algorithm for the assembly trees.

4.2 The heuristic function h_2: use of resources

It corresponds to an estimation of the time needed if only the remaining usage times of each machine are taken into account, further supposing the number of changes of configuration to be at a minimum. It can be defined as follows:

$$h_2(n) = \max_{M_i \in machines} \left(h_2(n, M_i) - e(n, M_i) \right) \tag{8}$$

where $h_2(n, M_i)$ is the minimum time of use of machine M_i without considering the task precedence constraints. If each configuration is associated with only one robot, the calculation of $h_2(n, M)$ is equivalent to the traveling salesman problem, when considering the configurations used by the tasks that still have not been included in n as the cities and an origin corresponding to the last-used configuration in the machine M:

$$h_2(n, M) = \left(\sum_{C_j \in M} \sum_{T_i \in cand(n)} h_2(T_i, C_j) \right) + \Sigma\left(n, \Delta_{cht}(M) \right) \tag{9}$$

with $h_2(T, C)$ the remaining time of usage of configuration C by task T and its successors. The term $\Sigma\left(n, \Delta_{cht}(M) \right)$ refers to the time needed for the changes of configuration. In the usual case that times for change of configurations do not depend on the types of configuration, it can be calculated easily. Without any precedence information, an in order to maintain the admissibility of the heuristic, it must be supposed that each remaining configuration will be established only once.

5. Combination of heuristics

The heuristics defined in the last section take into account different elements of the problem: h_1 uses the precedence constraints taken from the *And/Or* graph in order to estimate the most unfavourable path from an assembly task to a leaf assembly task, supposing that tasks from different branches, i.e. not related by precedence constraints, can be executed independently, that is, ignoring if they use the same machine. In the other way, h_2 ignores the precedence constraints and calculates the total usage time for each machine. The two heuristics have different effects and are incomparable. Depending on the machines used and the structure of the *And/Or* graph, one of them can obtain a better estimation than the other one. For example, if there is only one machine, there is no parallel execution of tasks, and h_2 will obtain a more accurate estimation. In the other way, if each assembly ask is executed in a different machine, h_1 collects all the information about the problem and its estimation is accurate.

In the previous section h_1 and h_2 were defined related to n, the expansion node. But the nature of the two heuristics are different: $h_1(n)$ is the maximum of the estimations of the candidate tasks, and $h_2(n)$ adds the time of usage of machines for all the candidate tasks. In order to combine properly the information from the two heuristics, we will use their estimations referred to the candidate tasks. For h_1 we have $h_1(T)$ defined in equations (5) to (7). For h_2 we can define $h_2(T)$ in a similar way than in (9):

$$h_2(T) = \max_{machines} \left(h_2(T, M_i) \right) = \max_{machines} \left(\left(\sum_{C_j \in M_i} h_2(T, C_j) \right) + \Sigma\left(T, \Delta_{cht}(M_i) \right) \right) \tag{10}$$

where $\Sigma\left(T, \Delta_{cht}(M) \right)$ refers to the time needed for the changes of configuration in M for the execution of T and its successors.

5.1 Heuristic h_3: refining h_1 using h_2

As $h_2(T)$ could be a better estimation than $h_1(T)$, both being optimistic, the first could be taken into account into the calculation of the second, since in the recursive expression for $h_1(T)$ it is required an estimation of the time needed for the execution of all the tasks in the subtree below T. The new heuristic that it is obtained, h_3, is defined based on equation (5), substituting h_1 for h_3 and considering h_2, as indicated. This way, a better estimation due to h_2 is propagated towards the predecessor tasks in the precedence tree. So, $h_3(T)$ is defined as:

$$h_3(T) = \max\left(dur(T) + \max_{T_i \in suc(T)} \left(h_3(T_i) + \tau_{mov}(T_i, T) \right), h_2(T) \right) \qquad (11)$$

The definition of $h_3(n)$ is similar to that of $h_1(n)$, (equation (4)), resulting a more informed heuristic than $h_1(n)$. However, $h_3(n)$ does not invalidate $h_2(n)$, because the last considers all candidate tasks in the expansion node n.

5.2 Heuristic h_4: estimating the intervals of machine usages

In the definition of $h_3(T)$, the time of usage of the most unfavourable machine, given by $h_2(T)$, is supposed that can take place during the execution of all the tasks of the subtree whose root is T. In some cases, it could be determined, by an analysis of the precedence tree, that the interval of use is smaller, so that the estimation of the total time for the execution of all tasks in the tree could be improved even more. Two new variables are defined, δ_b and δ_e, indicating the intervals, at the start and the end respectively, of the execution of all the tasks in the tree, in which the machine is not used.

The calculation of δ_b is done using its recursive definition:

$$\delta_b(T,M) = \begin{cases} 0 & \text{if } M = M(T) \\ dur(T) + \min_{T_i \in suc(T)} \left(\delta_b(T_i, M) + \max\left(\Delta_{mov}(\cdot), \Delta'_{cht}(T_i, T) \right) \right) & \text{if } M \neq M(T) \end{cases} \qquad (12)$$

where $\Delta_{mov}(\cdot) \equiv \Delta_{mov}\left(sa(T_i), M(T_i), M(T) \right)$ and $\Delta'_{cht}(T_i, T)$ represents the delay due to the possible change of configuration between the execution of T_i and T, defined by

$$\Delta'_{cht}(T_i, T) = \begin{cases} \Delta_{cht}\left(M(T), C(T_i), C(T) \right) & \text{if } M(T) = M(T_i) \\ 0 & \text{if } M(T) \neq M(T_i) \end{cases} \qquad (13)$$

In order to obtain a consistent definition, we take $\delta_b(T,M) = \infty$ when $M \neq M(T)$ and $suc(T) = \varnothing$. This way, when a machine is not used by any task belonging to a precedence subtree, the value of δ_b will be infinite.

In the other way, δ_e is calculated by means of its recursive definition:

$$\delta_e(T,M) = \begin{cases} \min_{T_i \in suc(T)} \left(\delta_e(T_i, M), h_4(T) - dur(T) \right) & \text{si } M = M(T) \\ \min_{T_i \in suc(T)} \left(\delta_e(T_i, M) \right) & \text{si } M \neq M(T) \end{cases} \qquad (14)$$

Again, for a consistent definition, we take $\delta_e(T,M) = \infty$ when $M \neq M(T)$ and $suc(T) = \varnothing$.

The definition of the new heuristic $h_4(T)$ has the same structure than $h_3(T)$, except that instead of using $h_2(T)$ alone, we take into account δ_b and δ_e. Moreover, it is necessary to separate the estimations of $h_2(T)$ for each machine, using $h_2(T, M)$:

$$h_4(T) = \max\Big(dur(T) + \max_{T_i \in suc(T)} \left(h_4(T_i) + \tau_{mov}(T_i, T) \right),$$

$$\max_{h_2(T, M_i) \neq 0} \left(h_2(T, M_i) + \delta_b(T, M_i) + \delta_e(T, M_i) \right) \Big) \qquad (15)$$

The definition of $h_4(n)$ is similar to that of $h_1(n)$, (equation (4)), resulting again a more informed heuristic than $h_1(n)$ and $h_3(n)$, but not necessarily better than $h_2(n)$, because the last considers all candidate tasks in the expansion node n.

5.3 Heuristic h_5: considering all machines in h_1, h_3 and h_4

In the definition of the heuristics h_1, h_3 and h_4 referring to a task T we have not taken into account the use of all the different machines, but only that of the machine used for the task T. In order to obtain this estimation we must define a new function related to the maximum delay that can be done in the use of each machine. Based on h_1, the new function, $\tau'(T, M, C)$, is defined as

$$\tau'(T,M,C) = \begin{cases} \Delta_{cht}\left(M,C(T),C\right) & \text{if } M = M(T) \\ \max_{T_i \in suc(T)} \left(h_1(T_i)+\tau'(T_i,M,C)-h_1(T)\right) & \text{if } M \neq M(T) \end{cases} \qquad (16)$$

and corresponds to the time before the execution of T at which the machine M must have configuration C in order to the execution of T and its successors does not finish after $h(T)$. Notice that this definition is similar to that of $\tau(T, M, C)$ (equation (7)), but now we can have negative values, indicating in that case a spare time for an eventual change of configuration that could be necessary, or simply that it is possible to have the configuration C in M after the execution of T has started, without altering the total execution time of T and its successors.

The same ideas used in defining the heuristics h_3 and h_4 can be employed in order to have a better estimation of τ' when $M \neq M(T)$, preserving the same expression when $M=M(T)$. This way, for h_3, $\tau'(T, M, C)$ can be defined, when $M \neq M(T)$, as

$$\tau'(T,M,C) = \max\left(\max_{T_i \in suc(T)} \left(h_3(T_i)+\tau'(T_i,M,C)-h_3(T)\right), \right.$$
$$\left. h_2(T)+\Delta''_{cht}(T,M,C)-h_3(T) \right) \qquad (17)$$

where

$$\Delta''_{cht}(T,M,C) = \begin{cases} 0 & \text{if } h_2(T,C)>0 \\ \min_{h_2(T,C_j)>0} \left(\Delta_{cht}(M,C,C_j)\right) & \text{if } h_2(T,C)=0 \end{cases} \qquad (18)$$

that shows that it will be needed a change of configuration if C is not used below T.

For h_4, $\tau'(T, M, C)$ can be defined, when $M \neq M(T)$, as

$$\tau'(T,M,C) = \max\left(\max_{T_i \in suc(T)} \left(h_4(T_i)+\tau'(T_i,M,C)-h_4(T)\right), \right.$$
$$\left. h_2(T)+\delta_e(T,M)+\Delta''_{cht}(T,M,C)-h_4(T) \right) \qquad (19)$$

The new heuristic $h_5(n)$ is defined as

$$h_5(n) = \max_{T_i \in cand(n)} \left(\max_{machines} \left(h(T_i)+\tau'\left(T_i,M_j,lastConf\left(n,M_j\right)\right)-e\left(n,M_j\right)\right)\right) \qquad (20)$$

where h refers to the heuristic used in the definition of τ', giving three different heuristic functions, named h_{51}, h_{53} and h_{54}.

6. Comparative results

There are different factors that affect the complexity of the problem proposed. Some of the more important are the number of parts, the size and structure of the *And/Or* graph, and the distribution of values for the durations and resources associated to the tasks.

As it is known, one of the most important problems in applying A* algorithms is the amount of memory wasted. In order to limit this consumption, the algorithm was adapted so that it used a depth-first search periodically for finding a new solution whose value could be

Table 1. Comparative results of the heuristics.

Heuristic	Nodes visited			Time (ms)			N-Df	N-F	% Error
	Ave	Max	Min	Ave	Max	Min			
h_1	30297	93376	32	13224	30930	0	11	15	0,985
h_2	4797	42775	32	668	6420	0	9	0	0,000
h_3	26414	88102	32	12408	30810	0	11	14	1,114
h_4	27046	87456	32	13321	30920	0	11	15	1,279
h_{51}	28745	92326	32	12892	31420	0	11	14	0,909
h_{53}	25641	81332	32	12598	30820	0	16	15	1,233
h_{54}	21698	54860	32	11462	30420	0	17	13	1,279
$\max(h_1, h_2)$	6008	71585	32	1453	30050	0	9	1	0,062
$\max(h_3, h_2)$	3267	23167	32	535	4230	0	8	0	0,000
$\max(h_4, h_2)$	4450	63996	32	1266	30050	0	6	1	0,041
$\max(h_{51}, h_2)$	5925	70432	32	1408	30150	0	8	1	0,062
$\max(h_{53}, h_2)$	2724	18254	32	465	4280	0	9	0	0,000
$\max(h_{54}, h_2)$	2459	18165	32	418	4280	0	8	0	0,000

used for pruning the search tree. Another improvement was done about detecting symmetries, so that redundant nodes are avoided in the expansion.

The results shown in Table 1, rather significant about the behaviour of the heuristics that have been defined, are based on a hypothetical product with 30 parts, with 396 Or nodes and 764 And nodes in the And/Or graph, so that the number of legal linear sequences is about 10^{21}. Each row of the table shows the results of 40 different problems solved using the corresponding heuristic, considering 10 different combinations on durations and resources among tasks, for each of four conditions in the resources used: 2 and 4 machines and 2 and 4 configurations/machine.

Table 1 shows, apart from the number of nodes and the time spent by the algorithm, how many times the optimal solution was found by a depth-first movement (N-Df), how many times the algorithm did not find the optimal solution in 30 seconds, when the available memory was exhausted (N-F), and the error rate. The results show the successive improvements that the heuristics have obtained. When analysing the results, it must be taken into account that the optimal solution can have been found through a depth-first movement, that is carried out from the best node just when this strategy is used, that explains the apparent contradiction in the comparative results between different heuristics, since the nodes used for the depth-first movements are (surely) different in each case. Another improvement came from the combined use of the heuristic h_2, of additive nature, with the others, which consider the most unfavourable candidate task for the calculation of the corresponding estimation for each expansion node.

7. Conclusions

Different heuristics have been defined for selecting optimal assembly sequences. The first two ones are based on both relaxed models of the problem, each one considering only a type of constraints, one related to the precedence constraints, and the other one to the use of shared resources. From them, other heuristics have been defined, combining both types of information, obtaining successive improvements, as it is shown in the results obtained.

Acknowledgements

This work has been partially funded by the Spanish Ministerio de Ciencia y Tecnología under grant DPI2003-07146-C02-01, and the European Regional Development Fund (ERDF/FEDER).

References

[1]   A. Bourjault. *Contribution à une Approche Méthodologique de l'Assemblage Automatisé: Elaboration Automatique des Séquences Opératoires*. Thèse d'état, Université de Franche-Comté, Besançon, France, 1984.
[2]   T.L. De Fazio and D.E. Whitney. Simplified Generation of All Mechanical Assembly Sequences. *IEEE J. Robotics and Automation*, Vol. 3, No. 6, pp. 640-658, 1987. Also, Corrections, Vol. 4, No. 6, pp. 705-708, 1988.
[3]   L.S. Homem de Mello and A.C. Sanderson. A Correct and Complete Algorithm for the Generation of Mechanical Assembly Sequences. *IEEE Trans. on Robotics and Automation*. Vol. 7, No. 2, pp. 228-240, 1991.
[4]   T. L. Calton. Advancing design-for-assembly. The next generation in assembly planning. *Proceedings of the 1999 IEEE Intl. Symp. on Assembly and Task Planning*, pp. 57-62, Porto, Portugal, July, 1999.
[5]   B. Romney, C. Godard, M. Goldwasser, G. Ramkumar. An Efficient System for Geometric Assembly Sequence Generation and Evaluation. *Proceedings of the 1995 ASME International Computers in Engineering Conference*, pp. 699-712, 1995.
[6]   R.H. Wilson, L. Kavraki, T. Lozano-Pérez and J.C. Latombe. Two-Handed Assembly Sequencing. *International Journal of Robotic Research*. Vol. 14, pp. 335-350, 1995.
[7]   L.S. Homem de Mello and A.C. Sanderson. And/Or Graph Representation of Assembly Plans. *IEEE Transactions on Robotics and Automation*. Vol. 6, No. 2, pp. 188-199, 1990.
[8]   J. Wolter. A Combinatorial Analysis of Enumerative Data Structures for Assembly Planning. *Journal of Design and Manufacturing*. Vol 2, No. 2, June 1992, pp. 93-104.
[9]   M.H. Goldwasser and R. Motwani. Complexity measures for assembly sequences. *International Journal of Computational Geometry and Applications*, 9:371-418, 1999.
[10] L.S. Homem de Mello and S. Lee (eds.) *Computer-Aided Mechanical Assembly Planning*. Kluwer Academic Publishers, 1991.
[11] C. Del Valle and E.F. Camacho. Automatic Assembly Task Assignment for a Multirobot Environment. *Control Engineering Practice*, Vol. 4, No. 7, pp. 915-921, 1996.
[12] C. Del Valle, M. Toro, E.F. Camacho and R.M. Gasca. A Scheduling Approach to Assembly Sequence Planning. *Proceedings of the 2003 IEEE Intl. Symp. on Assembly and Task Planning*, pp. 103-108, Besançon, France, 2003.
[13] J. Pearl. *Heuristics: Intelligent Search Strategies for Computer Problem Solving*. Reading, MA, Addison-Wesley, 1984.

Planning, Scheduling and Constraint Satisfaction: From Theory to Practice
L. Castillo et al. (Eds.)
IOS Press, 2005

Integration of Mission Planning and Flight Scheduling for Unmanned Aerial Vehicles

Elodie Chanthery, Magali Barbier, Jean-Loup Farges
ONERA, Toulouse Center - 2 av E. Belin - Toulouse, France

Abstract. This article presents the integration of on-line mission planning and flight scheduling for an unmanned aerial vehicle in military observation missions. Planning selects and orders the best subset of observations to be carried out and schedules the observations while accommodating time windows. The vehicle is subjected to speed, fuel supply and flight constraints in a uncertain and dynamic environment. The modeling of the problem and the algorithms implementation based on the exploration of a graph by an ordered depth-first search are presented. Mission planning and flight scheduling function is integrated in an on-board architecture based on Petri nets.

1 Introduction

Robots and unmanned vehicles have been used to perform missions in hazardous environment. Among these applications is the development of unmanned aerial vehicles (UAVs) for military observation missions in order to reduce human casualties. The autonomy of an unmanned vehicle is characterized by its level of interaction with the operator [6] : the more abstract the operator decisions are, the more autonomous the vehicle is. On-board mission planning and flight scheduling, computing a time-stamped itinerary for the vehicle in order to achieve the objectives of the mission, is one of the main challenges for intelligent UAV development in order to increase the autonomy level.

On-board functions for autonomous vehicles have to comply with three kinds of requirements : adaptability to a dynamical and, most of the time, uncertain environment, on-line problem solving and respect of real-time constraints for reactivity needs. Those functions thus should be integrated in an on-board mission management architecture including reactive capabilities. In this paper, the execution control function performs the global control of the execution of a mission. This includes the interaction with the physical system and the supervision of deliberative tasks. The main decisional component carries out the planning and scheduling function. The architecture makes it possible to react to degraded situations : the calculation of a new plan takes into account the new constraints. For this function, a long computation time only induces a degradation of the relevance of the plan with respect to the situation at the instant it becomes available but does not imply the vehicle destruction : mission planning problem is a soft real time problem.

The application context of the planning problem (including scheduling), its modeling, the planning algorithms implementation and the simulation results are provided in Section 2. Section 3 details the planning function integration in a real time architecture. The choice of intermixed planning and execution control is justified, the main concepts of the on-board architecture are presented, then the details of the planning integration are given. Section 4 concludes this work and presents a discussion of future work.

2   Planning Algorithms

2.1   *Observation Mission Planning Problem*

The context is a military observation mission for an autonomous aerial system in a three-dimensional, dynamic, uncertain and dangerous environment [2]. The environment of the mission includes an unsafe area where the vehicle carries out operations, that are the objectives of the mission. A mission is modeled by an origin waypoint, one or several end waypoints located outside the unsafe area and by the definition of a set of objective areas located inside the unsafe area. The information collected on an objective area may be transmitted either on line or at the exit of the area or at a transmission point, located in the range of the ground station and defined for all objectives that have their exit points outside this range. Transmissions are supposed to be instantaneous. Any collected information not already transmitted is obtained on the end waypoint. Danger zones are defined by the expected localization of potential threats. The mission constraints are due to the objectives, the environment and the engine. The planning function has to select and order the best sub-set of objectives and to determine the arrival date at each waypoint, maximizing observation profits and minimizing criteria on danger, fuel consumption and durations, while meeting the mission constraints.

Since there are few advantages and for the moment few means of anticipating replanning points (role of a prediction function), planning is performed *a priori* : the solution is based on probabilistic information on the future events. All useful information for planning is supposed to be known before computation.

2.2   *Previous Works*

Many planning problems for vehicles are described and solved in the literature. The scheduling of observations for an airborne telescope [4] requires making choices which lead to other choices later, and contains many interacting complex constraints over both discrete and continuous variables. It is similar to our problem except that there is no danger. The planning for mobile robot navigation in unknown terrain [11] is solved by a heuristic search method that repeatedly determines a shortest path from the current robot coordinates to the goal coordinates while robot moves along the path. There is only one goal while our objective includes several sub-goals that are the observation areas. These solutions are thus not suited for observation missions. It is necessary to implement algorithms adapted not only to the overall goal of the mission, but also to the danger of the mission and which are able to take into account various mission constraints including the finite fuel supply or the flight altitude. A real-time route planning named SAS route planner [17] generates mission-adaptable routes and takes into account various mission constraints cited above, but there is no scheduling.

Our planning problem can be seen as a more complex case of the Orienteering Problem with Time Windows (OPTW) [9], which is classified as NP-hard. The next section describes how our problem is modeled as an itinerary search in a graph with a costs optimization.

2.3   *Modeling*

In the chosen modeling [2], the vehicle takes off from the safe area at PO and comes back at an end waypoint PF. The unsafe area is defined by entrance points $\{PEZ\}$ and exit points $\{PSZ\}$. Each objective area is defined by a set of entrance points $\{PE\}$ and a set of exit points $\{PS\}$. With the transmission waypoints PT, these waypoints make it possible to define a directed graph as a set of nodes and a set of arcs. A node is an encapsulation of a 3D physical waypoint. The type of the node is related to the point which it represents among $(PO, PEZ, PSZ, PE, PS, PT, PF)$. An example of a mission map including two objective areas is given Figure 1. Figure 2 illustrates the data graph for this mission where the graph is represented by subsets of nodes having the same predecessors and the same successors.

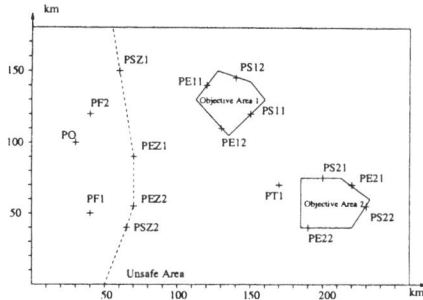

Figure 1: Mission map

Figure 2: Data graph example

One hypothesis denoted "cycles elimination hypothesis" reduces the number of possible paths in the graph : an entrance point of an objective area which objective was already carried out can not be crossed again.

The criterion to be minimized [2] is the difference between the costs and the profits obtained on the selected path. The modeled costs are relative to the consumption, the danger and the durations. The total profit can be seen as a reward associated with information obtained on objective areas. Costs and profit take into account uncertainties. The decision variables are the flight duration of each arc and a boolean variable expressing the fact that an arc is used in the itinerary or not. The components of the vector of flight durations for an itinerary is speeds related. The consumption and duration costs may be expressed as sums on the arcs of functions of these decision variables. The major difficulty is that profits and danger costs depend on the past route and on the optimized durations between each node. They can not be calculated by arc as for a traditional OPTW.

The problem presents linear and nonlinear constraints. Linear constraints, applied to arcs, depend on the characteristics of the vehicle (minimum and maximum speeds) and on the data graph : the date of arrival on some waypoints is included in a time window out of which the observations are not valid any more. Nonlinear constraints are global and are related to danger (loss of the vehicle) and consumption limits (maximum fuel quantity).

At the mission beginning, the aim of planning is thus to find an optimal path starting by PO, finishing by an end node via the arcs of the graph. During the mission, the planning function computes an optimal path beginning at a predicted vehicle position in the graph updated according to the objectives already carried out.

2.4   Planning Algorithms Description

The itinerary search is performed on the tree of possible ways. Proposed algorithms are based on an alternative of the ordered depth-first search [15] guided by a best-first strategy. These algorithms are different from the ones of the literature : for each developed node, the precise evaluation of the criterion requires an optimization of the speeds of the whole itinerary. The output is a path defined by an ordered list of nodes and a vector of optimized durations between each pair of nodes. The pruning function makes it possible to cut the branches of the exploration tree and thus to reduce the number of node expansions. The planning algorithm is adapted for on-line replanning and so is able to begin at any aerial point taking into account a new environment or new objectives. For each developed node, an optimization subproblem is solved. The nonlinear danger and fuel constraints are integrated in the criterion as penalty functions. The problem becomes the optimization of a nonlinear criterion under linear constraints (speed limits and arrival dates). The problem is solved by the Frank-Wolfe algorithm [5]. This basic algorithm [2] is called Algorithm 1.

In order to improve the guidance of the exploration in the tree of the possible paths and to improve the pruning function, Algorithm 1 is modified by implementing a cost evaluation of the itinerary from an unspecified node to an end node : the problem is solved with a constant speed on the itinerary. The selected value is the optimal value for a problem without constraint and danger. The calculation takes into account the transmissions differed at the transmission waypoints. The pruning of Algorithm 1 is improved by the calculation of a first path without optimization speeds and by developing only a limited number of nodes. Speeds are then optimized for this path, given a bounded value for the criterion. The only difference between Algorithms 2a and 2b is the pruning function. Algorithm 2a uses the pruning function of Algorithm 1. It has the advantage of not cutting a branch of the exploration tree containing the optimal path. Search will be better guided than for Algorithm 1 because of the evaluation of the cost path to an end point. However, the tree could be not pruned enough and search in all the possible paths would take time. Algorithm 2b uses an evaluation of the future cost for its pruning function. The disadvantage is that if parameters are badly selected, the branch containing the optimal path may be cut. The advantage is that it makes possible to cut a higher number of branches and thus to deal with problems of big size.

2.5   Results

The algorithms are implemented using C++ language. A military mission is defined for a Mean Altitude Long Endurance vehicle. The waypoints of the mission are shown on the map Figure 1. The transmission for the objective area 1 is done at an exit point of the area. The objective area 2 is located out of the range of the ground station, a transmission point PT1 is thus defined for the transmission of information concerning this area. The operator defines the mission by giving the set of waypoints (type, coordinates, time windows), the frontier between safe and unsafe areas and information about threats.

The first test is carried out without danger and with a total observability but with time constraints on each entrance point of the unsafe area. Optimal path is shown on Figure 3. The speed adapts to time constraints. For the second test, the quantity of fuel is limited.

For the third test, a threat $DG1$ is added ofter the entrance in the unsafe area. The profit is degraded compared with the first test because of the risk to lose the vehicle. The path bypasses the danger zone (Figure 4). The last test is an on-line replanning that occurs between the entrance in the unsafe area and the first objective area in the second test because a new threat has been detected. The autonomous system bypasses the new threat (Figure 4). This test highlights the vehicle ability to autonomously adapt to a new environment.

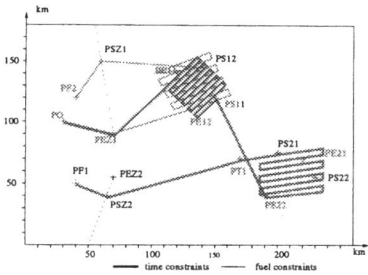

Figure 3: Results for time and fuel constraints

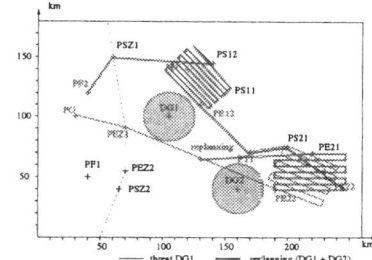

Figure 4: Results for threats and replanning

Table 1: Experiments results

case	time windows			fuel			threat $DG1$			replanning		
Algorithm	1	2a	2b	1	2a	2b	1	2a	2b	1	2a	2b
first admissible path	9	0	0	9	0	0	12	0	0	5	0	0
optimal path	173	0	0	9	0	0	70	0	0	234	8	8
algorithm end	449	170	148	192	162	23	122	60	28	286	114	105

Comparative results for the four tests, treated by the three algorithms, are shown on table 1. The values correspond to the number of developed nodes to obtain an admissible path, the optimal path and to end the algorithm. For Algorithms 1 and 2a, the total number of developed nodes to end the algorithm corresponds to the number of developed nodes to obtain the optimality proof of the best cost path obtained. For Algorithm 2, 0 indicates that a route is obtained after the search phase at constant speed. The average of CPU time for one node expansion is about 0.2s for a Sun Microsystems Sparc Ultra 5 processor.

A first advantage of the algorithms is that a suboptimal admissible solution is obtained after a few node expansions. For Algorithm 2, the first admissible path is obtained after 0.9s maximum. For all the tests, the number of developed nodes is lower than the maximum number of developed nodes without pruning (2103). Algorithm 2 is efficient for pruning and search guidance : the total number of developed nodes is less than for Algorithm 1 and the optimal solution is obtained more quickly. As expected, Algorithm 2b prunes more the exploration tree than Algorithm 2a. The optimal solution is always found by Algorithm 2b.

3   Planning and Scheduling Integration in a Real-Time Architecture

3.1   Intermixed Planning and Execution Control Choice

Recent studies on the links between the calculation of plans and their executions show a growing number of practical applications. The context of these studies casts doubt over the assumptions which are generally adopted in planning, that are a static environment and no failure. Indeed, new events can occur and invalidate the plan in progress; the execution of the planned actions can fail and the planning must modify the current plan. The execution controller of the mission must adapt in an asynchronous way to the update of the state of the vehicle.

Various types of links between the planning and the execution control exist in the literature.

A probabilistic or conditional planning such as the Markov Decision Processes (MDP) allows to control uncertainties relating to the state of the environment and the effects of the actions. A problem of exploration planning is solved in [18]. An hybrid approach between state space factorization and decomposition is proposed. The supervisor directly applies the strategy found by planning for the current state of the system. A library of plans calculated off line or in line [8] can describe the various behaviors of a vehicle. The supervisor starts the suitable plan according to its knowledge of the environment, its objectives and its intentions. New objectives or new environment are not taken into account. The IxTeT-eXEC planning system [12] interleaves planning and execution control. Its key component is a temporal executive which interacts with the planning system. It regularly updates the plan under execution, repairs the plan in case of failure and replans upon arrival of new goals. However, the plan is not optimized and the planner cannot deliver early a partial plan.

Our approach proposes to use a structure based on the combination of the planning algorithm described in the previous section with the ProCoSA execution controller [14]. The originality of ProCoSA is that it implements tasks scheduling and event handling strategies that are described with Petri nets [13]. Petri nets are directed graphs with two kinds of nodes, the places and the transitions. The marking of the graph is given by tokens in places. In ProCoSA, an automaton, called the Petri Player, manages the update of the Petri nets marking. The data-processing components of the deliberative part of the vehicle such as a planning algorithm are implemented as on-board software programs. The real-time level of this language will depend on the application; in this work, the architecture behaves like a soft real-time system. Indeed, there is no guarantee on time response mainly because ProCoSA internally uses a socket communication protocol and events treatments depend on the Petri Player state. An original functionality of the ProCoSA Petri nets is the possibility to assign events and requests to transitions. A transition is fired if the marking validates it and if an assigned event occurs. The crossing of this transition produces the assigned requests. These requests are either events towards other transitions or messages toward a software program. Finally, software programs can produce events towards ProCoSA. The Petri nets are developed off line by means of a convivial graphic user interface.

In the Petri nets that describe the vehicle behavior during the mission, places model the possible states of the vehicle and transitions model the changes between states: at any moment, the set of marked places describes the state of the vehicle.

3.2   The On-Board Architecture Concepts

Two things make it possible to reduce the complexity of on-board architectures. In compositional methods [16], the problem is broken up into a sequence of several small problems of manageable complexity; in distributed hierarchical architectures [10], the system is described by increasingly detailed elements. The on-board architecture presented in this paper has such an implementation (Figure 5) : software programs carry out the decisional and practical tasks, a set of Petri nets hierarchically models the logic of the vehicle behavior and a supervisor manages the update of the vehicle behavior and the communication with decisional tasks.

The architecture thus includes several software programs : the planning program; the trajectory computation program calculates the vertical profile between two mission waypoints; the guidance program calculates the controls sent to the vehicle by taking account its flight

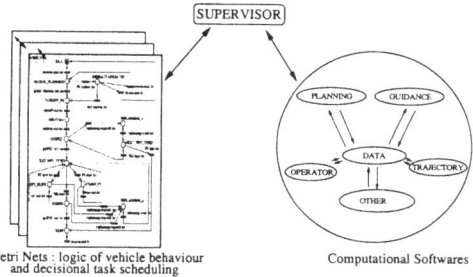

Figure 5: On-board architecture

dynamic characteristics; a data management program centralizes dynamic information necessary to all components; the operator program allows the ground operator to communicate high level decisions on the mission (abandon, new objective ...); a situation awareness program supervises the mission and the engine state and sends alerts events for replanning or operator information. Planning program is the one described in section 2. Both guidance and data management programs are described in detail in a first implementation [1]. The other programs are to be developed.

Petri nets detail the vehicle behavior during the mission in nominal mode and in degraded situations. The typical phases of an observation mission are : takeoff, navigation to the next waypoint as long as there remains one, return to the ground station and landing. Each phase is broken up in an increasingly detailed way. The low level of this decomposition is the highest level of piloting controls communicated to the engine. The Petri nets are developed in a hierarchical way according to this decomposition. An advantage of this architecture is to allow an easy integration of new behaviors. In addition, comprehension is easier for an operator located in a ground station.

The main Petri net "Mission" (Figure 6) describes the general behavior of the vehicle from its takeoff until its landing. The marked place in this Petri net indicates the phase in which the vehicle is or the high level action in progress (TAKEOFF_PO, GO2PEZ, OPE_PE2PS, TRANS_PT, GO2PSZ, GO2PF). These places correspond to the activation of a more detailed Petri net. At the beginning of the mission, the activation of the GLOBAL_PLANNING place indicates the global planning computation. If the optimal value of the criterion is negative, it means that costs are lower than profits. The path is then accepted and sent for treatment, the mission starts. On the contrary, if the criterion is positive, the mission is either abandoned or interrupted. During the mission, the places REPLANNING_s and REPLANNING_u detail the behavior of the vehicle during replanning either in the safe area (s), or in the unsafe one (u). Places OPE_PE2PS and TRANS_PT detail the operation between PE and PS and the data transmission. Specific transitions and the associated Petri nets control the reaction to operator and degraded events (eventually from situation awareness program).

The hierarchy of the Petri nets is presented Figure 7. The Petri net "Takeoff" describes the takeoff of the vehicle at the beginning of the mission, corresponding to the PO waypoint. The Petri net "Operation" activates the Petri net corresponding to the type of the operation. During this net, PE and PS of the mission area carried out are joined. "Transmission" describes the behavior of the aerial system during the data transmission to the ground station on a PT

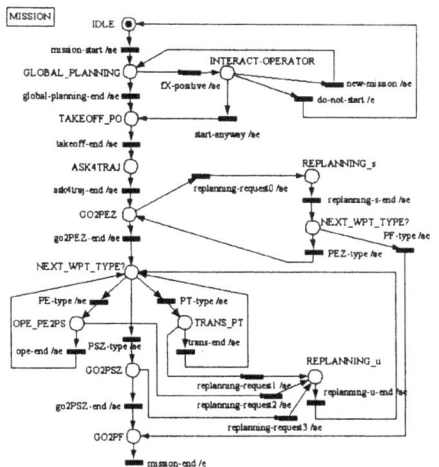

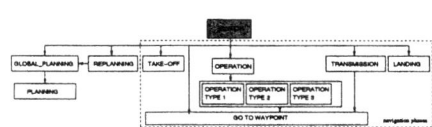

Figure 7: Hierarchy of the Petri nets

Figure 6: Mission Petri net

waypoint. The Petri net "Landing" describes the end of the mission on PF. The Petri net "Go to waypoint" specifies the behavior of the vehicle during the navigation phase to a specified waypoint. It is used by the net "Mission" for the waypoints of type PEZ and PSZ, by the net "Operation" and by the net "Transmission" to navigate to the transmission waypoint.

3.3 Planning Integration

Planning is integrated in the on-board architecture thanks to three Petri nets "Global_planning", "Planning" and "Replanning" that call the planning algorithm with different parameters. Figure 8 illustrates the links between these three Petri nets.

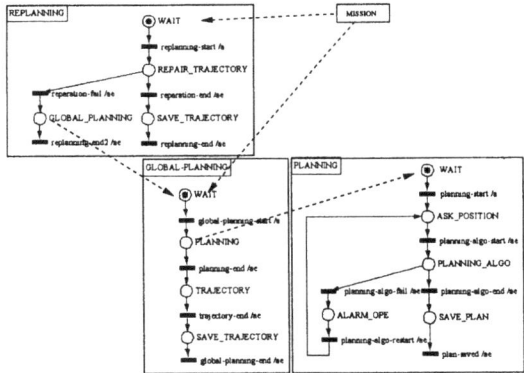

Figure 8: Planning integration in Petri nets

The Petri net "Global-planning" is run when the place GLOBAL-PLANNING of "Mission" is activated. The Petri net "Replanning" is run when one of the two places REPLAN-NING of "Mission" is activated.

Global planning consists in the determination of the best plan, resulting of the planning computation described in section 2, and then in the calculation of the trajectories between the waypoints of the plan. The net "Planning" asks for the current position of the vehicle, then runs the planning algorithm. If the computation fails, an alarm is sent to the operator via an Human Machine Interface. "Replanning" consists in trying to repair the trajectories. If it fails, it runs the global planning.

4 Conclusions and future work

This paper proposes the integration of on-line mission planning and flight scheduling for an unmanned aerial vehicle.

The planning problem is defined in the context of an observation mission in a three-dimensional, dynamic, uncertain and dangerous environment. The mission is modeled by a directed graph where each node is an encapsulation of a physical waypoint and edges represent feasible trajectories between waypoints. The goal of the planning is to find a path from the origin waypoint to one of the end waypoints and to schedule observations to accommodate time windows. The criterion to minimize is the sum of the consumption, danger and durations costs minus the profits obtained from the observations. The constraints are induced by the mission objectives, the environment and the autonomous aerial system. Three planning algorithms are proposed : they solve a shortest path search problem in the graph where costs are dynamic, either positive or negative, and take into account uncertainties. The tree exploration is based on an ordered depth-first search algorithm. For each node expansion, the speed is dynamically optimized for each edge of the path. Several tests show the good behavior of the algorithms with time and fuel constraints, in presence of dangers and in a replanning way.

The planning and scheduling function is integrated in a hierarchical architecture based on its combination with the ProCoSA execution controller. A user interface allows an operator to define various observation missions. The vehicle behavior is described by increasingly detailed Petri nets. The Petri net of the highest level illustrates the modeling of the mission. It exists a close link between the modeling of the mission (Section 2) and this Petri net. If an other modeling is chosen [1], the main Petri net "Mission" could be adapted. The advantage of this architecture is the hight abstraction level of Petri nets. They allow to specify every kind of modeling (space state and plan space planning). Three Petri nets are dedicated to the planning and replanning during the mission. They allow the specification of the planning function running using an intermixed approach between execution control and planning.

To conclude, the operator only defines the mission in terms of waypoints and constraints. The planning function gives a high autonomy level to the aerial vehicle. Moreover, the system is adapted to a dynamical and uncertain environment.

Future work will first concern the improvement of the tree exploration of the planning algorithm. A solution considering a factored tree where each objective is globally considered is under investigation. A second track will concern the test of the algorithm in a real time context. In that case and for a given computer technology, a trade-off has to be performed between the quality of the solution and the reactivity of the autonomous aerial system. This trade-off could be studied by limiting the number of node expansions by associating a reaction time to a number of node expansions and by observing the resulting vehicle behavior. Other research could be performed on the modeling assumption, the use of a weighted criterion, the use of penalty functions. The durations of transmission could be modeled and taken into account. Other types of threat may also be modeled. Petri nets may be used not only for specifying the behavior of the system, but also for modeling some constraints of the planning problem. An any-time planning approach [7] could face the problem of having a partial admissible solution at any time in urgency case. The final integration of planning and scheduling in the architecture is still in hand. Future work will finalize this implementation and simulations with the global architecture should be done in future months.

References

[1] E. Chanthery and M. Barbier, 'Functional modules for intermixed planning and execution of an observation mission', in *Proceedings of the 18th Bristol UAV Systems Conference*, (April 2003).

[2] E. Chanthery, M. Barbier, and J.L. Farges, 'Mission planning for autonomous aerial vehicles', in *IAV2004 - 5th IFAC Symposium on Intelligent Autonomous Vehicles*, (2004).

[3] G. B. Dantzig, *Linear Programming and Extensions*, Princeton University Press, 1963. Princeton, NJ.

[4] J. Frank and E. Kurklu, 'Sofia's choice: Scheduling observations for an airborne observatory', in *Proceedings of the 13Th International Conference on Automated Planning & Scheduling*, (2003).

[5] M. Frank and P. Wolfe, *An Algorithm for quadratic programming*, volume 3, Naval Research Logistic Quaterly, 1956.

[6] M.A. Goodrich, D.R. Olsen, J.W. Crandall, and T.J. Palmer, 'Experiments in adjustable autonomy', in *Workshop on Autonomy Delegation and Control*, Seattle WA, (August 2001). IJCAI 2001.

[7] N. Hawes. 'Anytime planning for agent behaviour', in *Proceedings of the Twelfth Workshop of the UK Planning and Scheduling Special Interest Group*, 157–166, (2001).

[8] F. Ingrand, R. Chatila, and R. Alami, 'An architecture for dependable autonomous robots', in *IARP-IEEE Workshop on Dependable Robotics*, Seoul, South Korea, (2001).

[9] M.G. Kantor and M.B. Rosenwein, 'The orienteering problem with time windows', *Journal of Operational Research Society*, **43**(6), 629–635, (1992).

[10] H. Jin Kim, R. Vidal, D. H. Shim, O. Shakernia, and S. Sastry, 'A hierarchical approach to probabilistic pursuit-evasion games with unmanned ground and aerial vehicles', in *IEEE Conference on Decision and Control*, Orlando, (December 2001).

[11] S. Koenig and M. Likhachev, 'Improved fast replanning for robot navigation in unknown terrain', Technical report, College of Computing, Georgia Institute of Technology, (2001).

[12] S. Lemai and F. Ingrand, 'Interleaving temporal planning and execution: Ixtet-exec', in *ICAPS 03 Workshop on Plan Execution*, (2003).

[13] T. Murata, 'Petri nets : properties, analysis and applications', in *IEEE*, pp. 77(4), 541–580, (1989).

[14] DCSD ONERA, 'http://www.cert.fr/dcsd/cd/procosa'.

[15] J. Reif, 'Depth-first search is inherently sequential', *Information Processing Letters*, **20**, 229–234, (1985).

[16] B. Sinopoli, M. Micheli, G. Donato, and T.J. Koo, 'Vision based navigation for an unmanned aerial vehicle', in *IEEE International Conference on Robotics and Automation*, (2001).

[17] R.J. Szczerba, P. Galkowski, I.S. Glickstein, and N. Ternullo, 'Robust algorithm for real-time route planning', *IEEE Transactions on Aerospace and Electronics Systems*, **36**(3), 869–878, (2000).

[18] F. Teichteil-Konigsbuch and P. Fabiani, 'An hybrid probabilistic model for autonomous exploration', in *Proceedings of RFIA 2004*, (2004).

Planning, Scheduling and Constraint Satisfaction: From Theory to Practice
L. Castillo et al. (Eds.)
IOS Press, 2005

Planning tourist visits adapted to user preferences

Susana Fernández
Univ. Carlos III de Madrid
sfarregu@inf.uc3m.es

Laura Sebastia
Univ. Politecnica de Valencia
lstarin@dsic.upv.es

Juan Fdez-Olivares
Univ. de Granada
faro@decsai.ugr.es

Abstract In this paper, we present a work that is part of a running project, SAMAP
[1]. The aim of the project is to make tourist plans for a user in an 'intelligent' way,
considering its preferences to propose a list of activities that better adjusts to its profile.
The application could displayed in any device with Internet connection capabilities,
such as Personal Digital Assistants (PDA) or mobile phones. In this paper, we focus
on the planning part of the project showing the difficulties that entail to solve a real
problem with AI planning and proposing a system that overcomes them.

1 Introduction

During the last years, global networks, such as the Internet, have experienced an important
growth. This is causing a social and economic impact in many aspects. For example, from
the commercial point of view, we can buy a different range of products through the Internet,
i.e., books and films, and we can even buy a plane ticket or book a hotel. The success of these
new commercial activities is related with the fact that we can use a PC or even new hardware
devices with connection capabilities, such as Personal Digital Assistants (PDA) or mobile
phones to access the Internet, to compare prices and to buy the product we are interested in.

Electronic tourism is one of the activities that have enjoyed an important success in the
Internet, not only from the commercial point of view but also from a social perspective. Many
sites provide information about places to visit in a city, activities to do during the travel,
restaurants, etc. But this information is always static in most cases, that is, it is presented to
all users in the same way. Moreover, the quantity of available information can be large and,
therefore, the user must select which pieces of information are interesting for him.

In this paper, we present an application that is able to compute a tourist plan for a user.
One of the most important features of this application is its ability of building a plan that
takes into account the user preferences. This way, the system presents to the user only the
information he is interested in. The following section gives an overview of this application.
Next sections focus on the planning part of this system as what we would like to outline is
that the planning task resulting from the analysis of this tourist problem is a difficult task,
which can make it unsolvable by existing planners. Section 3 introduces an example of this
planning problem and outlines its main features. Section 4 describes the suggested solution
which overwhelms the difficulties. Section 5 presents the preliminary experiments that we
have performed and their outcome. And, finally, Section 6 draws some conclusions from the
work.

---

[1]This work has been partially supported by the Spanish MCyT under project TIC2002-04146-C05

2 Overview of the application

The goal of this application is to compute a tourist plan for a user (any person with Internet access via a handy device, such as a PDA or a mobile phone). This system needs to have access to the following information:

- Information about the city, that is, the context that surrounds the user (i.e. monuments and interesting places in a city, etc.)

- Personal data, interests and preferences of the user, that is, type of activities that this user likes to do when he visits other cities (user model)

- Places that other people similar to our current user liked when they visited the same city (plans of other users)

- Basic services that the user requires for performing his activities (i.e. payment with credit card, use only taxi for movements, etc.)

Once we have all this information, the application computes a tour which contains the following elements:

- a selection of the most interesting places for this user according to his model

- indications about which transport he/she should take to move between different places

- recommendations about where to have lunch or dinner (restaurants, bars, etc.)

- proposals of places of leisure such as cinemas or theatres

Figure 1 shows a generic architecture of this application. The first step consists of **building the user model**. This requires the user to introduce information about itself, that is, his personal data and his interests and preferences about, i.e., art, monuments, meals, etc. This information can be gathered by using any device with Internet connection. In order to obtain more interesting data about the user, the system (by means of learning techniques, mainly classification techniques [7]) can use past information about the same user (provided it has used the application before).

The second step consists of the **analysis of the user model** in order to obtain a list of places it may like to visit according to its preferences. Each place in this list is associated with a number which indicates the utility that visiting this place might have for the user. This module uses both the user model and a repository which stores previous visits of other users. Therefore, the system compares previous visits to the same city of other users with a similar profile to the current user.

The last step is the **computation of the tourist plan** by taking into account only the visits that may be interesting for the user (that is, the output of the previous step). This planning task has several features that make it hard for current planners. These features are exposed in the next section and Section 4 explains how we have solved some of these difficulties in order to obtain a solution plan. Once the application has computed a plan, it must be showed to the user through its device.

We have developed an **ontology** to store all the information introduced by the user and generated by each module. We can distinguish the following parts in this ontology:

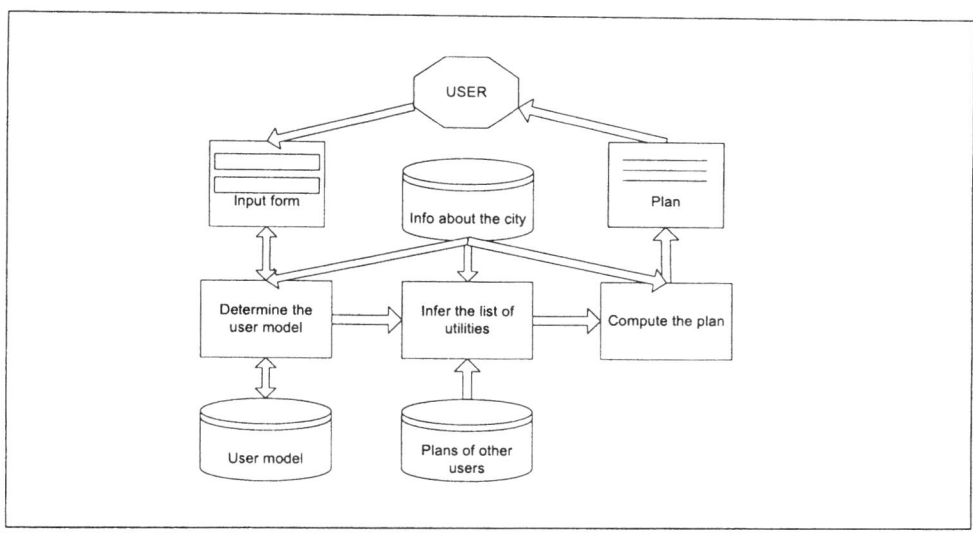

Figure 1: Application overview

- User information:

    - Personal data: name, language, place of residence, age, mobility, children, etc.

    - Device data: model, quantity of data per page, information that should be enfasized, etc.

    - Preferences: meals timetable, type of meal, payment, transport, budget, specific and generic activities, etc.

- City information:

    - Means of transport: bus, subway, taxi

    - Places: restaurants, museums, buildings, churches, parks, etc

    - Streets and their intersections

- Plan

    - Planning operators: attend a show, move between locations, have lunch or dinner, visit a place, etc

    - Selected activities joint with the feedback from the user (accepted or rejected activity)

In this paper, we will focus on the planning part, assuming that we get a list of activities that represent the places of interest for the user together with a number indicating their utility.

3 Problem characteristics

The development of planning systems for real world problems requires the use of additional techniques to manage duration of actions, numerical values, uncertainty, etc. There are several

Table 1: List of places to visit adapted to the user model. Duration is given in minutes and Utility is a value between 1 and 5.

Place	Duration	Utility	Price	Opening hours	Coordinates
City hall	45	3	free	All day	(725756.938, 4372347)
Cathedral	60	5	free	9 to 13 - 17 to 20	(725896.25, 4373109.5)
La Lonja	60	5	free	9 to 20	(725569.688, 4372920)
Modern Art Museum	120	4	5e	9 to 19	(725195.563, 4373554.5)
Central Market	90	3	free	8 to 15	(725575.188, 4372881.5)
...	...	...	...	....	
Restaurant					
La Papardella	75	4	12e	14 to 16.30	(725634.5, 4373123.45)
La Abadia d'Espi	90	5	18e	13.30 to 17	(725734.5, 4373248.2)
...	...	...	...	....	
Theatre					
Principal	90	3	12e	19 to 20.30	(725576.1, 4372876.59)
Talia	120	4	10e	21 to 23	(725570.1, 4372910.34)
...	...	...	...	....	

planning systems that include some of these techniques. However, our tourist problem has specific features that make it hard for these planners. This section describes these features.

First, let's introduce an example. Suppose that our application receives a requirement of a user who is visiting Valencia (Spain). He asks for a tour starting in his hotel (located at City Hall Square) at 9 and finishing not later than 8 in the afternoon in his hotel, too. His budget is 100 euros for the whole day. The system asks additional information necessary to compute the user model and, after analysing the user preferences, it determines the list of places to visit partly shown in Table 1.

Therefore, all this information makes up the initial state of the planning problem, together with data about the city. The goal of this problem cannot be specified easily, as we want to obtain a plan that accomplishes the following characteristics:

- **Referring to management of time:** The first condition is that the sum of the duration of the visits in the plan must fit into the available time of the user. Moreover, each visit should be scheduled according to the opening hours of each place. For example, we cannot visit the Central Market later than 15h.

- **Referring to management of numerical values:** The prices of the visits, meals and transports must not exceed the available budget.

- **Referring to locations:** The plan indicates how to go from one place to another, that is, which transport the user should take. In case it is preferable to walk, the plan indicates which route the user should follow. What implies the management of a great amount of knowledge and represents a trade-off for the planner complexity.

- **Referring to the goal:** We can specify three types of goals:

  - totally instantiated goals, i.e., visit the Modern Art Museum

  - partially instantiated goals, i,e., visit any museum

  - a goal indicating that the plan must maximize its utility.

Moreover, not all the places available must be visited.

Most of these features can be handled by most temporal planners. However, we will focus on the ones that are more specific:

1. **Each visit is scheduled according to the opening hours of each place.** This implies that we need an explicit management of the current time. In addition to the restrictions that existing temporal planners take into account when scheduling an action, our system must consider the current time because a place cannot be visited if it is closed. This also causes that there can be empty time points, that is, time points when no action is executed (from the point of view of the user, an empty time point is free time). This free time is not handled by temporal planners (every time point has an associated action).

2. **The plan indicates how to go from one place to another.** This task can be performed (theoretically) by any planner. But our system has to deal with all the means of transport (subway, bus, taxi, ...) in a city and the routes one can take to walk from one place to another.

3. **The objective of the problem contains partially instantiated goals.** This means that the planner must select only one specific place whose type is equal to the partially instantiated goal.

4. **The plan is computed in order to maximize the utility of the visits.** In a general planning problem, even when we deal with durative actions and numerical values, we specify the goal as a set of literals that must belong to the final state. However, in our case, there is not such a set of literals; our goal is to maximize the utility of the plan. This kind of problems were introduced in the International Planning Competition held in 2003 in the hard numeric track, but only few planners (MIPS [3], SHOP2 [6] and TLPlan [1]) were able to solve them.

4 Adopted solution

In the previous section, we have demonstrated the difficulty to use a simple planner for solving the planning part of the application. Therefore, we propose to build a system composed by a planner and other modules in order to reduce the workload of the planner. The input of the system is an original list of activities that represents the places of interest for the user (including eating and leisure places) together with a number indicating their utility, i.e the usefulness that visiting such site provides the user. Each activity can be totally or partially instantiated, as in visit museum of Modern Art or visit a museum. In addition there can also exist duplicated planned activities because a user can visit the same place twice in the same day. The output is one or more tourist plans including as many visits as possible, along with the indications about the transports needed to move between the different places (the transport subplans). The system also calculates the cost of the plans trying to maximize its quality according to the established metric. By default, the quality metric is to maximize the total utility, but it could be to diminish the cost, a combination of both or any other one. The ontology stores all the information: the static one, as well as the output of the different modules of the application, including the list of activities. So, the final step of the planning system is to store the generated plans into the ontology.

Figure 2 shows the proposed architecture, composed of five modules:

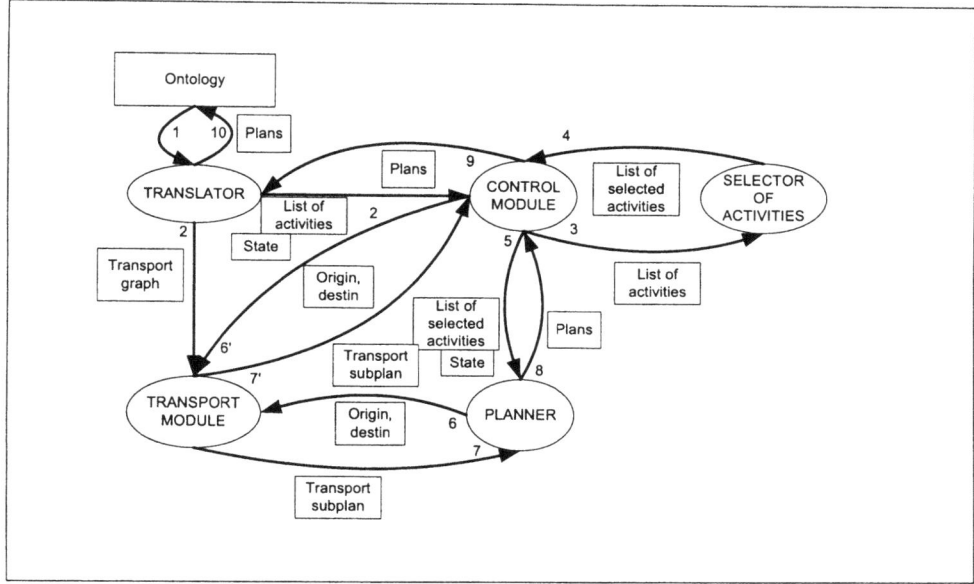

Figure 2: Planning System Architecture.

• **Translator** module: it is the module in charge of transforming the knowledge stored in the ontology into the knowledge (initital state and goals) required by the planner. As the ontology stores all necessary information as a hierarchy of frames (classes and instances), the predicates of the initial state are obtained from slot values of instances as triplets (`<slot> <object> <value>`). On the other hand, goals are translated from the list of activities (which also are slot values of ontology instances) to instances of the predefined predicate (`visited <place>`).The translator module also produces the transport graph, i.e, all the information related with the transportation (places, distances, means of transport, users preferences ...). In addition, it also transforms the solution plans into the corresponding instances of the ontology

• **Control** module: it coordinates the rest of modules providing the input that they need in the suitable format and gathering their output. It can invoke the Transport module or let the Planner module do it

• **Selector of activities** module: the aim of the system is to maximize the utility of the plan and/or to satisfy some specific or generic goals, but not to fulfil all the available activities. This module selects the most appropriate actions to be solved by the planner each time. This module should be designed to have a similar behaviour to a tourist. For example, it should select first those activities related to near places with the highest utility

• **Planner** module: it generates the plans. Its input is a domain planning problem (state + list of activities), a quality metric, a cost bound and a time bound. It tries to generate one or more plans that solve the problem during the time bound. The cost of the solutions cannot be greater than the cost bound, according to the quality metric. There can be more than one Planner module each with a different planning technique. The Control module compiles all the results. This module can directly communicate with the Transport module

- **Transport** module: it receives an origin and a destination point and returns the transport subplan for moving a person from the origin to the destination. It also returns the cost and time of the itinerary

So far, there is not feedback amoung modules. In case of failure, the Selector of activities simply provides a different list of actions to be solved without considering the failures. However, it would be interesting that the system was able to analyze the failures in order to exclude the actions that make it impossible to reach a solution.

As the crucial part of the system is the planner, in the next section we will focus on the features that it should have in order to planning a tourist visit.

5 Preliminary experiments

The preliminary experiments concern the Planner module. As the architecture is presently at an early stage we are not interested in efficiency issues, but in testing how a standard planner can make tourist plans considering the specific features shown in Section 3. Therefore, we have defined a domain that accomplish all the requirements and several simple problems to test it. So far, we have made the problems by hand but in the final system they will come from the Selector of activities module.

The planner used for these experiments is QPRODIGY, the version of PRODIGY that is able to compute the cost of the generated plans. We refer the reader to [2] for the details about it. In this paper it is enough to point out some of its characteristics that allows it to plan the tourist visits according to the layout introduced in the previous sections:

- PRODIGY uses a specific domain description language whose representation capabilities are similar or even better, in some issues, than the current planning standard PDDL2.1 [4]. A PDDL problem can be automatically translated into a PRODIGY problem

- PRODIGY enables to call any Lisp function in the domain description. This, among other things, facilitates the interaction with extern modules as the Transport one

- Although, it is a nonlinear planner, its behaviour can be easily modified to be linear by changing the value of a global variable. Planning a tourist visit is typically a linear problem; there is no interaction among goals

- QPRODIGY is able to compute complex quality metrics assigning different values to the same action depending upon the situation in which that action is applied. The total quality (cost) of a plan P is computed by adding the cost of the plan operators

- PRODIGY allows the introduction of control knowledge, described as a set of control rules, that guides the decision-making process. PRODIGY planning/reasoning cycle, involves several decision points: *select a goal* from the set of pending goals and subgoals; *choose an operator* to achieve a particular goal; *choose the bindings* to instantiate the chosen operator and *apply* an instantiated operator whose preconditions are satisfied or continue *subgoaling* on another unsolved goal. Decisions at all these choices are taken based on user-given or learned control knowledge to guide the search and convert it into an intelligent commitment search strategy. Control knowledge can *select, reject, prefer*, or *decide* on the choice of alternatives [8]. If no control knowledge is given, backtracking is usually required, thus reducing planning efficiency. An example of control rule for this domain is showed in figure 3. This rule avoids the planner to work in the goal of trying to update the current-time.

```
(control-rule reject-all-current-time
    (if (and (target-goal (current-time <user> <day> <time> ))
        ))
    (then reject goal (current-time <user> <day> <time>)))
```

Figure 3: Example of a control rule for reject working in goal current-time

As we said in Section 3, it is necessary an explicit management of the current time, for which, we perform a discretization of the time. We divide the time in units that correspond to a certain amount of minutes, e.g. 15. There is a predicate current-time that takes finite values corresponding with these units and represents the actual planning time for the user. It also tells the planning operators the possible times where the visits can start by means of a function that calculates the list of valid values according to the timetable of the place, the duration of the visit and the user available time. The loss of accuracy that this discretization entails is minimum since it is perfectly assumed that no action can take less minutes than the one we have established for one unit of time. Let see the following example to clarify it: there is a goal to visit a museum that closes at 8 p.m, the estimated duration of the visit is 2 hours and the current time is 5 p.m. We first convert all the hours into time units (considering unit 0 at 12 p.m and 1 unit is equal to 15 minutes), so current time is 68 $(17*4)$, the museum close time is 80 $(20*4)$ and the duration is 8 units $(2*4)$. The list of values for the variable <time> in the predicate (current-time <user> <day> <time>) would be:(68 69 70 71 72) because after 6 p.m (unit 72) the user wouldn't has enough time to finish the visit. Suppose the user needs 1 unit to move to the museum, so the first value that the planner could fix would be 69 and the current time would be updated to $69+8 = 77$ after the execution of the operator.

PRODIGY, like most planners, cannot achieve the same goal twice. Given that in this domain the user can visit the same place more than once in the same day, it is necessary to add another variable, <nth> which can have finite values (1, 2, 3 ...), to all the goal predicates. This causes the planner consider them as different goals. For example, if a tourist wants to visit bar twice , the goals of the problem would be (visited-bar 1 ...), (visited-bar 2 ...).

The operators defined in the domain are the following:

- MOVE: it calls the Transport module to compute the duration and cost of the tourist movements and it updates the current-time, money-available and location according to these results. It also adds the cost to the total cost of the plan

- There is a VISIT-*PLACE*: operator for each one of the possible types of places considered in the ontology. From visiting a museum (VISIT-MUSEUM), to eating in a restaurant (VISIT-RESTAURANT) or watching a film (VISIT-CINEMA). The only difference between all these operators is the type of the place (museum, restaurant, show_room ...)

and the partially instantiated goal that each one adds (visited-museum, visited-restaurant, visited-cinema . . .). There is a predicate visited <place> for the totally instantiated goal that is an effect of these operators as well, so a unique operator solves both kinds of goals. It also contemplates the possibility that goals can be repeated by adding the <nth> variable. As example, figure 4 showed the definition of the operator VISIT-MUSEUM

- PREPARE-VISIT: there are several common preconditions and effects to all operators VISIT-PLACE who group themselves in this operator, as the current-time, price, duration, started time and cost.

```
(OPERATOR VISIT-MUSEUM
        (params <nth> <u> <p> <day>)
        (preconds
         ((<u> USER)
          (<p> MUSEUM)
          (<day> DAY)
          (<nth> (and ENUMERATE (possible-enumerates))))
         (and (prepared-visit <u> <p> <day>)))
        (effects
         ()
         ((add (visited-museum <nth> <u> <day>))
          (add (visited <nth> <u> <p> <day>))
          (del (prepared-visit <u> <p> <day>)))))
```

Figure 4: Definition of operator VISIT-MUSEUM in PRODIGY

So far, we have tested our domains with some problems made by hand according to the places of Table 1. Considering the five first places (City Hall, Cathedral, La Lonja, Modern Art Museum and Central Market) in the initial state and varying the number of goals, Problem1 has as unique goal visited the City Hall; Problem2, visited the Cathedral as well; . . . . We have also considered that the goals can be totally or partially instantiated.

The metric used in all the problems is the user utility. Table 2 shows the results of running the planner with the above problems and using the control rule of figure 3. It displays the number of goals, the number of nodes generated for the planning process and the time (in seconds) until it finds the solution for both cases totally and partially instantiated goals, and the total cost of the reached plans.

Table 2: Results of the execution of PRODIGY in the tourist domain

Problem	GOALS	NODES/TOT.	SECONDS/TOT.	NODES/PAR.	SECONDS/PART.	COST
PROBLEM1	1	29420	25.14	29413	24.07	3
PROBLEM2	2	57400	52.27	57388	51.91	8
PROBLEM3	3	79648	79.02	79630	79.04	13
PROBLEM4	4	92570	95.95	92548	93.75	17
PROBLEM5	5	151854	190.07	86824	91.43	20

The results shows that PRODIGY can solve the problems and therefore the definition of the domain is apparently correct, but the number of nodes and time increases significantly with the number of goals. It will be probably necessary to add control knowledge to the planner.

There are not significant differences between totally or partially instantiated goals but this is probably because there are not many places to choose yet.

6 Conclusions

In this work we have introduced a planning application for assisting a tourist to plan the visits in a city using a PDA or a third generation mobile phone. These plans are adapted to the user preferences proposing only a list of activities that could be really interesting for it. It has been shown that the planning task resulting from the analysis of this tourist problem is a difficult task since several issues that appear in real world domains have to be adressed, namely: (1) satisfying multiple criteria about resources like time and money; (2) selecting the appropriate places to visit in order to maximize the utility of the planned visits; (3) incorporating transport subplans; (4) solving partially instantiated goals. We have performed by hand some preliminary experiments that show how a nonlinear planning system (QPRODIGY), that follows a means-ends analysis and that computes cost plans, can build tourist plans taking into account these issues. However, the time and space complexity is increased according to the number of goals, what demonstrates that solving this kind of problems is hard.

In order to reduce the problem solving complexity and with the aim of building a fully applicable planning system in the domain of interest, we have proposed an architecture composed by several modules: Translator module, Control module, Selector of activities module, Planner module and Transport module. In summary, this work has to be considered as a step forward in the development of such architecture. At present, we are working on the integration of these modules, and we are focused on the development of the Transport module (initially based on a A* algorithm), and on the improvement of the Selector of activities, in order to better adapt to the user preferences.

References

[1] F. Bacchus and M. Ady. Planning with resources and concurrency: A forward chaining approach. In *International Joint Conference on Artificial Intelligence (IJCAI-2001)*, pages 417–424, 2001.

[2] Daniel Borrajo, Sira Vegas, and Manuela Veloso. Quality-based learning for planning. In *Working notes of the IJCAI'01 Workshop on Planning with Resources*, pages 9–17, Seattle, WA (USA), August 2001. IJCAI Press.

[3] S. Edelkamp. Symbolic pattern databases in heuristic search planning. In *AIPS'02*. AAAI Press, 2002.

[4] Maria Fox and Derek Long. *PDDL2.1: An Extension to PDDL for Expressing Temporal Planning Domains*. University of Durham, Durham (UK), February 2002.

[5] Héctor Geffner. Perspectives on artificial intelligence planning. In *Eighteenth national conference on Artificial intelligence*, pages 1013–1023. American Association for Artificial Intelligence, 2002.

[6] D. Nau, H. Munoz-Avila, Y. Cao, A. Lotem, and S. Mitchell. Total-order planning with partially ordered subtasks. In *International Joint Conference on AI - IJCAI-2001*, 2001.

[7] W. Pohl, I. Schwab, and I. Koychev. Learning about the user: A general approach and its applicatio. In *Proceeding of IJCAI'99 Workshop "Learning About Users"*, 1999.

[8] Manuela Veloso, Jaime Carbonell, Alicia Pérez, Daniel Borrajo, Eugene Fink, and Jim Blythe. Integrating planning and learning: The PRODIGY architecture. *Journal of Experimental and Theoretical AI*, 7:81–120, 1995.

Planning, Scheduling and Constraint Satisfaction: From Theory to Practice
L. Castillo et al. (Eds.)
IOS Press, 2005

A Diagrammatic Inter-Lingua for Planning Domain Descriptions

Max GARAGNANI*
Department of Computing, The Open University
Walton Hall, Milton Keynes MK7 6AA – United Kingdom

Abstract. Sentential and diagrammatic representations are two different formalisms for describing domains and problems. Sentential descriptions are usually more expressive than diagrammatic ones, but tend to present a more complex and less intuitive notation. All modern planning domain description languages are sentential. The complexity of sentential formalisms has been of hindrance to the wider dissemination and take up of planning technology beyond the planning research community. As an alternative to such languages, this paper proposes a *diagrammatic* "inter-lingua" for planning domain descriptions based on setGraphs. SetGraphs represent actions, states and goals in terms of set- and graph-theoretic constructs. Through some examples, setGraphs are shown here to yield simpler and more intuitive domain encodings. An abstract formalisation of setGraphs illustrates how the representation can be easily specified using a formal language. SetGraphs are then proven to be at least as expressive as a standard modern propositional planning domain description language. The model proposed is intended to be used as a common "core" representation, suitable to be used across different levels of abstraction, and aimed at facilitating the elicitation, maintenance and re-use of planning domain descriptions during the processes of language development and domain knowledge engineering.

1 Introduction

During the past few years, research in AI planning has reached a stage of maturity that should have resulted in wide industrial and commercial take up. However, this has not generally happened. One of the causes of the gap between theory and applications lies in the fact that the remarkable capabilities of modern planning technology (and, perhaps, even the *existence* of the technology itself) are still largely ignored outside the planning community. This is not hard to believe, given the relatively young age of the field and the speed at which it has been developing. Indeed, many AI researchers who are not directly involved in planning research still consider this area as mostly concerned with STRIPS-like systems and problems.

In order for planning technology to find wider application, more awareness and a clearer understanding of what planning currently is and what it has to offer are required. The rather specialistic, predicate-logic notation that all modern domain description languages adopt appears to be one of the major obstacles to the technology dissemination and take up, particularly in non-academic environments. In fact, although AI researchers and practitioners are usually familiar with the concepts of states and goals and are well versed in formal logic,

---

*The author wishes to thank the UK EPSRC for the support given to this research (grant ref. GR/R53432/01).

users, knowledge engineers and domain experts are often discouraged when presented with the latest BNF formalisation of PDDL [14], and when required to express their problem in such terms. Paradoxically, in several cases PDDL still fails to offer the flexibility and expressiveness that is needed to accurately and completely describe the real problem at hand anyway.

In order to allow planning experts and non-experts to more easily represent, communicate and modify domain descriptions, we propose a *diagrammatic* (or analogical [15]) formalism based on the model of *setGraph* [4, 6, 5]. SetGraphs represent states, goals and actions in terms of directed graphs in which the vertices are sets of symbols. SetGraphs were introduced in [4] as a simpler and more efficient alternative to traditional, pervasive, *sentential* domain description languages. SetGraphs representations can be easily translated into more formal domain description languages. Furthermore, preliminary experimental evidence [6] suggests that planning problems represented in diagrammatic terms can be solved much faster (up to two orders of magnitude) than when described using a purely sentential language. This paper argues that setGraphs also yield simpler and more intuitive (yet flexible) domain descriptions, which can be more easily and quickly understood by non-planning experts and facilitate the process of domain knowledge engineering.

The paper is organised as follows: Section 2 introduces the main ideas behind setGraphs through simple examples; Section 3 presents setGraphs in more precise and formal terms, introducing numeric values in the model; in Section 4, setGraphs are proven to be expressively equivalent to a simplified version of the standard planning domain description language PDDL. Related work, limitations and future directions are discussed in the last section.

Before proceeding any further, it should be clarified that setGraphs are not claimed here to be "the" universal language which is fit for *all* application domains. Adopting the same view of Frank, Golden and Jonsson [3], we propose setGraphs as a common "core" representation for use in many planning domain description languages, sufficiently expressive for most simple, well-defined, problems, and easy to be extended to meet the different requirements of the various real-world situations. In addition, it should be pointed out that this paper is not concerned with the definition of a specific language for the computational encoding of the proposed diagrammatic representation. The representation described here constitutes a "meta-language", aimed at facilitating the processes of domain description language development and knowledge engineering, including domain knowledge elicitation, representation, modification and re-use. The task of specifying the actual syntax of a domain description language based on setGraphs, although relatively straighforward (setGraphs are built using basic concepts of set and graph theory), does not fall within the scope of this work[1].

2 A gentle introduction to SetGraphs

We start with a very simple representation, which is then progressively augmented with additional features. The formal description of the formalism is given in the next section.

A setGraph is essentially a directed graph in which the vertices are sets of symbols. For example, Figure 1.(a) shows a setGraph description of a Blocks World (BW) state with three blocks and a table, represented by symbols 'A', 'B','C', 'Table'. The vertices of the graph are depicted as ovals, labelled $V_1, \ldots, V_{10}$. In this example, the edges of the graph (arcs)

---

[1]However, see [6] for an example of BNF formalisation of a simple language based on a restricted version of the setGraph model.

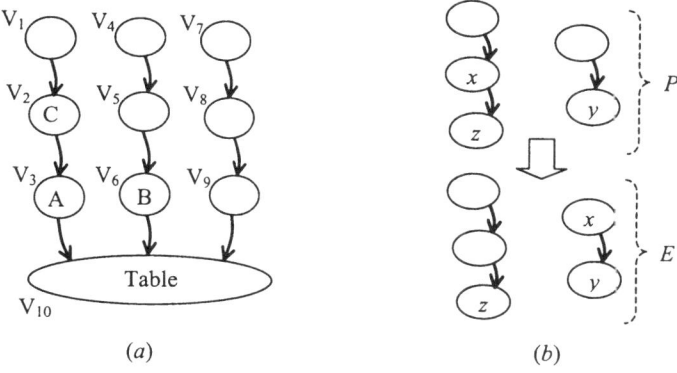

Figure 1: A SetGraph encoding of the Blocks World domain: (a) state representation; (b) $Move(x, y, z)$ operator (where $x \in \{A, B, C\}$ and $y, z \in \{A, B, C, Table\}$).

represent 'on' relations between spatial locations: if a vertex containing symbol x is linked to a vertex containing symbol y, then On (x, y) holds in the current state.

The symbols of a setGraph can be moved from one vertex (set) to any other through the application of diagrammatic operators, which specify the set of legal transformations of a state (setGraph). Figure 1.(b) depicts the *Move* operator for the BW domain. The operator preconditions P describe a specific arrangement of symbols in a part (sub-graph) of the current state; the effects E describe the arrangement of these symbols in the same sub-graph after the application of the operator. Intuitively, an operator $P \Rightarrow E$ is applicable in a state s iff each of the graphs contained in P can "overlap" with (be mapped to) a sub-graph of s having the same "structure", so that each variable corresponds to a distinct symbol, each vertex to a vertex, each edge to an edge, and: (1) if a variable is contained in a set (vertex), the corresponding symbol is contained in the corresponding set; (2) if an edge links two vertices, the corresponding edge links the corresponding sets; and (3) if a set is empty, the corresponding image is empty. When all of these conditions hold, we will say that the precondition setGraphs are *satisfied* in s. Notice that the variables can be of specific *types*, subsets of the universe of symbols. For example, variable x in the $Move(x, y, z)$ operator of Figure 1.(b) has type $Block=\{A, B, C\}$; this operator is applicable only if block x has an empty set on top of it (i.e., if x is clear).

The application of an operator to a state s causes the corresponding symbols in s to be rearranged according to the situation described in the effects E. For example, the $Move(x, y, z)$ operator can be applied to the state of Figure 1.(a) in several ways. One possible binding is x/C, y/Table, z/A; the application of $Move$(C,Table,A) would unstack block C from A and put it on the table (i.e., in set V_9 of Figure 1).

This simple representation can be easily extended with additional features. The following example illustrates the use of typed and symbol-to-symbol edges in setGraphs; in the next section, symbol-vertex edges and numeric quantities will be introduced. As discussed later, the addition of these features makes the formalism significantly more expressive.

Example 1 - Consider a variation of BW in which blocks have a specific weight, and the

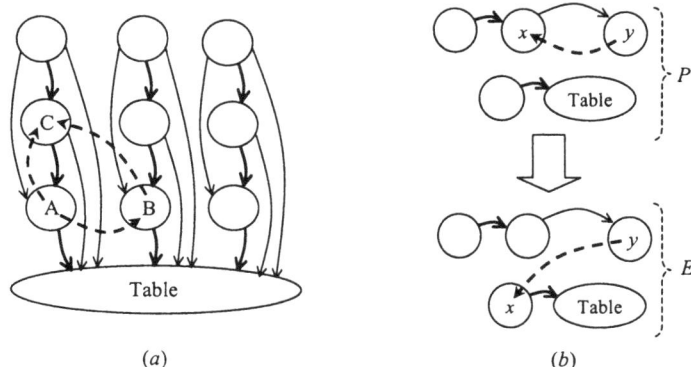

(a)   (b)

Figure 2: A richer diagrammatic model of BW: (a) current state; (b) *Unstack*(x, y) operator. Bold, thin and dashed arcs indicate, respectively, 'on', 'above' and 'heavier' relations (see Example 1 for details).

stacks are such that a block can be removed from the top only if the stack contains at least another block which is *heavier* than the one being removed. In order to encode this domain, two additional relations between objects (namely, the relation 'heavier' and 'above' between blocks) have to be represented. One possible way to obtain this is to introduce typed edges. Figure 2.(a) depicts different types of edges using different *styles* of arcs (although *labelled* arcs could also have been used). The state representation contains two new types of edges, identified by thin and dashed arcs. A thin arc linking a vertex containing symbol x to one containing symbol y denotes that block x is the n-th block above y (with $n > 1$); a dashed arrow linking symbol x to symbol y indicates that block x is heavier than block y. Figure 2.(b) depicts the diagrammatic version of the *Unstack*(x, y) operator (the *Stack*(x, y) operator is identical to the *Move*(x, y, z) operator of Figure 1.(b) with z=Table). The preconditions P require the existence of a block y such that both Heavier (y, x) and Above (x, y, n) hold. The effects E encode the new position of block x, now located on the table. We assume that when a symbol is moved, all arcs connected to it move with it.

Notice that the number of edges needed in a setGraph to represent relations between objects (like 'above' or 'heavier') grows only *polynomially* in the number of objects of the domain. Another interesting property of diagrammatic representations is that they allow the spatial relations existing between the "mobile" objects of a domain to be represented as *static* (or invariant) elements of the description, whenever the set of possible positions in which such objects can be (relatively to each other) is finite and predetermined. For example, it is easy to see that all the edges of the setGraph of Figure 2.(a) (representing spatial and weight relations between blocks) are static and remain unchanged throughout any plan execution, as they are not affected by any of the actions. Interestingly, this encoding could have been also "emulated" using a propositional language description. For example, if the vertices of the setGraph of Figure 2.(a) were considered as entities of the domain, then the BW state could be described also as follows:

$$I = \{ \; \text{On}\,(V_1, V_2)\,, \text{On}\,(V_2, V_3)\,, \text{On}\,(V_3, \text{Table})\,, \ldots \,, \text{On}\,(V_9, \text{Table})\,,$$
$$\text{Above}\,(V_1, V_3)\,, \text{Above}\,(V_2, \text{Table})\,, \ldots \,, \text{Above}\,(V_7, \text{Table})\,,$$
$$\text{Heavier}\,(A, B)\,, \text{Heavier}\,(B, C)\,, \text{Heavier}\,(A, C)\,,$$
$$\text{In}\,(C, V_2)\,, \text{In}\,(A, V_3)\,, \text{In}\,(B, V_6)\,,$$
$$\text{Empty}\,(V_1)\,, \text{Empty}\,(V_4)\,, \text{Empty}\,(V_5)\,, \ldots, \text{Empty}\,(V_9) \; \}$$

Predicate $\text{In}\,(x, y)$ indicates that symbol x is inside vertex y; $\text{Empty}\,(x)$ indicates that vertex x contains no symbols; $\text{On}\,(x, y)$, $\text{Above}\,(x, y)$ and $\text{Heavier}\,(x, y)$ denote the corresponding edges between vertices and symbols. Observe that in the state representation I, only the instances of the predicates $\text{In}\,(x, y)$ and $\text{Empty}\,(x)$ are subject to change; the rest of the literals are static. Although obtaining this propositional encoding from Figure 2.(*a*) appears to be a straightforward task, no planner would have been able to *automatically* generate state I from the original, propositional description of the BW domain.

Whilst this graph-based notation is capable to encode most of the "classical" benchmark domains, a more expressive formalism is required for most real-world domains. The next section contains a more precise and formal definition of setGraphs, in which the representation is further extended with numeric quantities and actions involving not only the movement (or removal) of symbols but also of vertices. As pointed out earlier, however, the main aim of this paper is not to build a domain description language suitable for encoding all possible real domains, but rather to introduce a common core, simple and intuitive diagrammatic formalism that can be easily extended with additional features according to the different domain specific requirements. In view of this, the description of the model has been kept intentionally abstract and stripped of any low-level syntactical detail, so as to avoid committing the representation to any particular language or paradigm.

3 Formalising setGraphs

The formal definition of setGraph is based on the concept of *multiset* [16]. A multiset is a set-like object in which the order of the elements is unimportant, but their multiplicity is significant. For example, C={1,1,0,0,0} denotes a multiset of integers containing two occurrences of 1 and three occurrences of 0. Since the order is unimportant, C is equivalent to {1,0,1,0,0}, but not to {1,1,0,1,0}. The empty multiset is denoted as { }. We will say that x is *contained* in C and write "$x \in$ C" to indicate that element x appears (occurs) at least once in multiset C.

The definition of a setGraph is based on that of *nodeSet*, specified recursively as follows:

Definition 1 (NodeSet, Node, Place). *Let W be a set of symbols (language). A NodeSet is either:*

- *a symbol $w \in W$ (in which case, the nodeSet is a* Node*), or*

- *a finite multiset of nodeSets (in which case, the nodeSet is a* Place*).*

A node is a symbol (string) of the language. A place is a "container" for both nodes and places. Nodes and places are nodeSets. In short, nodeSets are data structures consisting of multi-nested sets of symbols (strings) with multiply occurring elements and no limit on the level of nesting. Places can be labelled (possibly with identical labels). Given a nodeSet N,

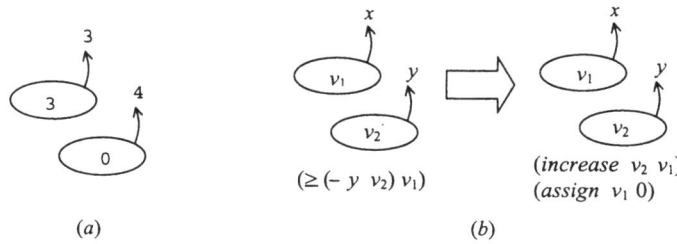

Figure 3: A diagrammatic model of the Water Jug domain: (a) initial state; (b) *Pour* operator.

$\wp(N)$ is defined as the multiset of all the nodeSets occurring in N (including N itself). For example, consider a language $W=\{A,B,C\}$. Let N_1 be the nodeSet $\{A, \{B\}, \{\{C\}\}\}$. Then, $\wp(N_1)= \{A, B, C, P_0, P_1, P_2, P_3\}$, where $P_0 = N_1, P_1 = \{B\}, P_2 = \{\{C\}\}$ and $P_3 = \{C\}$.

Definition 2 (SetGraph). *A* setGraph *is a pair* $\langle N, E \rangle$*, where N is a nodeSet and $E = \{E_1, \ldots , E_k\}$ is a finite set of binary relations on $\wp(N)$.*

If E contains only one relation E', we shall simply write $\langle N, E' \rangle$ instead of $\langle N, \{E'\} \rangle$. For example, let N_1 be the nodeSet $N_1=\{A,\{B\},\{\{C\}\}\}$. The pair $\alpha = \langle N_1, E_1 \rangle$ is a setGraph, where $E_1=\{(C, B), (\{B\}, \{\{C\}\}), (\{A,\{B\},\{\{C\}\}\}, A)\}$. The instances of the binary relation E_1, pairs of elements of $\wp(N_1)$, are the edges of the setGraph. Notice that if N_1 is specified using the notation $N_1=P_0\{A, P_1\{B\}, P_2\{P_3\{C\}\}\}$ in which all places are labelled, then E_1 can be specified simply as $\{(C, B), (P_1, P_2), (P_0, A)\}$ (refer to the previous example).

A complete treatment of the setGraph representation lies outside the scope of this paper, and can be found in [5]. The above description, however, illustrates how setGraph models can be formalised quite easily using set- and graph-theoretic constructs.

3.1   Actions with numeric and non-conservative effects

The simple planning operators introduced in Section 2 are limited to the movement of nodes from one place to another. Let us now augment the representation so as to allow the description of actions containing numeric preconditions and effects, and involving the movement, addition to, or removal from the setGraph of any element (nodeSet or edge).

Numbers are represented in setGraphs as *numeric nodes*. A numeric node is a string (symbol) of W of form "$n.m$" or "n", where n, m denote sequences of digits (possibly preceded by $+$ or $-$). Operators preconditions and effects will consist of two separate parts, diagrammatic and numerical. The diagrammatic preconditions and effects are lists of parameterised setGraphs. The numerical preconditions consist of a set of comparisons ($<, >, =, \leq, \geq, \neq$) between pairs of numerical expressions. Numeric expressions are built from the values of numeric nodes using arithmetic operators. Numeric effects can make use of a set of assignment operations that update the values of a numeric node; these include direct assignment and relative assignments (such as increase and decrease – see Figure 3 and example below).

The possible setGraph transformations considered here are: (i) addition or removal of a node, place or edge, (ii) movement of a nodeSet, and (iii) update of a numeric node. The movement and removal of elements in a setGraph is based on the following general rules: (1) if a node is moved (removed), all edges linked to it move (are removed) with it; (2) if a

```
(define (domain jug-pouring)
   (:requirements :typing :fluents)
   (:types jug)
   (:functions
        (amount ?j - jug)
        (capacity ?j - jug))

   (:action pour
        :parameters (?jug1 ?jug2 - jug)
        :precondition (>= (- (capacity ?jug2) (amount ?jug2))
        (amount ?jug1))
        :effect (and (assign (amount ?jug1) 0)
                     (increase (amount ?jug2) (amount ?jug1)));
   )
)
```

Figure 4: PDDL2.1 encoding of the Water Jug problem (*from* [2]).

place is moved (removed), all the elements contained in it and all edges linked to it move (are removed) with it. Any element not moved, removed or updated is left unaltered.[2]

Example 2 - In the well-known Water-Jug domain, the action *Pour* allows the water in one jug to be emptied into a second jug, provided that the capacity of the second jug is sufficiently large to hold the total volume of water currently present in the two jugs. One possible way to describe this domain using setGraphs consists of considering each jug as a place, *associated to* (i.e., linked by an edge to) a numeric node. The value of the node denotes that jug's capacity. Each jug will also contain a numeric node, representing the current volume of water in it. Figure 3.(*a*) encodes a possible initial state for this problem, in which two jugs of capacity 3 and 4 contain, respectively, 3 and 0 units of water. Figure 3.(*b*) encodes the *Pour* operator. This action has no effect on the arrangement of the nodes and places in the setGraph, as it only updates the numeric values of nodes v_1 and v_2. Figure 4 contains the sentential description of the Water-Jug domain, expressed in PDDL2.1 style [2]. When compared to sentential descriptions, diagrammatic representations appear to be simpler and more natural, less error-prone and easier to modify and re-use. As demonstrated in the next section, setGraph representations are also at least as expressive as modern propositional planning domain description languages.

4 Expressiveness of setGraphs

The expressiveness of setGraphs is assessed by comparing the representation against a propositional formalism that allows the use of numeric quantities and functor symbols. In particular, we adopt the same semantic model adopted in PDDL2.1 [2]. In short, the PDDL2.1 semantics is based on the idea of a state being composed of two separate parts, a *logical* state and a *numeric* state. While a logical state L consists of a set (conjunction) of ground atomic formulæ (the truth of an atom p depending on whether $p \in L$), the numeric state consists of a (finite)

---

[2]Movement and removal of elements in the i-th setGraph G_i of the preconditions P are encoded implicitly by the i-th setGraph G_i' of the effects E. The different nodeSets of G_i and their (possibly new) positions are identified in G_i' using the same identifiers that those elements have in G_i. However, since addition of elements is permitted, G_i' might also contain new nodeSets (associated to labels or values that do not appear in G_i) or new edges. Similarly, since removal is permitted, G_i might contain nodeSets or edges that do not appear in G_i'.

vector R of values in $\Re_\perp = \Re \cup \{\perp\}$, representing the complete set of *primitive numeric expressions* (PNEs) of the problem (values associated with tuples of domain objects by domain functions – see [2] for a more detailed explanation). An operator specifies a transformation of a state-pair $s = (L, R)$ into a new state-pair $s' = (L', R')$. In this analysis we consider *ground* (i.e., instantiated) operators of form $(P \Rightarrow E)$, in which the preconditions P contain a list of ground literals and a set of comparisons between pairs of numeric expressions (containing PNEs and numbers), while the effects E consist of list of ground literals and a set of numeric update operations (analogous to those adopted in setGraphs). Notice that any PDDL2.1 ("level 2", i.e., non-durative) action schema can be compiled into an *equivalent* set of (ground) operators of the above form [2].

The two main results concerning the expressiveness of setGraphs are presented below:

Theorem 1 (Expressiveness). *Every propositional* (PDDL2.1) *state* $s = (L, R)$ *can be represented as a setGraph.*

Proof Every state $s = (L, R)$ consists of a finite set L of ground atoms $p(x_1, \ldots, x_n)$ and a finite vector R of values y_j, each one representing the value in s of the j-th primitive numeric expression $f(x_1, \ldots, x_m)$ (where the $x_i \in C$ are symbols representing the objects of the domain). Let G be a setGraph containing the following: (1) three places, labelled *Pred*, *Obj* and *Funct*; (2) a node "x_i" in *Obj* for each symbol $x_i \in C$; (3) a node "p" in *Pred* and a set of labelled edges $\{e_1(p, x_1), \ldots, e_n(p, x_n)\}$ for each atom $p(x_1, \ldots, x_n)$ of L; and (4) a node "f" for each functor symbol f and a set of nodes $\{x_1, \ldots, x_m, y_j\}$ in *Funct* linked by a set of edges $\{(f, x_1), (x_1, x_2), \ldots, (x_m, y_j)\}$ for each value y_j of R. Then, the truth of an atom $p(x_1, \ldots, x_n)$ can be determined by checking if the setGraph $\langle \{Pred\{p, x_1, \ldots, x_n\}\}, \{e_1(p, x_1), \ldots, e_n(p, x_n)\}\rangle$ is satisfied in G. In addition, the value of the j-th PNE is identified by the value to which the numeric variable $w \in \Re_\perp$ has to be bound for the parameterised setGraph $\langle \{f, x_1, \ldots, x_n, w\}, \{(f, x_1), (x_1, x_2), \ldots, (x_m, w)\}\rangle$ to be satisfied in G.

Corollary *Every ground propositional (PDDL2.1, level 2) operator can be transformed into an equivalent setGraph operator.*

Proof sketch Given the encoding used in the proof of the above theorem, every sentential operator can be transformed into an equivalent setGraph operator as follows: each addition (removal) of an atom $p(x_1, \ldots, x_n)$ to (from) the logical state L corresponds to the addition (removal) of the corresponding node "p" and associated edges to (from) place *Pred*. Similarly, each update of a PNE $f(x_1, \ldots, x_m)$ in R is encoded through the update of the numeric node w at the end of the chain $(f, x_1), (x_1, x_2), \ldots, (x_m, w)$.

Notice that the transformation of sentential descriptions into setGraph models is *polynomial* (while the size of the result is *linear*) in the size of the original encoding[3].

5 Related work and Discussion

The aim of this paper was to propose a diagrammatic inter-lingua for planning domain descriptions, which would facilitate the process of language development and domain knowl-

---

[3]The measure of this size includes the size of R and the arity of the PNEs and predicates of the language.

edge engineering. The examples illustrated that setGraphs produce simpler and more intuitive domain descriptions, easier to understand for non-planning experts. This should allow researchers and practitioners outside the planning community to better understand modern planning technology, facilitating its dissemination and take-up, and hence reducing the existing gap between theory and real-world applications. At the same time, the setGraph formalism described was proven to be at least as expressive as a propositional language that allows the use of numeric quantities and functor symbols, and to be easily translated into formal, set- and graph-theoretic constructs. These characteristics make the model suitable to be used across different levels of abstraction (e.g., as a tool for knowledge elicitation and exchange between planning experts and domain experts, or, alternatively, as a basis for domain description language development). In particular, setGraphs can be used as a common core representation – in other words, as an underlying "platform" – for the development of different domain description languages having different syntax and/or additional components (see the requirements for a core language proposed by Frank et al. in [3]).

The development of tools for the automatic translation of setGraph descriptions into textual (or machine-readable) descriptions represents a natural continuation of this work. Notice that such a translation would not necessarily lead to a *propositional* domain encoding. Indeed, an example of textual, non-predicative language able to encode a restricted version of setGraphs is presented in [6]. Such *analogical* language preserved the ability of setGraphs to closely mirror the spatial and topological aspects of the real domain. Experimental evidence obtained with a simple prototype planner [6] indicates that *Move* problems (involving the movement of objects subject to several constraints) are solved much faster (between two and one hundred and sixty times) if encoded using this language rather than propositionally.

SetGraphs borrow ideas from various works in the area of analogical representations [7, 9], qualitative reasoning [1], set and graph theory [8] and semantic networks (in particular, conceptual graphs [17]). However, the use of diagrammatic representations in *planning* had never been investigated before. The work by McCluskey, Liu and Simpson [13], although sharing with it some of the underlying motivations, bears no particular relation to this proposal: GIPO is a graphical user interface that helps the user build a domain description using diagrams, but the diagrams which are built are not *analogical models* of the real domain; furthermore, the final product is still a propositional (although object-centred) encoding [11].

Interestingly, the work of Fox and Long on the automatic extraction of generic types [12] fits nicely with the present proposal. As Fox and Long demonstrated, although not overtly described as such, some domains are *isomorphic* to and can be treated as "transportation" or "construction" problems [12]. After automatically recasting a domain in terms of movement or manipulation of (possibly abstract) objects, the propositional description thus obtained could be further (automatically) transformed into a more efficient, analogical representation based on setGraphs. Unfortunately, only few, simple domains can be entirely represented using just analogical (diagrammatic) representations. Indeed, most real domains typically involve a "mixture" of diverse components, only part of which are conveniently captured by diagrams; several aspects of the real world (e.g., the value of non-spatial attributes, such as colour or temperature) still seem to be most "naturally" described using predicates. To address this shortcoming, a *hybrid* domain representation model for the integration of analogical and sentential descriptions is proposed in [5], in which the conditions for the construction of *sound* analogical (setGraph) and hybrid representations are also formally identified. These conditions extend those for sentential models of sound action described by Lifschitz in [10], still at the basis of current propositional planning description languages [14].

Finally, two important aspects of action modelling that have not been dealt with here and that require further investigation concern the specification of *concurrent* and *durative* (analogical) actions, particularly when coupled with other features such as conditional and continuous effects.

References

[1] K. Forbus. Qualitative Spatial Reasoning: Framework and Frontiers. In *[7]*, chapter 6, pages 183–202. 1995.

[2] M. Fox and D. Long. PDDL2.1: An extension to PDDL for expressing temporal planning domains. *Journal of Artificial Intelligence Research*, 20:61–124, 2003.

[3] J. Frank, K. Golden, and A. Jonsson. The loyal opposition comments on plan domain description languages. In *Proceedings of 13th International Conference on Automated Planning and Scheduling (ICAPS'03) - Workshop on PDDL*, pages 39–48, Trento, Italy, June 2003.

[4] M. Garagnani. Model-Based Planning in Physical domains using SetGraphs. In M. Bramer, A. Preece, and F. Coenen, editors, *Research and Development in Intelligent Systems XX (Proc. of AI-2003)*, pages 295–308. Springer-Verlag, December 2003.

[5] M. Garagnani. A Framework for Hybrid and Analogical Planning. In I. Vlahavas and D. Vrakas, editors, *Intelligent Techniques for Planning*, chapter II, pages 35–88. Idea Group, Inc., 2004.

[6] M. Garagnani and Y. Ding. Model-based planning for object-rearrangement problems. In *Proceedings of 13th International Conference on Automated Planning and Scheduling (ICAPS'03) - Workshop on PDDL*, pages 49–58, Trento, Italy, June 2003.

[7] J. Glasgow, N.H. Narayanan, and B. Chandrasekaran, editors. *Diagrammatic Reasoning*. AAAI Press/The MIT Press, Cambridge, MA, 1995.

[8] D. Harel. On Visual Formalisms. *Communication of the ACM*, 13:514–530, May 1988.

[9] Z. Kulpa. Diagrammatic representation and reasoning. *Machine GRAPHICS & VISION*, 3(1/2):77–103, 1994.

[10] V. Lifschitz. On the semantics of STRIPS. In M.P. Georgeff and Lansky, editors, *Proceedigns of 1986 Workshop: Reasoning about Actions and Plans*, 1986.

[11] D. Liu and T.L. McCluskey. The OCL Language Manual, Version 1.2. Technical report, Department of Computing and Mathematical Sciences, University of Huddersfield (UK), 2000.

[12] D. Long and M. Fox. Automatic synthesis and use of generic types in planning. In S. Chien, S. Kambhampati, and C.A. Knoblock, editors, *Proceedings of the 5th International Conference on AI Planning and Scheduling (AIPS'00)*, pages 196–205, Breckenridge, CO, April 2000. AAAI Press.

[13] T.L. McCluskey, D. Liu, and R. Simpson. GIPO II: HTN Planning in a Tool-supported Knowledge Engineering Environment. In E. Giunghiglia, N. Muscettola, and D. Nau, editors, *Proceedings of 13th International Conference on Automated Planning and Scheduling (ICAPS'03)*, Trento, Italy, June 2003. AAAI Press.

[14] D. McDermott, C. Knoblock, M. Veloso, D. Weld, and D. Wilkins. PDDL – the planning domain definition language. Version 1.7. Technical report, Department of Computer Science, Yale University (CT), 1998. (Available at www.cs.yale.edu/homes/dvm/).

[15] K. Myers and K. Konolige. Reasoning with analogical representations. In B. Nebel, C. Rich, and W. Swartout, editors, *Principles of Knowledge Representation and Reasoning: Proceedings of the Third International Conference (KR92)*, pages 189–200. Morgan Kaufmann Publishers Inc., San Mateo, CA, 1992.

[16] S. Skiena. *Implementing Discrete Mathematics: Combinatorics and Graph Theory with Mathematica*. Addison-Wesley, Reading, MA, 1990.

[17] J. Sowa. *Conceptual Structures: Information Processing in Mind and Machine*. Addison-Wesley, Reading, MA, 1984.

Planning, Scheduling and Constraint Satisfaction: From Theory to Practice
L. Castillo et al. (Eds.)
IOS Press, 2005

AI Planning for Automatic Generation of Customized Virtual Courses

NÉSTOR DARÍO DUQUE MÉNDEZ
Professor
Universidad Nacional de Colombia, Campus Manizales
nduque@nevado.manizales.unal.edu.co
CLAUDIA JIMÉNEZ RAMÍREZ
Professor
Universidad Nacional de Colombia, Campus Medellín
csjimene@unalmed.edu.co
JAIME ALBERTO GUZMÁN LUNA
Professor
Universidad Nacional de Colombia, Campus Medellín
jaguzman@unalmed.edu.co

Abstract.

This article presents a goal-oriented model for generating virtual adapted courses according to the academic trajectory of each student and for offering multiple activities or knowledge unities that can be associated to a specific learning style. High level of detail impedes the generation of a course manually. That is why the decision of using intelligent planning techniques was taken. It is shown how the course composition problem can be viewed as a planning problem. We present our preliminary vision model for translating course elements into Hierarchical Task Network (HTN) environment, in particular SHOP2, to make possible the automatic generation of virtual customized courses.

1. Introduction

The possibilities offered by new information and telecommunication technologies have not been enough exploited for virtual education systems. The customization of the teaching–learning process is rarely offered using these new tools and it is a key factor for improving the effectiveness of the process.

Current poor effectiveness of e-learning environments is manifested by opting for conventional courses when it can be possible. This could be happening because contents or activities programmed for virtual courses are fixed, without considering learning styles LS, and the student's academic trajectory does not offer different alternatives to fulfill an educative goal. Because of that, students can feel neglected for being successful in their studies and can feel the activities proposed, in a course, are not accommodated to their style of learning. If they are well accommodated, it can result in improved attitudes toward learning and an increase in productivity, academic achievement, and creativity. On the other hand, it must also be considered that a student could have fulfilled some goals in previous courses and there is no reason to repeat them.

This proposal is oriented to the automatic generation of customized virtual courses using intelligent planning techniques according to the academic trajectory of each student and offering multiple activities or knowledge unities. These alternatives must be ranked according to the educative goal, the student is going to work on and his (her) preferred learning style. The idea is to offer virtual customized courses using an AI planner that can choose the goals to be fulfilled by a specific student and can rank the different alternatives to meet by each student according to his (her) preferred style of learning. There are other proposals oriented to build virtual customized courses, like [1], [3], [4] and [5] that the reader can consult; but they do not consider AI planning techniques.

The model presented in this article, will be implemented in a social network system for education, that we are currently working on, called FORHUM (acronym for "FOrmacion HUMana). FORHUM is a project conceived to maintain and facilitate academic interchange and collaboration between four educative institutions from Bolivia, Ecuador, Peru, and Colombia.

The rest of this his document is organized in the following way: Section 2 presents the Virtual Course Model Adapted to the Student Profile. In Section 3, the background knowledge about HTN (Hierarchical Task Network) is given, and the aspects of how SHOP2 can help us to generate customized courses in an automatic way are also described. Section 4 includes our vision model, translating the customized virtual courses generating elements into SHOP2 environment. Then in Section 5, a simplified example to illustrate the process to be carried by the planner, is presented . And finally, we present some conclusions.

2. A Virtual Course Model Adapted to the Student Profile

The model presented in this article considers individual characteristics like the academic history and learning styles to generate customized virtual courses. It is based on the educative goals that must be satisfied by the student during a course. These goals can be achieved with different activities and knowledge unities and they can be associated to a specific psycho pedagogic profile.

The manual or semiautomatic customization of courses is a complex and expensive task because of the effort needed to select the educative objectives for a particular learner taking a virtual course and to choose the appropriated academic activities to fulfill that objectives according to his (her) preferred learning styles. But this process can be automatized by using intelligent planning assistance if the academic records and student characteristics are available. Besides, automatic generation could be simpler if teaching materials are defined with a high granularity in such a way they can be reused for other courses [6].

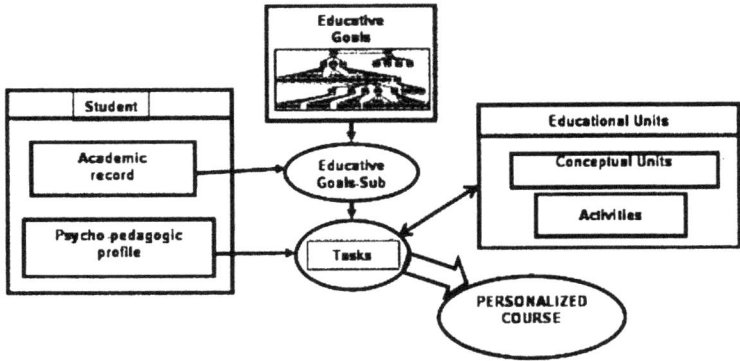

Figure 1. Customized Courses Generating Model

Figure 1 presents the proposed model in a schematic way. The educative goals pertaining to the general course and the academic records determine the subgroup of goals that must be fulfilled by an individual student. Once these goals have been selected, it is necessary to choose the adequated tasks for that student. The tasks could be readings, exercises, simulations or interviews, etc. They should be specially created attending different learning styles. The academic record represents the knowledge acquired by students and it is consigned in terms of achieved goals. And the psycho pedagogic profile is defined by means of the preferred learning style.

A learning style is a student consistent way of responding to and using stimulus in the context of learning [10]. There are many kinds of classifications of learning styles, that can be seen in [9], [12], [13], and [15]. We consider VARK model for our project. This model considers four kinds of learning styles: Visual, Auditory, Read/Write, and Kinesthetic.

On the other hand, Educational Unities (EU), conformed by contents or activities, are needed to define the tasks that a student has to do to achieve his (her) subgroup goals. Our proposed model considers a *m:n* relationship between the EU and the atomic educative goals meaning that a specific atomic goal can be fulfilled by doing different tasks and a specific EU can be used for achieving different atomic goals. This fact facilitates the customization of courses and the reusability of the materials previously performed.

The graphical representation of our proposed data model appears in Figure 2, using UML notation.

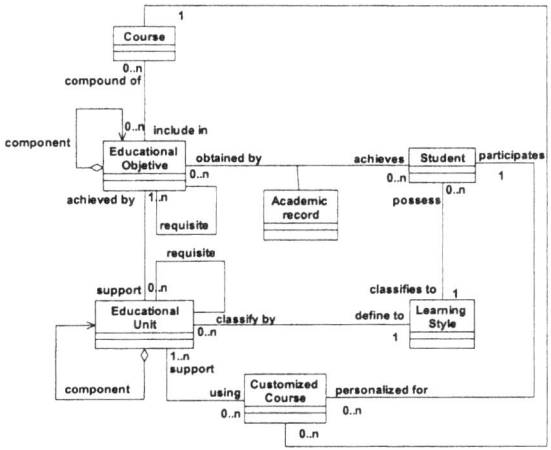

Figure 2. Customized Courses Class Diagram

Unfortunately, a high level of detail impedes the generation of a course manually. That is why the decision of using intelligent planning techniques that have been useful to synthesize complex problems giving an initial state, and a representation that specifies objectives and a set of possible transitions of states, was taken.

3. Background

The generic structure of a flexible course is more complex than a mere sequence of tasks, because it is an oriented graph without cycles meaning that a student would not repeat tasks while taking a   course. It can also be seen like a tree structure, and that is why an approximation to hierarchical planning, in particular Hierarchical Task Network [7], seems to be the best alternative for our proposal. We believe that HTN is promising for our purpose, because the task network is very similar to the course structure, in terms of educational objectives (see, figure 3). Moreover, from experimental studies, hand-tailorable planners have quickly solved planning problems orders of more complicated magnitude than those typically solved by "fully automated" planning systems in which the domain-specific knowledge consists only of the planning operators [14].

In order to obtain such structure, it is required an action model of an intelligent planner for customized courses generation and a mechanism for the translation. Proposals in other fields can be seen in [2], [15] and [17], but our work is novel as a means of performing planning in domains which until now were beyond the reach of state of the art in planning systems.

3.1. Hierarchical Task Network HTN Planner

HTN (Hierarchical Task Network), is an AI planning methodology that creates plans by task decomposition. An HTN planner decomposes tasks into smaller and smaller subtasks, until primitive tasks are found so that can be performed directly [8]. The description of a planning domain includes a set of operators and a set of methods (a prescription about how to decompose a task into subtasks). The description of a planning problem will contain an initial state and a partially ordered set of tasks to accomplish (but instead of goal formula).

3.2. Simple Hierarchical Ordered Planner 2 (SHOP2)

We adopt SHOP2 (Simple Hierarchical Ordered Planner 2), a domain-independent HTN planning system by generating the steps of each plan in the same order that those steps will later be executed (instructional plan) [14].

In order to do planning in a given planning domain, SHOP2 needs to be given the knowledge about that domain. A SHOP2 knowledge base consists of operators and methods. Each operator is a description of what needs to be done to accomplish some primitive task, and each method tells how to decompose a compound task into partially ordered subtasks [11].

A SHOP2 *operator* is an expression of the form $(h(v)$ Pre Del Add) where $h(v)$ represents a primitive task with a list of input parameters v. Pre, Del, Add represent the operator's preconditions, delete list, and add list respectively.

A SHOP2 *method*, indicates how to decompose a compound task into a partially ordered set of subtasks; is an expression of the form $(h(v)$ Pre T), more generally may have the form $(h(v)$ Pre_1 T_1 Pre_2 T_2 . . . Pre_n $T_n)$. Where $h(v)$ represents a compound task with a list of input parameters v, Pre_n represents the $operator_n$ preconditions, and T_n represents a partially ordered list of subtasks which are the decomposition of $h(v)$.

A *planning problem* for SHOP2 is a triple (S, T, D), where S is initial state, T is a task list, and D is a domain description. By taking (S, T, D) as input, SHOP2 will return a plan $P=(p_1p_2...p_n)$, a sequence of instantiated operators that will achieve T from S in D [11].

4. From Course Model Environment to SHOP2

Translating course generating problem into planning environment, implies the definition of the operators, methods, and the planning problem in SHOP2 terms.
Procedures for knowledge transferring to a planning environment
In similar way as suggested by Wu *et al* [17]:

The initial State, *S*, is represented by the Educative Objectives, EO, previously obtained from a specific student (academic profile) and his/her learning style (psycho pedagogic profile), LS.

The partially ordered set of tasks to accomplish represent the EO that are hoped to obtain in course or thematic area.

The *Operators* represent the Educational Unities, EU required for achieving goals.

M*ethods* reflect the decomposition of objectives into sub-objectives (achievement indicators).

EU_O: EU into a Operator:
Input: EU.   Output: SHOP2 Operator of the form *(h(v) Pre Del Add)*
Procedure:
1. *h* : name or identifier of the Educational Unity, *EU.id*
2. *Pre*: Conjunct of prerequisite of EO (*Pre_EO$_n$*) for EU,
       prerequisite of EU, *EU.pre*
3. *Del*: ϕ (empty)
4. *Add*: associates goal with EO for EU, EO$_n$, represented by *EU.oe*
5. Return (operator) $O=(EU_{id}$ *(f(EU.oe) EU.pre)* ϕ *EU.oe*)
       Where *f(EU.oe)* is a function and returns *Pre_EO$_n$*

EO_M: Composite EO into a Method:
Input: EO.   Output: SHOP2 Method M of the form $(h(v)$ *Pre$_n$ T$_n$))*
Procedure:
1. *h:* name or identifier of the Educative Objective, *EO.id*
2. Pre$_n$: prerequisite of EO, *Pre_EO$_n$*
3. T= Educational Sub-objectives (Sub_EO$_1$, Sub_EO$_2$,..., Sub_EO$_n$)
4. Return *M=(EO.id Pre_EO$_n$* (Sub_EO$_1$, Sub_EO$_2$,..., Sub_EO$_n$))

EU_M : Several EU for single EO into a Method:
Input: EU   Output: SHOP2 Method M of the form *(h(v) Pre$_1$ T$_1$ Pre$_2$ T$_2$ . . . Pre$_n$ T$_n$)*
Procedure:
1. *h:* name or identifier of the EO, *EU.oe*
2. Pre$_n$: Learning Style associated to EU$_n$, *LS$_n$*.
3. T$_n$= EU$_n$
4. Return *M=(EU.oe* LS$_1$ EU$_1$ LS$_2$ EU$_2$ ... LS$_n$ EU$_n$)

EUc_M: Composite EU into a Method:
Input: EU   Output: SHOP2 Method M of the form $(h(v)$ *Pre$_n$ T$_n$))*
Procedure:
1. *h:* name or identifier of the EU, *EU.id*
2. Pre: prerequisite of EO, *Pre_EO$_n$*
3. T= Educative Sub-unities, (Sub_EU$_1$, Sub_EU$_2$,..., Sub_EU$_n$)
4. Return *M=(EU.id f(EU.oe)* (*Sub_EU$_1$, Sub_EU$_2$,..., Sub_EU$_n$*))
       Where *f(EU.oe)* is a function and returns *Pre_EO$_n$*

Course Domain into a SHOP2 Domain
Input: EU and EO collection.   Output: SHOP2 Domain *D*
Procedure (Dmn):
1. D = ϕ
2. For each EU , execute EU_O(EU)

3. For each compound EO execute EO_M
4. For each group of EU for one EO, execute EU_M
5. For each composite EU, execute EUc_M
6. Return D

Course generating problem into a SHOP2 planning problem.
Output: SHOP2 planing problem of form (S, T, D)
Procedure:

1. $S = ((EO_{L1}, EO_{L2},..., EO_{Ln}) LS)$, $EO_n \subseteq EO$
Where EO_{Ln}: EO obtained by student, and LS is his/her learning style.

2. T: EOs expressed in terms of the set of tasks to accomplish $(EO_1, EO_2,..., EO_n)$

3. D: execute algorithm Dmn.

4. By taking (S, T, D) as input, SHOP2 will return a plan P=(p_1 p_2...p_n), a sequence of instantiated operators that will achieve T from S in D.

5. Example

Suppose the topic to be taken by a specific student is: "Analysis of Computer Assisted Audit Techniques", associated with the Educational Objective identified by EO42. Because we consider VARK model for our project, the students are going to be classified as Visual, Auditory, Read/Write or Kinesthetic. Educational Units in its property, LS, will have one of these values, too. Figure number 3 shows the general course structure represented by Educational Objectives.

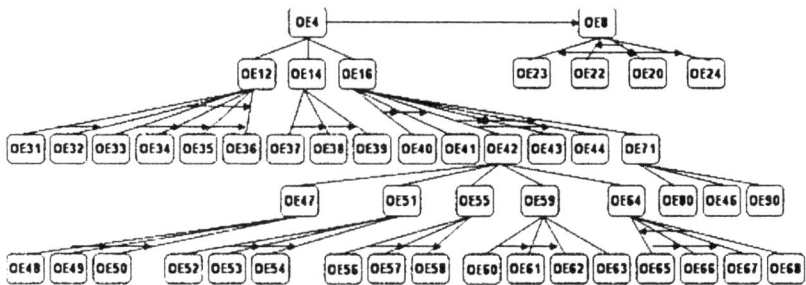

Figure 3. General Course Structure.

Tables 1 and 2 presents relevant attributes for the composition of the customized course, in terms of the Educational Units and the Educational Objectives.

Transferring course domain to a planning environment

EU_O: EU into a Operator:
$O=(EU_{id}$ $(f(EU.oe) EU.pre)$ ϕ $EU.oe)$
         Where $f(EU.oe)$ is a function and returns Pre_EO_n
     Then, for EU325:
(EU325 (Pre_EO48 ϕ) ϕ EO48) ==> (EU325 (ϕ ϕ) ϕ EO48)
         In terms SHOP2:
(:operator (UE325)

( )
( )
((OE48))

)

And so forth, (see, Table 3).

Table 1. Educational Units

Id	Educational Units – Description	EO	Format	LS
EU325	Test Data Techniques. Concepts.	EO48	T	R
EU326	Test Data Techniques. Concepts.. Diagram	EO48	G	V
EU327	Test Data Techniques. Concepts. Animation	EO48	AN	V
EU336	Test Data Techniques. Advantages Disadvantages	EO49	T	R
EU340	Test Data Techniques. Considerations in the use.	EO50	S	V
EU341	Test Data Techniques. Considerations in the use.	EO50	T	R
EU350	Integrated Test Facilities (ITF). Concepts	EO52	T	R
EU351	Integrated Test Facilities (ITF). Concepts. Diagram.	EO52	G	V
EU380	Integrated Test Facilities (ITF). Concepts. Animation.	EO52	AN	V
EU381	Integrated Test Facilities (ITF). Advantages Disadvantages	EO53	T	R
EU391	ITF. Considerations in the use.	EO54	S	V
EU427	ITF. Considerations in the use.	EO54	T	R
EU429	Audit Software. Concepts.	EO60	T	R
EU431	Audit Software. Concepts. Graphic.	EO60	G	V
EU440	Audit Software. Advantages Disadvantages	EO61	T	R
EU556	Audit Software. Considerations in the use.	EO62	S	V
EU559	Audit Software. Considerations in the use.	EO62	T	R
EU573	Audit Software. Operation.	EO63	T	R
EU596	Audit Software. Simulation.	EO63	SI	K

T: Text   G: Graphic   AN: Animation   SI: Simulation   S: Slide

Table 2. Educational Objectives and their pre-requisites

EO_{id}	Pre_EO_n	EO_{id}	Pre_EO_n
EO8	EO4	EO43	EO42
EO22	EO20	EO49	EO48
EO23	EO20	EO50	EO49
EO24	EO20	EO53	EO52
EO32	EO31	EO54	EO53
EO34	EO33	EO57	EO56
EO35	EO34	EO58	EO57
EO36	EO35	EO61	EO60
EO36	EO32	EO62	EO61
EO38	EO37	EO66	EO65
EO39	EO38	EO67	EO66
EO41	EO40	EO65	EO68
EO42	EO41	EO71	EO43

Table 3. Operators

Id	Precondition	Delete list	Add list	Id	Precondition	Delete list	Add list
EU325	ф	ф	EO48	EU391	EO53	ф	EO54
EU326	ф	ф	EO48	EU427	EO53	ф	EO54
EU327	ф	ф	EO48	EU429	ф	ф	EO60
EU336	ф	ф	EO49	EU431	ф	ф	EO60
EU340	EO49	ф	EO50	EU440	EO60	ф	EO61
EU341	EO49	ф	EO50	EU556	EO61	ф	EO62
EU350	ф	ф	EO52	EU559	EO61	ф	EO62
EU351	ф	ф	EO52	EU573	ф	ф	EO63
EU380	ф	ф	EO52	EU596	ф	ф	EO63
EU381	EO52	ф	EO53				

EO_M: Composite EO into a Method:

$M=(\,EO.\text{id}\ Pre\_EO_n\ (\text{Sub\_EO}_1,\text{Sub\_EO}_2,...,\text{Sub\_EO}_n))$

Then:

Table 4. Methods from Composite EO

Task	Precondition	Subtasks
EO47	φ	EO48,EO49,EO50
EO51	φ	EO52,EO53,EO54
EO55	φ	EO56,EO57,EO58
EO59	φ	EO60,EO61,EO62,EO63
EO64	φ	EO65,EO66,EO67,EO68
EO42	EO41	EO47,EO51,EO55,EO59,EO64
EO71	EO43	EO80,EO46,EO90
EO12	φ	EO31,EO32,EO33,EO34,EO35,EO36
EO14	φ	EO37,EO38,EO39
EO16	φ	EO40,EO41,EO42,EO43,EO44,EO71
EO8	EO4	EO23,EO22,EO20,EO24
EO4	φ	EO12,EO14,EO16

EU_M : Several EU for single EO into a Method:

$M=(\,EU.oe\ \text{LS}_1\ \text{EU}_1\ \text{LS}_2\ \text{EU}_2\,...\,\text{LS}_n\ \text{EU}_n\ )$

Then:

Table 5. Methods from Several EU for single EO

Task	Precondition/Subtask		Precondition/Subtask		Precondition/Subtask	
EO48	R	EU325	V	EU326	VK	EU327
EO50	V	EU340	R	EU341		
EO52	R	EU350	V	EU351	VK	EU380
EO54	V	EU391	R	EU427		
EO60	R	EU429	V	EU431		
EO62	V	EU556	R	EU559		
EO63	R	EU573	K	EU596		

The previous steps allowed transferring Course Domain into a SHOP2 Domain.

Course generation problem into a SHOP2 planning problem.

SHOP2 planning problem of form (S, T, D)

T: Course OEs: OE4, OE8; For instance, T : OE42

D: Operators and Methods obtained above.

S: EO obtained from student: EO55, EO59, and EO64. Learning Style, LS: Visual, V

SHOP2 will return a plan P = (p1 p2...pn), a sequence of instantiated operators (Educational Units) that will achieve T (Educational Objectives) from S (achieved goals) in D. The outcome for applying SHOP2 planning procedure [14], is similar to the shown in table 6.

Therefore, the instructional plan is: EU326, EU336, EU340, EU351, EU381 and EU391.

EU326. Test Data Techniques. Concepts.. Diagram

EU336. Test Data Techniques. Advantages Disadvantages

EU340. Test Data Techniques. Considerations in the use

EU351. Integrated Test Facilities (ITF). Concepts. Diagram.

EU381. Integrated Test Facilities (ITF). Advantages Disadvantages.
EU391. ITF. Considerations in the use.

Table 6. Output from executing SHOP2

I	Pr	T₀	M	T	S	A	P
EO42		EO42		EO42	V , EO55, EO59,EO64		
EO42	F		EO47,EO51, EO55EO59, EO64	EO47, EO51, EO55 EO59, EO64	V , EO55, EO59,EO64		
EO47	F	EO47,EO51, EO55 EO59,EO64	EO48,EO49, EO50	EO48, EO49, EO50, EO51,	V , EO55, EO59,EO64		
EO48	F	EO48	EU326	EU326, EO49, EO50, EO51	V , EO55, EO59,EO64		
EU326	T	EU326		EO49, EO50, EO51	V , EO55, EO59, EO64 EO48	EU326	EU326
EO49	F	EO49, EO51	EU336	EU336, EO50, EO51	V , EO55, EO59, EO64 EO48		
EU336	T	EU336		EO50, EO51	V , EO55, EO59, EO64 EO48, EO49	EU336	EU326 EU336
EO50	F	EO50, EO51, EO59	EU340	EU340, EO51			
EU340	T	EU340		EO51	V , EO55, EO59, EO64 EO48, EO49, EO50	EU340	EU326 EU336 EU340
EO51	F	EO51, EO59	EO52,EO53, EO54	EO52, EO53, EO54			
EO52	F	EO52	EU351	EU351, EO53, EO54	V , EO55, EO59, EO64 EO48, EO49, EO50		EU326 EU336 EU340
EU351	T	EU351		EO53, EO54	V , EO55, EO59, EO64 EO48, EO49, EO50, EO52	EU351	EU326 EU336 EU340 EU351
EO53	F	EO53	EU381	EU381, EO54			
EU381	T	EU381		EO54	V , EO55, EO59, EO64 EO48, EO49, EO50, EO52, EO53	EU381	EU326 EU336 EU340 EU351 EU381
EO54		EO54	EU391	EU391			
EU391	T	EU391			V , EO55, EO59, EO64 EO48, EO49, EO50, EO52, EO53, EO54	EU391	EU326 EU336 EU340 EU351 EU381 EU391

6. Conclusions and comments

AI planning techniques can be valuable tools to automate the process for customized course generation. HTN planning incorporates substantial expressive power into planning systems, that is why we consider it the best alternative for solving the problem we are dealing. Although this work is not finished yet, we realized that planning techniques could be very useful in educative domains. The model, presented here, is our first approach to automatic generation of customized courses. We are now working on the design phase and we are making some proofs for the implementation, using SHOP2 which permits the refinement of the proposed model. We are also working on algorithms to transfer information from the information system to the planning module treated in this document.

The biggest obstacle found when using AI planning techniques while we were solving this problem, was the difficulty when transferring the different components of the course model to the planning environment, which implies a strictly definition of the relevant elements in the personalization and the transferring algorithms.

Talking about the implementation of the customized courses according to the students profiles, the difficulty resides in changing the way to build them. On one side changing the courses oriented by the teaching materials to a vision guided by the educative objectives; and on the other side the effort taken to work with objectives and educative unities with a high level of detail and also the necessary introduction of data to the metadata which plays a significant role in the model. In spite of that, the teachers and students´s opinions are in favor to the customized courses which foretells success for making of the proposal a reality.

References

[1] Brusilovsky, P And Vassileva, J. *Course sequencing techniques for large-scale web-based education.* Engineering Education and Lifelong Learning. 2003, vol. 13, nos. 1 y 2, pp. 75-94. Available from: http://julita.usask.ca/Texte/BrusilovskyVassileva-print.pdf
[2] Carman, M., Serafin, L., and Traversa Paolo. *Web Services Composition as Planning.* Workshop on Planning for Web Services. Trento, Italy. June 2003.
[3] Carmona C, Bueno D, Guzmán E, Conejo R. *SIGUE: Making Web Courses Adaptive.* Second International Conference, AH 2002.
[4] Carro R.M., Pulido E., Rodríguez P. *Creación de Cursos Adaptativos en TANGOW.* Revista de Enseñanza y Tecnología. Dic 2001.
[5] Castells P., Macías J. A. *Diseño interactivo de cursos adaptativos.* 2000. Available from: http://www.ii.uam.es/%7Ecastells/publications/siie2000.pdf
[6] Duque Méndez, Néstor Darío. Jiménez Ramirez, Claudia. *Modelo de Generación de Cursos Virtuales Adaptados al Perfil del Estudiante.* Exposed in LatinEduca2004.: www.latinEduca2004.com
[7] Erol, K., Nau, D. and Hendler, J. *HTN planning: Complexity and expressivity.* In AAAI-94. 1994.
[8] Erol K., Hendler, J., and Nau, D. *Semantics for hierarchical task network planning,* 1994.
[9] Felder and Soloman. *Learning Styles and Strategies.* Available from: http://www2.ncsu.edu/unity/lockers/users/f/felder/public/ILSdir/styles.htm
[10] Hazel Paul. *What Can We Learn From Learning Styles?.* 2002. Available from: http://www.paulhazel.com/docs/styles.htm#intro
[11] Hendler, J., Wu, D., Sirin, E., Nau, D. and Parsia, B. *Automating DAML-S Web Services Composition Using SHOP2.* 2003.
[12] Honey, Peter. *Learning Styles – their relevance to training courses.* Available from: http://www.peterhoney.co.uk/Article/55
[13] Kolb, D.A. *Experiential Learning: Experience as the Source of Learning and Development.* Prentice Hall, N.J. 1984.
[14] Nau *et al. SHOP2: An HTN Planning System.* Journal of Artificial Intelligence Research 20. 2003. Available from: http://www.cs.cmu.edu/afs/cs/project/jair/pub/volume20/nau03a.pdf
[15] Peer, Joachim. *Towards automatic Web Service composition using AI Planning Techniques. First draft.* 2003.
[16] VARK - *A Guide to Learning Styles.* Available from: http://www.vark-learn.com/
[17] Wu, D., Hendler, J., Sirin, E., Nau, D. and Parsia, B. *Automatic Web Services Composition Using SHOP2.* Presented en ICAP-2003.

Planning, Scheduling and Constraint Satisfaction: From Theory to Practice
L. Castillo et al. (Eds.)
IOS Press, 2005

149

Knowledge and plan execution management in planning fire fighting operations

Marc de la Asunción, Luis Castillo, Juan Fdez-Olivares,
Oscar García-Pérez, Antonio González, Francisco Palao
siadex.dev@decsai.ugr.es
Departmento de Ciencias de la Computación e Inteligencia Artificial.
E.T.S. Ingenieria Informatica.
Universidad de Granada (Spain)

Abstract. This work introduces SIADEX [1], a planning framework intended to assist human experts in the design of forest fire fighting plans. Issues about how to engineer planning knowledge for such a system, how to monitor the execution of fighting plans and how to patch unfeasible plans are discussed in detail.

1 Introduction

AI planning techniques have shown to perform very efficiently in providing human experts with valuable tentative plans and strategies either in military [15] or civil [2] domains. These AI planning techniques are only the core of more complex architectures that may also involve knowledge management techniques and their plans might be directly scheduled for real execution or adapted by domain experts before their execution. The proposed system, SIADEX [7], is a planning framework that falls into this category of AI planning systems. It is being developed under a research contract with the Andalusian Regional Government (Regional Ministry of Environment) [7]. It is conceived as a distributed planning application and it is intended to assist technical staff in the design of forest fire fighting plans.

Thus, in order to achieve an adequate development of such a system, apart from the development of an adequate core planning engine, one has to focus on other planning related techniques. On the one hand, it is necessary to previously perform a knowledge engineering process in order to define an operational framework where to model and represent the knowledge managed by domain experts, planning experts and the own planning engine. In this sense, we have established a methodology that allows to reach "planner-readable" planning domain and problems from the knowledge currently managed by experts or knowledge engineers (planning experts). This methodology assumes that the modeling language (a high-level language, able to support a user-friendly introduction close to the expert understanding) is different from the language used by the planner (low-level language).

On the other hand, in order to obtain a useful system able to be applied in the real world, techniques about the execution and monitoring of temporal plans in a real framework, and techniques devoted to manage the response to unexpected situations have to be developed.

---
[1]This work has been partially supported by the Spanish MCyT under project TIC2002-04146-C05-02 and the Andalusian Regional Ministry of Environment contract n. NET033957/1

Thus, we also describe a monitoring and replanning process able to (1) reschedule part of a temporal plan in the case that a delay occurred during its execution, but maintaining the causal structure of the plan; and (2) in the case of an unfeasible delay, patch the plan in a human centered approach.

2   Overall Architecture

The core of the SIADEX architecture, (Figure 1), is a *planning server* that obtains and serves temporally extended plans following a hierarchical planning algorithm. The input to the planning server comes from the *ontology server* (called BACAREX), that is capable of integrating and "distilling" knowledge from different formats and sources (legacy GIS and external databases). It also serves the necessary knowledge (world objects and their properties, world states, temporal constraints, actions and tasks), represented in a standard (PDDL-compliant) planning language, in order to generate fire fighting plans: a chronologically ordered sequence of actions, where every action has a *time stamp* that refers to the time at which it should be executed. These plans are executed under the supervision of the *monitoring module* and a human operator. The communication between these modules is performed using the XML-RPC Protocol[2], a standard protocol that allows complex data structures to be transmitted, processed and returned using XML as encoding and HTTP as transport layer.

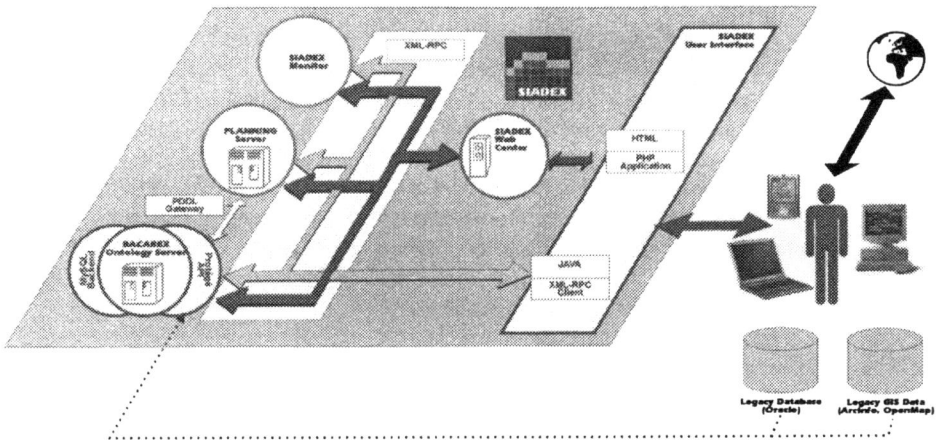

Figure 1: The architecture of SIADEX

This also allows the user to communicate with the system under a TCP/IP connection (OS independent), through a personal computer, a laptop or even a PDA device. All these operations are coordinated by the *WebCenter* module that interfaces all of the interactions between SIADEX and the outer world: it receives planning requests by the user (through the User Interface), and ask the planning server for new plans ; it gathers information on

---

[2]XML: Extensible Markup Language http://www.w3.org/XML. XML-RPC: XML Remote Procedure Call http://www.xmlrpc.com

the execution of the plan, and it launches execution orders, or raises alerts about possible execution failures to a human operator (upon notification of the monitor).

As can be seen, this architecture aims to be a distributed, stand-alone planning application, that implies the development of different planning techniques (hierarchical planning, plan monitoring and replanning, user interaction) that have to be integrated with time and resources management (scheduling). In addition, a stand-alone application as SIADEX cannot be built without developing appropriated planning and scheduling knowledge engineering techniques. All these issues will be discussed in the following sections.

3 BACAREX: the knowledge base of SIADEX

BACAREX is an ontology of planning objects conceived as a stand-alone module. It is, thus, responsible of providing the knowledge required by the planning process, but it is also an open platform to a continuous update and query by (domain or planning) experts. The ontology has an interface with legacy databases so that the flexibility and efficiency of data storage is guaranteed and multiple users/processes in parallel are also allowed. It also provides both offline and online access facilities. Offline access allow planning experts accessing the knowledge and carry out maintenance and validity checking operations with full operability. Online access is done through a web access service, and it is devoted to domain experts that do not have skills on knowledge representation for planning but may painlessly access the knowledge in a web browsing fashion by means of a hierarchy of objects and activities close to their understanding of the problem.

The operating requirements of such a knowledge base, the great amount of knowledge managed and its different categories, requires to consider methodologies and tools as standard and planner-independent as possible. We have realized that it is possible to adapt CommonKADS [16] to model and represent some parts of the knowledge base (later detailed). With respect to choosing a modeling language, this depends also on the existence of a tool for representing and editing the planning knowledge. Although some planning-specific tools and modeling languages can be found in the literature [13, 15, 17] they are either not planner-independent [15, 17], or they do not fit to real-world expressiveness requirements [13]. Thus, for the sake of standardization we have opted for Protégé [3], a widely recognized tool in the field of knowledge based systems development, and we have defined our planning modeling language and planning knowledge acquisition and validation process on this framework.

Thus, the knowledge engineering process that we have carried out has lead to the definition of an ontology of planning knowledge (BACAREX) and a validation process for such ontology. In addition, different actors in the management of this knowledge have been considered: the user (usually a domain expert), the knowledge engineer (a planning expert) and the planner; and different techniques have been developed according to every actor needs and operating requirements.

3.1 Engineering planning knowledge

In the development of BACAREX (see Figure 2) we have had to faced with the modeling, representation and management of several categories of knowledge.

---

[3] http://protege.stanford.edu. It also allows to easily develop online and offline access to the knowledge base.

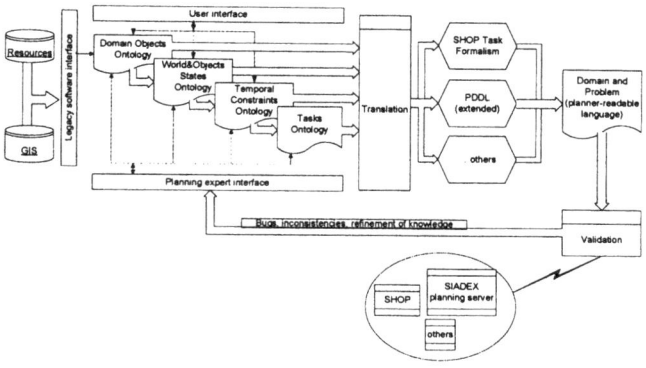

Figure 2: The modeling, representation and validation process followed in SIADEX

Domain objects. Objects (like geographical points, squads, vehicles, etc.) , their properties (like coordinates, number of components, avalaibility) and relations between objects (position, components, etc.) have to be identified, modeled and represented. In addition additional and relevant data like GIS information or weather forecasting already exists in legacy databases (Oracle databases for resource management, and GIS like ArcInfo for cartographic information, are used by technical staff) and they have to be incorporated also as domain objects. This knowledge is modeled and represented in the *domain objects ontology*, a part of the ontology that structures domain objects as a hierarchy of classes and instances. There are standard methodologies, like CommonKADS, that can be adapted [4] for helping to obtain that part of the ontology, but this is not the case for others parts.

World and objects states. Dynamic properties and relations between objects (like position or different states for resources), and their transitions, that are needed to define the dynamics of the domain, and required by the own planning process, have also to be modeled and represented. The *world and objects states ontology* represents the predicates (relations) necessary to define the domain dynamics, and it also allows the definition of deductive axioms in order to derive other states from logic combinations of more simple predicates. Some relations (i.e. predicates) can be automatically obtained, from domain objects slots, but there are other relations that appear to be necessary to represent only when a detailed analysis of actions requirements and effects is done in the validation stage.

Temporal and resources (scheduling) constraints. Apart from the necessary time representation for every dynamic property or relation, there is also information about weather forecasting (temperature, humidity and wind speed and direction) with attached time constraints. In addition, the use of resources is subject to legal temporal regulations, thus one has to consider: periods of availability of resources, legal safety constraints (maximum number of hours

---

[4]See [9] for a detailed description about adapting CommonKADS to the development of SIADEX

of flight for aircrafts), and schedule of the shifts of workers, by contracting agreement. The *temporal and resources constraints ontology* is devoted to this category of knowledge, and it associates time constraints (time points or intervals) to properties and relations described in the previous parts of the overall ontology.

Actuation guidelines and standard operating protocols. This category includes knowledge about the tasks that have to be accomplished in a fire fighting episode. These tasks are classified as strategy, logistics, attack, deployment and withdrawal procedures. In addition to this tasks knowledge, heuristics about the use of resources and conditions about the use of procedures in specific situations have also to be represented. This knowledge is modeled and represented in the *task ontology* , that is defined as a class-hierarchy of tasks where the representation of tasks follows a HTN standard: tasks may be primitive or compound, every compound task is associated to a set of methods that represents different ways to accomplish a task, and every method is a collection of (primitive or compound) tasks [14]. Tasks (compound or primitive) are represented with a name, arguments whose types are extracted from the domain objects ontology, and temporal constraints (a duration, and start and end time points). Primitive tasks contains preconditions and effects, represented by standard logical expressions. Every method, represented as a (possible unordered) task list, also contains a precondition that defines their application conditions (useful to encode user heuristics).

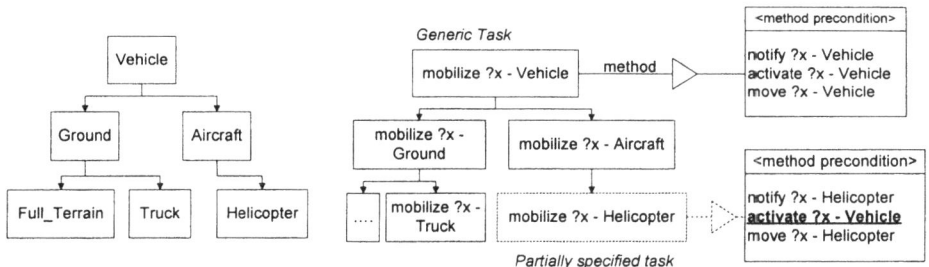

Figure 3: Tasks hierarchy with partially specified tasks

Apart from this basic representation, tasks are organized as a class hierarchy following the idea of an *object oriented foundation class*. This allows a planning expert to carry out knowledge management operations as the definition of generic tasks performed on abstract resources, and the specialization of such generic tasks performed on more concrete resources. The use of this kind of ontology has several advantages since it allows to maintain tasks even if they are partially specified. These kind of tasks are useful to describe cases in which the knowledge elicited (form documents or experts) is not at a sufficient level of detail to be considered fully operational; but it might be introduced to the planner server in a validation process in order to be refined by the interaction with domain and planning experts.

Though part of this modeling language is inspired by the HTN paradigm, it is important to notice that it is not a planner-readable language, and that it supports several modeling operations that are not offered by standard planning languages, but necessary if one want to develop a real-world planning application. These functionalities include: task organization by subject (strategy-definition tasks, logistics operations tasks, deployment tasks, attack tasks, withdrawal tasks, etc.), knowledge inheritance operations (tasks specialization by inheritance of either methods or precondition and effects) and generic tasks management. This splits knowledge engineering operations (domain modeling and validation) from proper planning operations.

3.2 Planner-independent validation

The knowledge stored in BACAREX is not directly recognizable by the planner module. This is not a drawback, but an added value. This allows to define a planner-independent validation process, which starts from a translation of the domain modeling and representation language to a planner-readable language. At present, we have developed some "plug-ins" that translates the BACAREX knowledge into the task formalism of SHOP [14] and an extension of PDDL [12] able to manage hierarchical tasks. Its main features are the following ones:

- Predicates are easily translated from the world and objects states ontology, and the classes hierarchy of the domain objects ontology are also translated as a hierarchy of types in the PDDL domain description. Deductive axioms are translated as *derived predicates* in PDDL 2.2.

- Slots in the domain objects ontology that contain numerical values that may change during a planning episode, mainly numerical resources like the level of fuel of a vehicle, are declared like fluents in the PDDL domain, so that the use of arithmetic operations and functions are allowed over them.

- The temporal knowledge related to durations and delays of tasks, like subgoals with deadlines, the maximum make-span allowed for a plan, durations of actions or any other temporal constraints defined between actions, are translated into the formalism described in [4], that extends the expressiveness of the level 3 of PDDL devoted to durative planning actions. Other temporal constraints in the *temporal constraints ontology* (like work shifts or weather forecasting) are translated into *timed initial literals* in PDDL 2.2.

- Primitive tasks are translated as PDDL 2.2 durative actions (with the time formalism extended as described in [4]). Compound tasks, their time constraints, and their associated methods are translated into a hierarchical extension of PDDL (inspired in the SHOP task formalism). In order to avoid a high branching factor in the planner, only the most specific tasks (leafs of the task hierarchy) are translated into the planning domain.

The result of the translation process is a planning domain and/or problem ready to use for a planning engine. This output is used in a validation process based on querys and answers performed against the planning server. These query and answer transactions are defined over a XML-RPC protocol that allows to use any planning engine that supports this protocol. That process allows to detect different kinds of mistakes usually produced in domain modeling and writing: syntactical bugs, semantical inconsistencies, and partially specified tasks.

4 The Planner

The planning module is still under development so we may not show performance or efficiency data here but it is a planner based on the HTN paradigm [11] over the ideas previously developed in our non-hierarchical temporal planner MACHINE [4] and our hybrid hierarchical planer HYBIS [3].

- The initial state is obtained from the world and states ontology by querying the ontology about the main slots of the instances of classes like facilities, human resources, vehicles, water points, etc. The domain is also extracted from the ontology, through the translation process explained above.

- The goal is interactively defined as a situation assessment of the episode made up of instances of the ontology that describe the desires of the technical staff. Then, the goal of a problem is defined in the following terms (by extending the PDDL representation of goals):

  - Geographical deployment of the episode (GIS information): situation of the episode, main fire lines, main focuses, water discharging areas, defense lines (grouped by sectors each of which has a fighting director that is responsible of it), command area and waiting areas.

  - All the items related to fire fighting activity have a slot that defines its intensity, that is, a numeric evaluation of the power of resources that should be assigned to it and that is fixed by hand by the fire fighting director. From the intensities, the planner may pre-select several combinations of resources, that are submitted to the fight director who finally selects one of them. Later, the planner will select a specific set of instances of resources that fits within the selected combination of resources.

  - The fire director also assigns different tasks to be carried out at each item with fire fighting activity (among the available tasks in the ontology) and, since every task is preconditioned with the type of resource that is able to develop it, the planner automatically assigns resources to tasks.

Finally, thanks to the expressive power of using Temporal Constraints Networks as the underlying formalism to represent temporal knowledge, the planner is able to obtain approximate temporal plans, that are plans whose time-line is flexible and may be scheduled in several different ways to adapt to unexpected delays, but this is discussed in the following section (for more details, see [4, 5]).

5 Monitoring and Replanning

Up to now, we have described a batch process that starts with the knowledge stored in the ontology server and ends with the raising of one (or more) approximate temporal plans ready for execution. This section describes the monitoring process and the replanning process (the role of the replanner is also played by the same planning module since it is an incremental planner able to plan an replan over the same episode [10]) whose interaction is sketched in Figure 4 and described below.

The monitoring algorithm [4, 10] is a real time algorithm that follows the execution of the temporal plan at the highest level of detail since temporal plans still represent the time at which every effect of every action is achieved. It checks that everything executes as predicted, otherwise, it may detect and, in some cases repair, some of the problems[5]. The type of problems and their possible solutions are the following ones:

---

[5]Clearly, the user may also interrupt the execution of the plan at any moment.

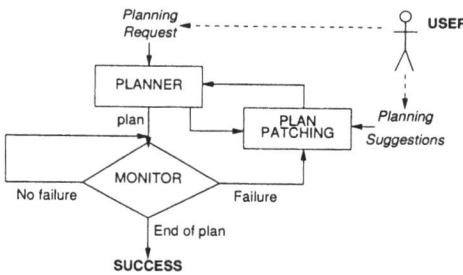

Figure 4: The monitoring user-centered replanning processes

Unexpected delays. These are detected when an action exceeds the time predicted to achieve one of its effects. In this case, it must be taken into account that a temporal plan encodes many temporal constraints between its actions like deadlines, relative constraints and time windows for execution and that most of these temporal constraints come from the cause/effect relationships between actions in the plan. For example, let us consider that action a_1 executes at time t and it produces an effect e at time $t + \delta_e$. Let us suppose again that action a_2 requires the effect e to be true before its execution and that it must be executed before the deadline $t + \delta_{a_2}$. This means that action a_2 must be necessarily executed in the time window $[t+\delta_e, t+\delta_{a_2}]$ and that any delay in the achievement of the effect e would also delay a_2 and even more, it might put in risk a correct execution of action a_2. Therefore, there may be three different situations.

- Local delays. They are delays that only affect locally to an isolated branch of the temporal plan without affecting the remaining actions. This is the easiest case since it could not affect deadline goals or makes-pans which depend on more global temporal constraints. In these cases, a new reschedule may be found[6] only for the actions of the affected branch leaving the remaining schedule unaltered.

- Global delays. They are more important since they might affect all of the remaining actions and deadline goals or makes-pans might also be affected and hence, a whole new reschedule might be needed.

- Infeasible delays. When an action a_j has been delayed beyond its limits, then no reschedule is possible and the possibility of replanning should be considered. In the previous example, if the effect e takes too much time to be achieved (when $\delta_e > \delta_{a_2}$) then a temporal inconsistency would rise and the temporal plan would not be valid.

Execution failures. These situations mean a real fail of execution of an action and they are very serious since, as a consequence of the failure, the cause/effect relationships between actions could have been damaged and the plan could fail to achieve its goal. Therefore, they are situations that necessarily imply some replanning decisions to be taken and that may be as easy as re-executing the failed action or as complex a re-designing a whole branch of the plan. These execution failures may be due to one of the following reasons:

---

[6]The rescheduling process is described in [8] and it consists of propagating the detected delay among all the actions that have not executed yet and detecting possible inconsistencies in the propagation.

- Missing condition. A condition that was previously achieved by the execution of a previous action has disappeared. For example, a defense line that was open by a bulldozer to protect an area but that the fire has jumped over it and now the protected area is threatened.

- Missing effect. An effect of an action under execution would never be achieved. For example, when an aircraft breaks down and it is not able to drop a discharge of water that had been previously scheduled.

- Unexpected condition. A condition that was not previously known suddenly raises. For example an unforeseen increase in the speed of the wind that impedes the flight of helicopters.

In any of these cases, the revision and redesign of the failed branch is carried out in a close interaction between the technical staff and the planning module in a "user centered" plan patching episode [10] like that outlined in Figure 4. Its main features are the following ones.

On the one hand, this episode allows the interaction with the user, that is, during this plan patching episode, the user may edit the plan and either delete and suggest conditions or actions to reflect his strategy to resume the execution of the plan or even define a new assessment of the situation by deleting goals and introducing new goals for the planner. This is a very important point since in critic situations, where there may be lives in danger, a completely automated process is not very realistic and the skills of human operators could not be substituted. After the patching of the failed plan, the own planning algorithm is able to regenerate a new plan adapted to these changes of the user and then submitted again to the technical staff for consideration until an appropriate solution is found and scheduled for execution.

On the other hand, this regeneration process is strongly based on local changes made on the failed plan, so that no radical changes are introduced and only the failed branches are redesigned, leaving the remaining of the plan unaltered. This issue is very important since otherwise, a global redesign of the plan could produce dramatic changes on the resources and their tasks and a chaotic migration from the older plan to the new one that would be unrealistic.

6   Final remarks

Specifically in the field of forest fire fighting there are several approaches in the literature. PHOENIX [6] (1989-1993) or CHARADE [1] (1992-1995) are good examples, but they have failed in their application as assistants to real fire fighting scenarios. The reasons for these unsuccessful approaches are: (1) They have neglected the development of appropriated planning knowledge engineering techniques; (2)The lack of deliberative planning techniques able to generate new plans for a situation without the requirement of having a predefined skeleton or general plan previously stored, monitoring of plan execution and replanning techniques to allow flexibility and responsiveness in the execution of the plan; (3) They consider user interaction at edition level, not allowing users and the planner to collaborate in the resolution of the same problem.

The knowledge modeling and validation process here described has to be considered as a step forward in the development of a standard tool, based also on a widely recognized representation language for engineering planning knowledge. In addition, the temporal reasoning framework described is devoted to primitive tasks, more work have to be done in order to fully extend the Temporal Constraint Networks reasoning process to a hierarchical planning algorithm.

References

[1] P. Avesani, A. Perini, and F. Ricci. Interactive case-based planning for forest fire management. *Applied Intelligence*, 13(1):41–57, 2000.

[2] B.Schattenberg and S.Biundo. On the identification and use of hierarchical resources in planning and scheduling. In *Proceedings of the 6th International Conference on AI Planning and Scheduling, Toulouse, France, April 2002, AAAI Press, Menlo Park, California*, 2002.

[3] L. Castillo, J. Fdez-Olivares, and A. González. On the adequacy of hierarchical planning characteristics for real world problem solving. In *Proc. of VI European Conference of Planning*, 2001.

[4] L. Castillo, J. Fdez-Olivares, and A. González. A temporal constraint network based temporal planner. In *Workshop of the UK Planning and Scheduling Special Interest Group, PLANSIG 2002*, pages 99–109, 2002.

[5] L. Castillo, J. Fdez-Olivares, and A. González. Some issues on the representation and explpoitation of imprecise temporal knowledge in an AI planner. In *Knowledge-Based Intelligent Information and Engineering Systems*, Lecture Notes in Artificial Intelligence, LNAI-2774, pages 1321–1328. Springer-Verlag, 2003.

[6] P.R. Cohen, M.L. Greenberg, D.M. Hart, and A.E. Howe. Trial by fire: understanding the design requirements for agents in complex environments. *AI Magazine*, 10(3):32–48, 1989.

[7] M. de la Asunción, L. Castillo, J. Fdez-Olivares, O. García-Pérez, A. González, and F. Palao. SIADEX: Assisted Design of Forest Fire Fighting Plans by Artificial Intelligence Planning techniques. http://siadex.ugr.es, 2003.

[8] M. de la Asunción, L. Castillo, J. Fdez-Olivares, O. García-Pérez, A. González, and F. Palao. Handling fuzzy temporal constraints in a planning framework. Submitted to the special issue of Annals of Operations Research on Personnel Scheduling and Planning, 2004.

[9] M. de la Asunción, L. Castillo, J. Fdez-Olivares, O. García-Pérez, A. González, and F. Palao. Siadex: A real-world planning approach to forest fire fighting. In *STAIRS 04*, 2004.

[10] Marc de la Asunción, Luis Castillo, Juan Fernández-Olivares, Oscar García-Pérez, Antonio González, and Francisco Palao. Local (human-centered) replanning in the SIADEX framework. In L. Castillo and M.A. Salido, editors, *Conference of the Spanish Association for Artificial Intelligence, II Workshop on Planning, Scheduling and Temporal Reasoning*, pages 79–88, 2003.

[11] K. Erol, J. Hendler, and D. Nau. UMCP: A sound and complete procedure for hierarchical task-network planning. In *AIPS-94*, 1994.

[12] D. Long and M. Fox. PDDL2.1: An Extension to PDDL for Expressing Temporal Planning Domains. *Journal of Artificial Intelligence Research*, 20:61–124, 2003.

[13] T. L. McCluskey, D Liu, and R. Simpson. GIPO II: HTN planning in a tool-supported knowledge engineering environment. In *Proceedings of the International Conference on Automated Planning and Scheduling, June, 2003 AAAI press. (ICAPS'03)* , 2003.

[14] D. Nau, T. Au, O. Ilghami, U. Kuter, J. W. Murdock, D. Wu, and F. Yaman. SHOP2: An HTN planning system. *Journal of Artificial Intelligence Research*, 20:370–404, 2003.

[15] H. Mu noz Avila, D. W. Aha, L. Breslow, and D. Nau. HICAP: An interactive case-based planning architecture and its application to noncombatant evacuation operations. In *Ninth Conference on Innovative Applications of Artificial Intelligence*, pages 879–885. AAAI Press, 1999.

[16] G. Schreiber, H. Akkermans, A. Anjewierden, R. de Hoog, N. Shadbolt, W. Van de Velde, and B. Wielinga. *Knowledge Engineering and Management – The CommonKADS Methodology*. The MIT Press, 1999.

[17] A. Tate, B. Drabble, and R. Kirby. O-PLAN2: An open architecture for command, planning and control. In M. Zweben and M. Fox, editors, *Intelligent scheduling*. Morgan Kaufmann, 1994.

Planning, Scheduling and Constraint Satisfaction: From Theory to Practice
L. Castillo et al. (Eds.)
IOS Press, 2005

Web Services for Adaptive Planning

G. Tsoumakas, G. Meditskos, D. Vrakas, N. Bassiliades, I. Vlahavas

Dept. of Informatics, Aristotle University of Thessaloniki, 54124 Greece

Abstract. This paper presents the design and development of an adaptive planning system using the technology of Web services. The Web-based adaptive planning system consists of two modules that can work independently. The first one is called HAP-WS and is the Web service interface to the domain independent planner HAP (Highly Adjustable Planner) that can be customized through the adjustment of several parameters, either manually or automatically. In the manual mode, the user itself adjusts planner parameters giving explicitly the values. In the automatic mode, the second subsystem, called LAMP-WS, computes the values of the planning parameters of HAP. LAMP-WS is the Web service interface to the learning system LAMP (Lazy Adaptive Multicriteria Planning) that can automatically configure a planning system using instance-based learning on past performance data of that system. The two subsystems are implemented as independent Web services, which can be used stand-alone and reside in different servers in potentially different geographical locations.

1 Introduction

Web services are the fundamental building blocks in the move to distributed computing on the Internet. Open standards and the focus on communication and collaboration among people and applications have created an environment where Web services are becoming the platform for application integration. Applications are constructed using multiple Web services from various sources that work together regardless of where they reside or how they were implemented.

Planning has an important role to play in the orchestration of Web services. It can be used to construct efficient execution plans of multiple Web services for the achievement of a complex task, by viewing service composition as a planning problem [4]. By doing so, various already available planning techniques and systems can be used to tackle Web service composition, probably with the addition of a few new techniques. The ability to perform automated service composition would revolutionize many application areas for Web service technology including e-commerce and systems integration.

Within this scenario, planning systems could also be deployed themselves as Web services, allowing their interoperation with other information integration Web services and incorporation into larger Web Information Management Systems. To the best of our knowledge, no planner has yet been provided as a Web service, with the exception of O-Plan [10]. Although O-Plan offers its functionality to users and programs on the World Wide Web, it uses the outdated technology of CGI scripts. Therefore, O-Plan cannot be dynamically discovered and invoked by users or other programs. They would have to know apriori its Internet address and the specifications of its input and output. Inevitably, bridging theory to practice requires the use of technology that is based on open standards, such as those adopted by the Web services architecture.

This paper presents the design and development of a Web-based system for Adaptive Planning that utilizes the technology of Web services. The system consists of two independent Web services: HAP-WS is a Web service interface to the HAP (Highly Adjustable Planner) planning system [14]. A user or program can directly use HAP-WS by providing it the planning domain and problem definition files, and optionally the values for its 7 planning parameters. LAMP-WS is a Web service interface to the LAMP (Lazy Adaptive Multicriteria Planning) learning system [12] that predicts a configuration for the planning parameters of HAP based on the characteristics of the given planning problem. LAMP-WS can also be used directly by a user or program for consultation on a suitable parameter configuration for the HAP planner. For automatically configuring HAP, a combination of the two services is required, which can be easily handled by a suitable client application. Such an application example developed in ASP.NET is also presented in this paper.

The rest of the paper is organized as follows. Section 2 presents a brief reference to the technologies that the Web service architecture entails. Section 3 introduces the concept of Adaptive Planning and related work. Section 4 describes the Web services that were developed for the purposes of Adaptive Planning and Section 5 presents an example ASP.NET application that uses these Web services. Finally the last section concludes this work and points areas for improvements.

2 Background

A Web service is a software system identified by a URI (Uniform Resource Identification), whose public interfaces and bindings are defined and described using XML. Its definition can be discovered by other software systems. These systems may then interact with the Web service in a manner prescribed by its definition, using XML based messages conveyed by Internet protocols [5].

The use of the Web services paradigm is expanding rapidly to provide a systematic and extensible framework for application-to-application (A2A) interaction, built on top of existing Web protocols and based on open XML standards. Web services aim to simplify the process of distributed computing by defining a standardized mechanism to describe, locate, and communicate with online software systems. Essentially, each application becomes an accessible Web service component that is described using open standards. The basic architecture of Web services includes technologies capable of:

- Exchanging messages.

- Describing Web services.

- Publishing and discovering Web service descriptions.

2.1 Exchanging messages

The standard protocol for communication among Web services is the Simple Object Access Protocol (SOAP) [2]. SOAP is a simple and lightweight XML-based mechanism for creating structured data packages that can be exchanged between network applications. SOAP consists of four fundamental components: an envelope that defines a framework for describing message structure, a set of encoding rules for expressing instances of application-defined data types, a convention for representing remote procedure calls and responses, and a set of rules for using SOAP with HTTP. SOAP can be used with a variety of network protocols, such as HTTP, SMTP, FTP, RMI/IIOP, or a proprietary messaging protocol.

SOAP is currently the de facto standard for XML messaging for a number of reasons. First, it is relatively simple, defining a thin layer that builds on top of existing network technologies such as HTTP that are already broadly implemented. Second, it is flexible and extensible, because rather than trying to solve all of the various issues developers may face when constructing Web services, it provides an extensible, composable framework that allows solutions to be incrementally applied as needed. Thirdly, it is based on XML. Finally, SOAP enjoys broad industry and developer community support.

SOAP defines four XML elements:

- *env:Envelope* is the root of the SOAP request. At the minimum, it defines the SOAP namespace. It may define additional namespaces.

- *env:Header* contains auxiliary information as SOAP blocks, such as authentication, routing information, or transaction identifier. The header is optional.

- *env:Body* contains one or more SOAP blocks. An example would be a SOAP block for RPC call. The body is mandatory and it must appear after the header.

- *env:Fault* is a special block that indicates protocol-level errors. If present, it must appear in the body.

2.2   Describing Web services

The standard language for formally describing Web services is Web Services Description Language (WSDL) [6]. WSDL is an XML document format for describing Web services as a set of endpoints operating on messages containing either document-oriented or procedure-oriented (RFC) messages. The operations and messages are described abstractly, and then bound to a concrete network protocol and message format to define an endpoint. Related concrete endpoints may be combined into services. WSDL is sufficiently extensible to allow description of endpoints and their messages regardless of what message formats or network protocols are used to communicate. A complete WSDL definition of a service comprises a service interface definition and a service implementation definition, as depicted in Figure 1.

A service interface definition is an abstract or reusable service definition that may be instantiated and referenced by multiple service implementation definitions. A service interface definition can be thought of as an IDL (Interface Definition Language), Java interface, or Web service type. This allows common industry standard service types to be defined and implemented by multiple service implementers.

In WSDL, the service interface contains elements that comprise the reusable portion of the service description: binding, portType, message and type elements. In the portType element, the operations of the Web service are defined. The operations define what XML messages can appear in the input, output and fault data flows. The message element specifies which XML data types constitute various parts of a message. The message element is used to define the abstract content of messages that comprise an operation. The use of complex data types within the message is described in the types element. The binding element describes the protocol, data format, security and other attributes for a particular service interface (portType).

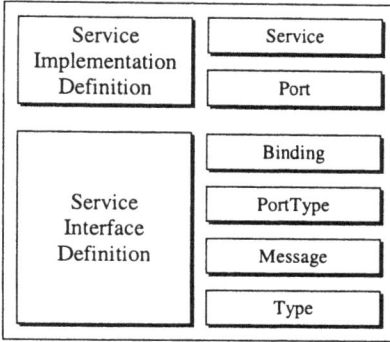

Figure 1: WSDL service implementation and interface definitions.

The service implementation definition describes how a particular service interface is implemented by a given service provider. It also describes its location so that a requester can interact with it. In WSDL, a Web service is modelled as a service element. A service element contains a collection of port elements. A port associates an endpoint (e.g. a network address location) with a binding element from a service interface definition.

2.3   Publishing and discovering Web services

While there are some established standards for Web service description and communication, the publishing and discovery of Web services can be implemented with a range of solutions. Any action that makes a WSDL document available to a requestor, at any stage of the service requestor's lifecycle, qualifies as service publication. In the same way, any mechanism that allows the service requestor to gain access to the service description and make it available to the application at runtime qualifies as service discovery.

The simplest case of publishing a Web service is a direct publish. This means that the service provider sends the service description directly to the service requestor. This can be accomplished using an email attachment, an FTP site, or even a CDROM distribution. Slightly more dynamic publication uses Web Services Inspection Language (WSIL) [3]. WSIL defines a simple HTTP GET mechanism to retrieve Web services descriptions from a given URL. Another means of publishing service descriptions available to Web services is through a Universal Description, Discovery and Integration (UDDI) registry [1]. There are several types of UDDI registries that may be used depending on the scope of the domain of Web services published to it. When publishing a Web service description to a UDDI registry, complete business context and well though out taxonomies are essential if the service is to be found by its potential consumers.

3   Adaptive Planning

Domain independent heuristic planning relies on ingenious techniques, such as heuristics and search strategies, to improve the execution speed of planning systems and the quality of their solutions in arbitrary planning problems. However, no single technique has yet proved to be the best for all kinds of problems. Many modern planning systems incorporate more than one such optimizing techniques in order to capture the peculiarities of a wider range of problems. However, to achieve the optimum performance these planners require manual fine-tuning of their run-time parameters.

We call Adaptive Planning the enhancement of Planning systems with Machine Learning techniques, in order to perform automatic configuration of their Planning parameters. Adaptive Planning can assist in the task of creating flexible Planning systems that can automatically adapt themselves to each problem, achieving best performance.

Two adaptive planners that were build upon the HAP planning system [14] are HAP_{RC} [15] and HAP_{NN} [13]. Both are capable of automatically fine-tuning the planning parameters of HAP based on features of the problem in hand. The tuning of HAP_{RC} is performed by a rule system, the knowledge of which has been induced through the application of rule learning over a dataset containing performance data of past executions of HAP. The tuning of HAP_{NN} is performed through instance-based learning that enables the incremental enrichment of its knowledge and allows users to specify their level of importance on the criteria of plan quality and planning speed.

The LAMP (Lazy Adaptive Multicriteria Planning) system [12] uses a generalization of the learning methodology of HAP_{NN} that can be utilized by any modern parameterized domain-independent planning system. In addition, it incorporates a feature weighting approach.

4 Web Services for Adaptive Planning

This section describes the two Web services and the way they can be combined in order to perform adaptive planning. The implementation of the Web services and additional information can be found in [11].

4.1 HAP-WS

HAP-WS is a Web service interface to the HAP (Highly Adjustable Planner) planning system [14]. The customization of HAP is feasible through 7 parameters that are outlined in Table 1.

Table 1: The seven planning parameters and their value sets

Name	Value Set
Direction	$\{0, 1\}$
Heuristic	$\{1, 2, 3\}$
Weights (w_1 and w_2)	$\{0, 1, 2, 3\}$
Penalty	$\{10, 100, 500\}$
Agenda	$\{10, 100, 1000\}$
Equal Estimation	$\{0, 1\}$
Remove	$\{0, 1\}$

The first one refers to the planning direction, which can be either backward (0) or forward (1). The second parameter allows the user to select one of the three available heuristic functions in order to use it as a guide during the search. The third parameter sets the values for the weights used during planning in the weighted A^* search technique. The fourth parameter sets the penalty put on states violating pre-computed fact orderings, while the next one sets the size of the planning agenda (maximum number of states in the frontier set). The last two parameters enable or disable techniques for overcoming plateaus in the search space and simplifying the definition of sub problems, respectively.

Here HAP is deployed as a planning Web service. The output of HAP-WS is a string containing the solution of the given problem. Apart from the 7 planning parameters, HAP-WS requires two additional string inputs, one for the domain of the problem and another for the problem itself, both in PDDL format. In the future we will replace string inputs with XML ones, following the XML syntax of PDDL [8], should the latter is stabilized. This will allow for automatic validation checks through commodity XML software. Figure 2 depicts an excerpt from the WSDL file of HAP-WS, showing the inputs.

```
<s:element name="HAP">
  <s:complexType>
    <s:sequence>
      <s:element minOccurs="0" maxOccurs="1" name="domain" type="s:string" />
      <s:element minOccurs="0" maxOccurs="1" name="problem" type="s:string" />
      <s:element minOccurs="0" maxOccurs="1" name="inputs" type="s0:HAP_Inputs" />
    </s:sequence>
  </s:complexType>
</s:element>
```

Figure 2: HAP-WS input description.

Note that the planning parameters are organized as a separate complex type, because they are optional. Figure 3 shows another excerpt from the WSDL file of HAP-WS defining the complex type of the parameters. As we see, the WSDL file also informs potential clients about the default values of these parameters.

```
<s:complexType name="HAP_Inputs">
  <s:sequence>
    <s:element minOccurs="0" maxOccurs="1" default="0" name="direction" type="s0:directionType"/>
    <s:element minOccurs="0" maxOccurs="1" default="1" name="heuristic" type="s0:heuristicType"/>
    <s:element minOccurs="0" maxOccurs="1" default="2" name="search" type="s0:searchType"/>
    <s:element minOccurs="0" maxOccurs="1" default="10" name="penalty" type="s0:penaltyType"/>
    <s:element minOccurs="0" maxOccurs="1" default="100" name="agenda" type="s0:agendaType"/>
    <s:element minOccurs="0" maxOccurs="1" default="1" name="closer" type="s0:closerType"/>
    <s:element minOccurs="0" maxOccurs="1" default="0" name="remove" type="s0:removeType"/>
  </s:sequence>
</s:complexType>
```

Figure 3: HAP-WS parameters complex type.

We also notice that the type of each parameter is further specified (directionType, heuristicType, etc.). This ensures that potential clients know the allowed values of each parameter. An example of such a type about the direction parameter is given in Figure 4.

```
<s:simpleType name="directionType">
  <s:restriction base="s:int">
    <s:enumeration value="0"/>
    <s:enumeration value="1"/>
  </s:restriction>
</s:simpleType>
```

Figure 4: HAP-WS direction type.

4.2 LAMP-WS

LAMP-WS is a Web service interface to the LAMP (Lazy Adaptive Multicriteria Planning) learning system [12]. LAMP automatically configures the parameters of a planner (such as search direction and agenda size) based on 26 measurable characteristics of planning problems (such as number of actions per operator and mutual exclusions between facts).

Learning data are produced by running the planner under consideration off-line on several planning problems using all combinations of values for its parameters. When LAMP is faced with a new problem, it first retrieves the recorded performance (execution time and plan length) for all parameter configurations of the k nearest problems. It then selects the configuration with the optimal performance.

Optimality is however susceptible to user preferences. Usually the most important performance metric is plan quality, i.e. a shorter plan is preferred over a longer cne, but there are cases (e.g. real time systems) where the planner must respond promptly even at the expense of the quality of the resulting plan. LAMP tries to mitigate these two mostly contradicting metrics by combining them into an overall score, using the Weighted Sum multicriteria method [9]. Users can specify the weights of plan quality and planning speed, reflecting their relative preference to either of the criteria. LAMP computes the overall score for each configuration according to the user specifications and recommends the one with the highest score.

Experimental results on the automatic configuration of the HAP [14] and LPG [7] planners have shown that LAMP manages to improve the performance of their default configurations by 10 and 6 percent respectively. In addition, setting the weights in favor of either the performance criteria has the expected effect on the planner performance.

There are various interesting discussion issues on LAMP. A first one is whether the 26 features manage to model effectively the different properties of planning problems. The experimental results show that they work, but perhaps there are additional features that should be included. This requires further work in terms of knowledge engineering for planning.

A second one is whether the *space* of different planner configurations (864 for HAP and 72 for LPG) is large enough for covering all the different properties of a planing problem. A first impression is given from the experimental results. HAP has a larger space of configurations than LPG and it was also the planner with the highest performance profit. It seems plausible that the higher the configuration space, the better the adaptation. However, a larger configuration space imposes a higher computational cost for collecting training data.

Here, LAMP is deployed as a Web service for the automatic configuration of HAP. The output of LAMP-WS is a structure containing the values for the 7 parameters of HAP. The inputs to LAMP-WS are the planning domain and problem files and the multicriteria weights for plan steps (ws) and planning time (wt). An excerpt from the WSDL file of LAMP-WS showing its input is given in Figure 5.

```
<s:element name="LAMP">
  <s:complexType>
    <s:sequence>
      <s:element minOccurs="0" maxOccurs="1" name="domain" type="s:string"/>
      <s:element minOccurs="0" maxOccurs="1" name="problem" type="s:string"/>
      <s:element minOccurs="1" maxOccurs="1" name="ws" type="s:double"/>
      <s:element minOccurs="1" maxOccurs="1" name="wt" type="s:double"/>
    </s:sequence>
  </s:complexType>
</s:element>
```

Figure 5: LAMP-WS input description.

4.3   Using the Web Services

Having obtained the WSDL documents of the Web services, a user or program can create proxy classes in order to establish a communication medium with them. As far as HAP-WS is concerned, a program can use it directly by providing the planning domain and problem definition files and optionally the values for its 7 planning parameters. Default values are used for the unset parameters. LAMP-WS can also be used directly by a user or program for consultation on a suitable parameter configuration for the HAP planner.

For automatically configuring HAP, a combination of the two services is required. First LAMP-WS must be called with the problem and domain description files and the multicriteria weights for plan steps and execution time. Then, HAP-WS is called passing as parameters the values that were returned by LAMP-WS. This process is shown in Figure 6.

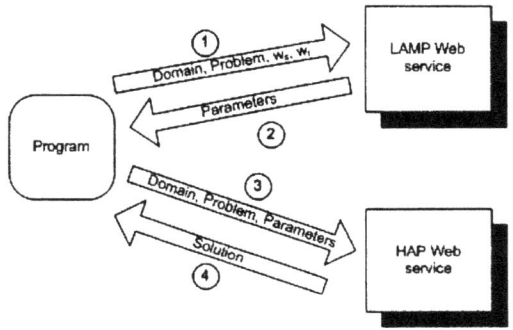

Figure 6: Combination of the two Web services for Adaptive Planning.

5   Web-based Client Application

For the purpose of testing the Web services, a Web-based client application has been developed as an ASP.NET Web page. Figure 7 depicts the layout of this page that plays the role of the application users would create for communicating with our Web services.

Users can provide the PDDL domain and the problem files by clicking the corresponding Browse buttons at the top of the page. They can then either manually configure HAP's options themselves or utilize the LAMP-WS Web service. Manual configuration is available by default, allowing users to change any of the 7 parameters of HAP through the corresponding input boxes. In each parameter, the default value is initially selected in order to inform the user about the default values of the planner and decide whether he/she wants to change the value or not. For automatic parameter configuration the corresponding check-box must be checked. This disables the input boxes for the 7 parameters.

Having finished with the configuration of the planner parameters (either manual or automatic), users can click the Solution button in order to obtain the problem solution. In the case of manual configuration, the ASP application calls HAP-WS passing the parameter values that the user has selected. In the case of automatic configuration, the application first calls LAMP-WS, then gets back the selected parameter values and finally calls HAP-WS with these values. In both cases HAP-WS returns the solution for the submitted problem and the ASP application displays it in the area of the page named Solution.

Select domain and problem files

Domain C:\domain.pddl   [Browse...]
Problem C:\problem.pddl   [Browse...]   [Help]

Options

Parameters configuration. [Help]

☐ Automatic Parameter Configuration

Insert weights for plan steps and planning
time depending on your priorities.   [Help]

Plan step weight [   ]
Planning time weight [   ]

Select planner parameters. [Help]

Search Direction: Default(Backward) ▼
Heuristic: Default(Initial Heuristic) ▼
Search Strategy: Default(w1=2, w2=1) ▼
Violations Penalty: 10
Agenda Size: 100

Strategy for equally estimated states:
Default(Prefer states close to I) ▼
Strategy for achieved sub-goals:
Default(Leave them in problem) ▼

Click 'Solution' button to retrieve the solution.
[Solution]   [Reset to defaults]

Solution

```
Plan:
------------------------------------
1) walk JIM BENCH1 STORE1
2) pick-iron JIM STORE1 IRON1
3) walk JIM STORE1 BENCH1
4) putdown-iron JIM BENCH1 IRON1
5) walk JIM BENCH1 STORE1
6) pick-plastic JIM STORE1 PLASTIC1
7) walk JIM STORE1 BENCH1
8) putdown-plastic JIM BENCH1 PLASTIC1
9) assembly JIM BENCH1 IRON1 PLASTIC1

Steps: 9
Elapsed time: 50
```

Figure 7: ASP.NET Web page

6 Conclusions and Future Work

This paper demonstrated the deployment of an Adaptive Planning system on the Web using the technology of Web services. Adaptive Planning successfully bridges domain-independent problem-solving theories to practical problems with specific properties. In general, we trust that Machine Learning will continue to play a prominent role in the development of effective planning systems. In addition, we believe that developing planning Web services is a step forward towards Planning for Web service composition and towards bridging the theory of Planning to its practical use as a component in larger AI systems and the Semantic Web.

From a technical point of view, delivering an existing (planning) system as a Web service is not very hard, once one becomes familiar with this technology. The task becomes much easier if the system is implemented using Object Oriented Programming, because Web services are based on this software model. Otherwise, there are two solutions. The first is to port the code of the system to an Object Oriented Programming language, which could be quite labor intensive. The second is to build an Object Oriented wrapper of the executable of the system. This is much more simple to implement but is platform-dependent and adds another layer of execution with potential computational complexity and security overheads. We followed the first solution for LAMP and the second for HAP.

As future work, we intend to develop a distributed adaptive planning system, loosely connected with different distributed planning Web services, that would be dynamically invoked and perhaps combined in order to solve a specific problem in an optimal way according to some user-specified performance criteria. We would also like to explore the application of our planning Web service to the problem of composing and orchestrating multiple general purpose Web services to achieve a complex task on the Semantic Web.

Acknowledgements

This work is partly funded from the eCONTENT FP5 European Programme under the EUROCITIZEN project, contract No. 22089.

References

[1] T. Bellwood, L. Clement, D. Ehnebuske, A. Hately, M. Hondo, Y. L. Husband, K. Januszewski, S. Lee, B. McKee, J. Munter, and C. von Riegen. UDDI version 3.0. http://uddi.org/pubs/uddi-v3.00-published-20020719.htm, July 2002.

[2] D. Box, D. Ehnebuske, G. Kakivaya, A. Layman, N. Mendelsohn, H.F. Nielsen, S. Thatte, and D. Winer. Simple Object Access Protocol (SOAP) version 1.1. http://www.w3.org/TR/SOAP/, May 2000.

[3] P. Brittenham. An Overview of Web Services Inspection Language. http://www.ibm.com/developerworks/webservices/library/ws-wsilover, 2001.

[4] M. Carman, L. Serafini, and Traverso P. Web service composition as planning. In *ICAPS 2003 Workshop on Planning for Web Services*, pages 1636–1642, Trento, Italy, June 2003.

[5] M. Champion, C. Ferris, E. Newcomer, and D. Orchard. Web Services Architecture. http://www.w3c.org/TR/ws-arch/, November 2002.

[6] R. Chinnici, M. Gudgin, J. Moreau, and S. Weerawarana. Web Services Description Language (WSDL) version 1.2 working draft. http://www.w3c.org/TR/wsdl12/, July 2002.

[7] A. Gerevini and I. Serina. LPG: a Planner based on Local Search for Planning Graphs with Action Costs. In *Proceedings of the 6th International Conference on Artificial Intelligence Planning Systems, AIPS02*, pages 13–22, 2002.

[8] J. Gough. Xpddl v.0.1. http://www.cis.strath.ac.uk/ jg/, March 2004.

[9] C.L. Hwang and K. Youn. *Multiple Attribute Decision Making - Methods and Applications: A State of the Art Survey*. Springer-Verlag, New York, USA, 1981.

[10] A. Tate and J. Dalton. O-Plan: a Common Lisp Planning Web Service. In *Proceedings of the International Lisp Conference 2003*, pages 12–25, New York, USA, October 2003.

[11] G. Tsoumakas. Web Services for Adaptive Planning. http://lpis.csd.auth.gr/systems/wsap/, May 2004.

[12] G. Tsoumakas, D. Vrakas, N. Bassiliades, and I. Vlahavas. Lazy Adaptive Multicriteria Planning. In *Proceedings of the 16th European Conference on Artificial Intelligence, ECAI04*, pages 693–697, Valencia, Spain, 2004.

[13] G. Tsoumakas, D. Vrakas, N. Bassiliades, and I. Vlahavas. Using the k nearest problems for adaptive multicriteria planning. In *Proceedings of the 3rd Hellenic Conference on Artificial Intelligence, SETN04*, pages 132–141, Samos, Greece, 2004.

[14] D. Vrakas. The Highly Adjustable Planner (HAP). http://lpis.csd.auth.gr/systems/hap/, September 2002.

[15] D. Vrakas, G. Tsoumakas, N. Bassiliades, and I. Vlahavas. Learning rules for Adaptive Planning. In *Proceedings of the 13th International Conference on Automated Planning and Scheduling, ICAPS03*, pages 82–91, Trento, Italy, 2003.

Planning, Scheduling and Constraint Satisfaction: From Theory to Practice
L. Castillo et al. (Eds.)
IOS Press, 2005

169

Planning and Scheduling for workflow domains

María D. R-Moreno [1], Daniel Borrajo [2], Angelo Oddi [3], Amedeo Cesta [3] and Daniel Meziat [1]

[1] *Departamento de Automática. Universidad de Alcalá.*
Carretera Madrid-Barcelona, Km. 33,600. 28871 Alcalá de Henares (Madrid), Spain.
{mdolores, meziat}@aut.uah.es

[2] Departamento de Informática. Universidad Carlos III de Madrid.
Avda. de la Universidad, 30. 28911 Leganés (Madrid), Spain.
dborrajo@ia.uc3m.es

[3] ISTC-CNR-Italian National Research Council
Viale Marx 15, I-00137 Rome, Italy.
{a.oddi, a.cesta}@istc.cnr.it

Abstract

One of the main obstacles in applying AI planning techniques to real problems is the difficulty to model the domains. Usually, this requires that the people that have developed the planning system carry out the modeling phase, since the representation depends very much on a deep knowledge of the internal working of the planning tools. Since, in Business Process Reengineering (BPR), there has already been some work on the definition of languages that allow non-experts to enter knowledge on processes into the tools, we propose here the use of one of such languages to enter knowledge on the organisation processes.

As instances of this domain, we will use the workflow modeling tool SHAMASH, where we have exploited its object oriented structure and rule-base approach to introduce the knowledge through its user-friendly interface. Then, we have used a translator to transform it into predicate logic terms. After this conversion, real models can be automatically generated using a planner that integrates Planning and Scheduling, IPSS. We present results in a simplified real workflow domain, the TELEPHONE INSTALLATION (TI) domain.

1 Introduction

Nowadays the efficiency of the internal workings of organisations strongly depends on the efficient management of company's resources and processes. Enhancing any organization processes is the main objective of BPR. Once the organization has been studied in depth from a process and resources perspective, corresponding models are generated in order to handle processes and resources computationally. Business processes are usually represented as workflow, that is, computerised models within which all the parameters needed for the completion of the processes can be defined: resources involved, orders, tasks, conditions, goals, quality criteria, information flow, etc. Workflow Management Systems have been widely deployed in sectors like insurance, banking, accounting, manufacturing, telecommunications, administration and customer service [10].

Although there have already been many approaches to the computer-aided design of processes, very few have focused on the automatic generation of process models that have in mind the organization resources as well as their capabilities and availability. Recently, there has been considerable interest in the application of AI techniques to Workflow Management (WM) Systems [3]. Most of these tools rely on process libraries as in [2, 9]. Instead, we will focus on how to model processes using AI P&S systems as automatic models generator instead of using processes generated by hand by the user and then saved them in libraries of processes.

In AI P&S some of the main concerns are how to represent the information and the problem solving techniques. The aims that we want to achieve with the integration proposed in this paper is two-fold: on one hand, given that the majority of BPR tools are based on objects and rules, we propose to translate this knowledge on models into the PDDL2.1 language, and on the other hand, we propose an integrated P&S system for solving the problems. We believe that systems that integrate AI P&S, as IPSS [14], are the best suitable candidates.

The paper is structured as follows: section 2 briefly describes the main concepts that Workflow Management (WM) and AI P&S systems share. Next, section 3 introduces two instances of both domains, SHAMASH and IPSS, explaining how the integration can be possible with a simple example of installing a new telephone line in a telecom company. Then, section 6 shows some results of IPSS against state of the art planners. Finally, section 7 outlines the conclusions and future work.

2 Workflow Management and AI Planning and Scheduling

The first step for the use of P&S for WM is to identify points in common by understanding the way WM and AI P&S work. The Process Model is the first stage in the adoption of a Workflow solution and involves the crucial task of revealing and recording all of the manual and automatic internal business processes of an organization. From there, the user designs, models, optimises and simulates the organisation's processes through user friendly interfaces. We include in this stage the design of the process templates that can be instantiated and enacted by a workflow system. Then, it comes the Process Planning where the activities required to achieve some user goals are instantiated, resources assigned, and a preliminary scheduling performed. This two stages are included in the Process Definition interface of the workflow architecture proposed by the Workflow Management Coalition (WFMC) [1]. Next, the enactment/execution stage, where agents (software or humans) carry out the activities, with the workflow system co-ordinating execution. The monitoring stage is conducted concurrently with Enactment/Execution. The system enacting the workflow is monitored, with status information being made available to human operators. Exceptions, such as deviation from the plan, and subsidiary processes are initiated to rectify problems.

In AI Planning systems the following phases can be identified: domain modelling, planning and scheduling, execution and monitoring.

Table 1 outlines at a high level the concepts that AI P&S share with the Workflow community (for a more detailed description we refer to the PLANET roadmap [3]).

---

[1] www.wfmc.org

Table 1: Concepts mapping between AI P&S and workflow.

AI P&S	Workflow
Modeling+Planning and Scheduling	Modeling and Scheduling
Execution	Enactment
Operators	Activities, tasks, ...
Initial State	Organisation, resources
Goals	Business goals, service provision, ...

3   The SHAMASH tool

Once the different stages between both areas have been identified, in this section we describe the features of a real workflow modeling tool, SHAMASH, and then, we make the connection between AI P&S and workflow modelling tools more precise, by describing first how to translate an organisation model described in terms of SHAMASH into a planning domain model for IPSS, how IPSS can produce the desired plan (model), and how this is translated back into SHAMASH.

3.1   The SHAMASH system

SHAMASH [1], a R&D project funded by the EU IV Esprit Program, generated a process modeling tool that allows simulation, modeling and optimisation of business processes taking into account a realistic model of the organisation.

This aspect combined with the features that the tool embodies, make SHAMASH a powerful tool for BPR. Very few tools allow its rich semantic model view of processes and resources. The richer modelling capabilities allow among others, modeling of organisation standards and rules of procedures, business goals, automatic validation and optimisation of the models, or generation of HTML/TEXT output, that allows people from the organisation to freely browse the processes in which they intervene. Basically the SHAMASH tool consists of 4 subsystems. The **Author Subsystem** that provides a user-friendly interface that enables definitions of three types of knowledge: on standards, on processes and on the organisation. The **Simulation and Optimisation Subsystem** checks the syntactic (statistically based simulation) as well as the semantic (rule-based) behaviour of the processes that the user creates. Also it is able to automatically perform an optimisation phase by which new better models are generated by searching the space of process models and using business goals as search metrics. The **Text Generation Subsystem** is responsible for maintaining coherence between the graphical and the text versions. Finally, the **Workflow Interface Subsystem** generates WPDL (Workflow Process Description Language, the standard generated by the WFMC as output of the process representation and be used as an input to any workflow engine.

Once the user defines all the organization knowledge (activities of processes, organisation structure, standards, ...) that will be part of the processes, s/he should specify how the activities are connected to each other. In the case of big processes, this stage is usually quite tedious and error prone for the user (not only from the syntactic point of view, but also from the semantic one). The focus of our work is to automatically generate the model, making sure that the established connections among activities conform a valid and efficient (according to resources usage and business goals) sequence of activities. After the model has been automatically generated, the user can simulate and optimise the process using SHAMASH. Figure 1 shows a high level view of SHAMASH architecture together with the proposed integration with an AI P&S system, IPSS.

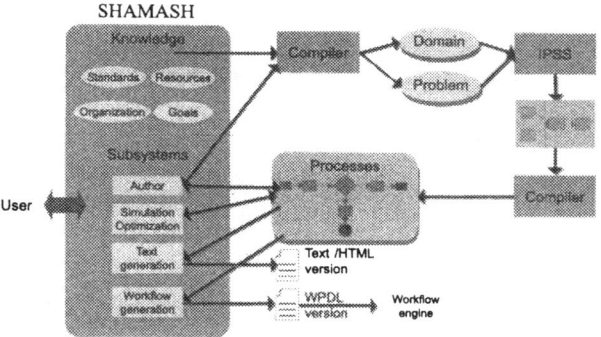

Figure 1: SHAMASH and IPSS integration.

3.2 The automatic model generation

To automate the process models generation, we need to translate the rich semantic representation of SHAMASH (objects and rules) into an AI planning language (operators, states and goals). The translation presented in this section could serve to any planner that uses logical formulae. A first step for the automatic process generation was to use the QPRODIGY planner [4]. But the disadvantages of using this planner were: the needs of domain dependent coded functions for the time reasoning, not explicit language for time and resources, and the output was given as a Total Order plan.

To overcome the drawbacks of the PRODIGY planner, we have used IPSS because it can reason about parallel actions, time and resources, or minimise the makespan at the same time as improving another quality metric, as these domains require. The automatic process generation using IPSS is as follows (see Figure 1): first, the system translates the SHAMASH objects and rules into the IPSS language. Then, IPSS produces a parallel plan of activities. And later, this sequence is translated back into SHAMASH to be presented graphically to the user. The translation has in mind the different semantics of BPR and AI planning concepts as well as their similarities.

4   IPSS: An integrated planning and scheduling system

In the present work we use the IPSS that is discussed in [14]. The planner extends the capabilities of the non-linear HSP metric planner QPRODIGY [4], integrating CSP-based scheduling abilities. IPSS works according to bi-partite architecture shown in Figure 2. Two main modules interact during problem solving: (a) IPSS-P that corresponds to the planning reasoner (it is composed of the QPRODIGY planner and a deordering algorithm that transforms the total ordered (TO) plan produced by QPRODIGY into a parallel plan the scheduling component reasons upon); (b) IPSS-S that corresponds to the scheduling reasoner (it is composed of a Temporal Constraint Network (TCN) that represent the current plan as a STP [12] and a resource reasoner that analyzes resource conflicts according to the algorithm proposed in [16]).

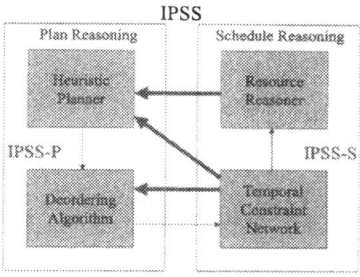

Figure 2: IPSS architecture.

The planning and the scheduling parts interleave information during the solving process. The planning module performs a bi-directional search: it begins by performing backward search from the goals, selecting respectively which goals to achieve, which operator to use to achieve the corresponding goal, and which bindings to use for its variables. Then, the de-ordering algorithm starts computing the link that satisfies the the preconditions of the operator that is going to be added to the TCN and must be supported by the effects of an operator that is already in the TCN. To compute the links, our algorithm starts searching from the first operator applied (origin) until the last one. The operator and the computed links are then added to the TCN.

The TCN layer represents the set of temporal constraints as a Simple Temporal Problem. Significant events, as start/end time of operators are represented as temporal variable tp_i called time points. And each temporal constraints has the form $a \leq tp_i\text{-}tp_j \leq b$, where tp_i - tp_j are time points and a and b are constants. The output from the deordering layer is trasformed in a STN that is checked for consistency. In case of inconsistency, feedback is given first to the deordering layer, to ask for a different deordering (for the sake of complexity the deordering algorithm is incomplete), then to the planner for rejecting the last choices.

The resource reasoner currently implement the conflict analysis for binary resources proposed by Smith and Cheng citesmit-chen-93. The algorithm iteratively imposes ordering constraints for solving resource conflicts between activities that require the same resource. When there is more than one possible order it chooses as heuristic the link following the planner logical order. Again, in case of an unsolvable resource conflict (e.g., no precedence posting can solve the contention) a failure for resource inconsistency is sent to the planner that backtracks the last decision.

5 A workflow domain: installing a new telephone line

We have used in this paper a simplified version of a real workflow domain, the Telephone Installation domain, which comes from analysis of some BT processes [11]. In this domain, among other process related issues, a customer (e.g. Mary Thompson) contacts a telecom company customer service for a new telephone line. If the customer is asking a line for the first time, a spare pair of wires must be available from the house to make a connection from the Distribution Point (DP, e.g.: telegraph pole). If no pair is available, then a new cable must be built. Then, it is necessary to check that there is a spare line card available in the exchange (in that case it is reserved/allocated). If none is available, its installation must be arranged. Installation involves making the connection at the DP (connecting a drop wire to the pair of wires that lead back to the exchange). Then, someone must: contact the customer to arrange a visit to the house to fit new network terminating equipment (NTE); arrange for an engineer to turn up on the right day/time to test the line end to end and install the NTE; allocate a telephone number to the new line and configure the exchange; update the exchange, line plant and customer records; and check with customer that s/he is happy with the service.

In this process there are several activities to perform: build a cable (BUILD-CABLE), set the spare pair of wires available (SET-SPARE-AVAILABLE), check if there is a spare line card available in the exchange (CHECK-LINE), contact the customer to fit the NTE (FIT-NTE), test the line (TEST-LINE), allocate a telephone number (ALLOCATE-NUMBER) and update customer data (UPDATE-DATA).

When the user specifies each activity in SHAMASH, s/he describes attributes specific to the activity (types of resources to be used, cost of the activity, ...), information and material elements used by the activity (data of the user, invoice, ...) as well as rules for describing pre-/post-conditions and its behaviour. An example of rule syntax in pseudocode is shown in Figure 3. This rule says that if there is a Spare Line with attributes *IsCable* equal to *No* and *Available* equal to *Yes*, and exist an Employee with *hours-left* greater or equal to three, then after the execution of the activity the field *IsCable* will be modified to *Yes* and the employee will have in its activities list to build the cable. Figure 4 shows the corresponding IPSS operator translated by the system automatically from the rule.

```
Rule Bill with properties ruleset behaviour
    If Exists a SpareLine of type MetaClassElement named var sp0
        with IsCable = ( FALSE )
        with Available = ( TRUE )
        with At-spare = ( Exists Zone of type MetaClassElement named var z0 )
    and
        Exists a Worker of type resource named var w0
            assigning to var z0 its At-worker
    Then Modify object sp0
        with IsCable is ( TRUE )
```

Figure 3: Example of a BUILD-CABLE activity rule in SHAMASH.

With respect to the problem definition, the initial conditions are generated automatically from the organisation information. This includes issues such as who works in each unit *(Assignedto Engineer-Unit Tom)*, the cost per hour of the employees belonging to a given category *(Cost Technician 548Euro)* and other information related to the details of the line *((Building-cable 3 hours))*. In the problem, we also need to specify the goals that IPSS needs to accomplish. For example, to allocate the line with identifier number 3 *(Allocated Line3 TRUE)*. With these conditions IPSS generates a plan, with resources, units and roles needed in that process.

```
(OPERATOR BUILD-CABLE
   (params <sp0>)
   (preconds ((<w0> WORKER) (<sp0> SPARELINE) (<z0> ZONE))
      (and (IsCable <sp0> FALSE) (Available <sp0> TRUE)
           (At-spare <sp0> <z0>) (At-worker <w0> <z0>)))
   (effects ((del (IsCable <sp0> FALSE))
             (add (IsCable <sp0> TRUE))))
   (costs
           ((<unit> TIME)
            (<duration> (and (DURATION
                                      (cost-from-pred (BuildingCable <duration> <unit>)))))
           ((TIME <duration>)))))
```

Figure 4: IPSS operator corresponding to the BUILD-CABLE rule of Figure 3.

6 Experiments

In this section the different IPSS configurations are explained and the comparison against some state of the art planners in the TI domain will be presented.

6.1 IPSS *configurations used*

We have used in this paper 3 IPSS configurations. IPSS bases its search in the QPRODIGY search integrated with the algorithm that converts incrementally the partial TO plan generated by QPRODIGY during the planning process into a partial PO plan. Then, the *Ground*-CSP layer checks its consistency and provides the temporal information back to the search. IPSS-R is equal to the previous one, but including some resource leverage heuristic. The resource reasoning component (*Meta*-CSP) tells the planner what are the less used resources, and the planner selects these for assigning resources to operators. The -Q extension allows to search for more than one solution using a branch and bound procedure. The planner does not stop when it finds the first plan, but after the time bound has exceeded.

6.2 *The* TI *domain*

All the operations in this domain need to be executed by a human worker, and any worker can perform any action if s/he is not doing something else. There are some restrictions to consider: one worker cannot perform two operations at the same time; and a cable must be built if the spare card is not available. To perform the tasks, the worker should move to the zone where the spares or lines are, in order to accomplish the work that has to be done. This implies that there are two subtypes of planning problems within this domain: a path planning problem (moving to zones from others) and task planning (setting up lines). To relax the problem and exploit its potential parallelism, we will consider that in any case we have to allocate the line, so this can be done in parallel to any other activity instead of waiting that everything is done to allocate the line.

The modeling of the domain does not consider if the worker is or not occupied doing something else. So, apart from planners that provide serial solutions, as, for example, FF [8] or QPRODIGY [4], the solution given by other planners as LPG [6] or MIPS [5] is not correct. In order to compare not only TO planners against our approach, we have also coded this domain having in mind the availability of the chosen agent for performing the corresponding action. In this case, each action (operator) requires the worker not to be busy on performing some actions. After the execution of the action, the agent (worker) is freed by a dummy action (the *free-agent* action). This forces the planners that reason about parallel actions not to consider parallelizing two actions that require the same worker. We have called this domain the TI_OCCU domain and the original TI. The set of problems for the TI_OCCU domain is exactly the same as in the TI domain, but in all problems the availability of the worker must be explicitly set to *not-occupied*.

6.3 Experimental setup

We have generated 160 problems, distributed in four groups of forty problems. Each group has a fix number of workers: two (G2), five (G5), eight (G8) and eleven (G11). Each set of forty problems is subdivided in four subsets of ten problems each, with the following features: 4 lines and spare cards to allocate, in 4 different zones and from 2 to 4 goals; 14 lines and spare cards to allocate in 9 different zones and from 5 to 7 goals; 24 lines and spare cards to allocate, in 14 different zones and from 10 to 12 goals; and 34 lines and spare cards to allocate, in 19 different zones and from 15 to 17 goals.

Table 2 shows the planners used for TI domain. The top part of the table shows the planners that were run using the TI version (FF, and IPSS-R and QPRODIGY (QP), with and without control rules. The bottom part shows the planners that use the TI_OCCU version as they reason about activities in parallel (MIPS, IPSS and LPG). Since LPG is non-deterministic, we run it five times and then show the results of the best (LPG-MIN), worse (LPG-MAX), and median (LPG-MED).

Table 2: Number of problems solved by each planner in the TI domain with a time bound of 180 seconds.

Name	G2	G5	G8	G11	Problems solved	Percentage
IPSS-R	30	30	32	31	123	77%
QP	30	31	33	32	126	79%
FF	40	40	40	40	160	100%
IPSS	29	29	33	31	122	76%
MIPS	22	19	20	24	85	53%
LPG	40	40	40	40	160	100%

From this table we can see that FF and LPG solve all the problems. Then QP, IPSS-R and IPSS. Table 3 shows the accumulative makespan (MS) obtained for all the planners in problems solved by all in the given time limit (180 seconds). We see that IPSS-R finds the best global makespan for the 160 problems in the TI domain. Then LPG-MIN and the IPSS configurations. MIPS finds better solutions than the worse LPG run, and finally, the TO planners, as the makespan is equal to the number of operators: first FF and then the QP configurations.

If we let the planners (just LPG, QP and IPSS are able to) to search for more than one solution during 180 seconds, the results are shown in the second column of Table 3. Again,

Table 3: Accumulative Makespan (MS) and Time by each planner in the TI domain.

Name	MS No Q-version	MS Q-version	Total Time
IPSS-R	347	326	28,58
QP	699	685	11,49
FF	615	–	1,83
IPSS	425	413	25,82
MIPS	486	–	38,61
LPG-Min	346	331	3,99
LPG-Med	417	349	4,05
LPG-Max	515	351	4,14

IPSS-R-Q configuration finds the best solutions although very similar to the one found by LPG-Q.

Even if we do not show the results here, with regards to the number of operators in the solutions, FF finds the shortest solutions and IPSS configurations and LPG the longest. With respect to the execution time, FF is the faster as the third column of Table 3 shows. Due to the low percentage of problems solved by MIPS, there were some problems were IPSS-R found the solution faster than IPSS. In this table, these problems were not solved by MIPS. Because we have plotted only problems solved by all configurations, they are not considered so that is why IPSS-R obtains worse results than IPSS. But, in general, they show the superiority of the integration of the P&S approach against the rest. Also pointing out that from our experience in this kind of domains, it is better to obtain good solutions than fast and bad ones.

7 Conclusions and future work

In this paper, we have focused on P&S for real domains, in particular in workflow domains. We have described the advantages of using a planner that integrates P&S for modeling processes in SHAMASH, a Knowledge Based System that uses an object oriented and rule-based approach. The SHAMASH rules and objects are translated into types and operators to produce a plan that correspond to a process instance (tasks dependency). Each plan will vary depending on the resources available, elements that flow through the process and the different tasks that the organisations can introduce to adapt their processes to the market changes. With this approach the models generated are automatically validated avoiding inconsistencies in linking activities and saving time to the user.

Also outline what AI planners can gain with this approach. Generally, to specify the domain theory, a deep understanding of the AI planners terminology is needed. However, if we use a tool like SHAMASH, the description language is closer to the user and allows an automatic verification of the syntax through a friendly interface. In this integration we could have also used the PDDL2.1 language instead. Then, any planner that supports PDDL2.1 could exploit the advantages mentioned in the paper. Although the planner we have used has some features that makes it specially fit for real domains as to impose a makespan for the solutions or separate the resource reasoning from the causal reasoning (feature that is not available in most of the state of the art planners). This shows that it is a viable alternative for solving the modelling phase of workflow domains.

Acknowledgements

The SHAMASH project was funded by the EU as project number 25491 (IV Esprit programme). A complementary grant was given by the Spanish research commission, CICYT, under project number TIC98-1847-CE. We thank the partners of this project: UF, SAGE, SEMA GROUP, WIP, and EDP. We would specially like to thank all the UC3M team, the PLANET people and Paul Kearney. Through talks with him we have outlined many ideas. This work has also been partially funded by grant CICYT TAP1999-0535-C02-02 and TIC2002-04146-C05-05. Cesta and Oddi work is partially supported by ASI (Italian Space Agency) project ARISCOM.

References

[1] R. Aler, D. Borrajo, D. Camacho, and A. Sierra-Alonso. A knowledge-based approach for business process reengineering, SHAMASH. *Knowledge Based Systems*, 15(8):473–483, 2002.

[2] P. M. Berry and B. Drabble. SWIM: An AI-based System for Organizational Management. In *Procs. of the 2nd NASA Intl. workshop on Planning and Scheduling for Space. San Francisco, California.*, 2000.

[3] S. Biundo, R. Aylett, M. Beetz, D. Borrajo, A. Cesta, T. Grant, L. McCluskey, A. Milani, and G. Verfaille. *Technological Roadmap on AI Planning and Scheduling.* PLANET, 2003.

[4] D. Borrajo, S. Vegas, and M. Veloso. Quality-Based Learning for Planning. In *Working notes of the IJCAI'01 Workshop on Planning with Resources. IJCAI Press. Seattle, WA (USA)*, 2001.

[5] S. Edelkamp and M. Helmert. On the Implementation of MIPS. In *AIPS Workshop on Model-Theoretic Approaches to Planning.*, 2000.

[6] A. Gerevini, A. Saetti, and I. Serina. Planning through Stochastic Local Search and Temporal Action Graphs. *Jounal of Artificial Intelligence Research*, 20:239–290, 2003.

[7] M. Hammer and J. Champy. Reengineering the Corporation. In *Reengineering the Corporation. Harper Business Press, New York.*, 1993.

[8] J. Hoffmann. The Metric-FF Planning System: Translating Ignoring Delete Lists to Numerical State Variables. *Journal of Artificial Intelligence Research*, 2002.

[9] P. Jarvis, J. Moore, P. Chung, I. McBriar, J. Stader, M. Ravinranathan, and A. Macintosh. Applying Intelligent Workflow Management in the Chemicals Industries. In *The Workflow Handbook 2001, L. Fisher (ed), Published in association with the Workflow Management Coalition (WfMC)*, 2000.

[10] T. Lydiard, P. Jarvis, and B. Drabble. Realizing Real Commercial Benefits from Workflow: A Report from the Trenches. In *AAAI-99 Workshop on agent-Based Systems in The Business Context.*, 1999.

[11] MD. R-Moreno and P. Kearney. Integrating AI Planning with Workflow Management System. *International Journal of Knowledge-Based Systems. Elsevier*, 15:285–291, 2002.

[12] R. Dechter, and J. Pearl. Directed Constraint Networks: A Relational Framework for Casual Modelling *Procs. of IJCAI' 91.*, 1991.

[13] MD. R-Moreno, A. Oddi, D. Borrajo, A. Cesta and D. Meziat. IPSS: A Hybrid Reasoner for Planning and Scheduling. *The 16th European Conference on Artificial Intelligence, ECAI04*, 2004

[14] MD. R-Moreno. Representing and Planning Tasks with Time and Resources *PhD thesis. Dpto. de Automática, Universidad de Alcalá*, 2003.

[15] M. Veloso, J. Carbonell, A. Pérez, D. Borrajo, E. Fink, and J. Blythe. Integrating Planning and Learning: The PRODIGY Architecture. *Journal of Experimental and Theoretical AI*, 7:81–120, 1995.

[16] S. F. Smith, and C. Cheng. Slack-Based Heuristics for Constraint Satisfaction Scheduling. *Procs. of the 11th National Conference on AI (AAAI-93)*, 1993.

Planning, Scheduling and Constraint Satisfaction: From Theory to Practice
L. Castillo et al. (Eds.)
IOS Press, 2005

Using a scheduling domain ontology to compute *user-oriented* explanations

Stephen F. Smith [1], Gabriella Cortellessa [2], David W. Hildum [1], Christian M. Ohler [1]

[1] The Robotics Institute Carnegie Mellon University
5000 Forbes Avenue - Pittsburgh PA 15213
{sfs,hildum,ohler}@cs.cmu.edu

[2] ISTC-CNR National Research Council of Italy
Viale Marx 15, I-00137 Rome, Italy
corte@istc.cnr.it

Abstract. One broad source of difficulty in transitioning automated planning and scheduling theories and algorithms into practical application systems is the need to integrate with user decision-making processes. Both user acceptance of system decisions in successful problem solving episodes and effective user involvement in circumstances where the system reaches a problem solving impasse require that the system be comprehensible, and this requirement, in turn, implies that the system be capable of explaining its decisions in user-understandable terms. Unfortunately, most current work in explanation instead forces users to understand the system's underlying search models. In this paper, we consider this problem of bridging the gap between user and system models in the context of a constraint-based scheduling system. Previous work has proposed the use of a scheduling domain ontology as a basis for translating user problem specifications into internal system models. Here we propose the complementary use of a domain ontology as a means of computing user-oriented explanations of system decisions. We focus specifically on the problem of explaining temporal constraint conflicts that may arise in the course of either solving a given scheduling problem or integrating new state information with a previously computed schedule. The central idea is to use domain ontology knowledge (1) to isolate those constraints that are meaningful to and can be manipulated by the user, and (2) to identify various constraint relaxation options that the user might consider to resolve the conflict at hand. Using the COMIREM planner/scheduler [10] as a reference model, we show examples of how this approach can generate effective user-level explanations of constraint conflicts from low-level descriptions of detected cycles in a temporal constraint graph. Along the way, we discuss the broader implications from the standpoint of mixed-initiative scheduling system design.

1 Introduction

One major obstacle to the practical application of new planning and scheduling theories and algorithms is the gap between these automated models and human planning and scheduling processes. Although there are certainly some exceptions, total automation of decision-making is not an appropriate goal in most practical domains. More typically, it is the case that experienced users and automated planning/scheduling technologies bring complementary problem-solving strengths to the table, and the goal is to synergistically blend these combined strengths. Often the scale, complexity or general ill-structuredness of practical domains overwhelms the solving capabilities of automated planning and scheduling technologies, and some sort of problem decomposition and reduction is required to achieve solver tractability. Likewise, human planners often have deep knowledge about a given domain which can provide useful strategic guidance, but they are hampered by the complexity of grinding out detailed plans/schedules. In such cases, successful technology application requires effective integration of user and system decision-making. However, this is complicated by the fact that users do not reason about plans and schedules at the level of search spaces and temporal constraint graphs; the system must somehow bridge the gap between user and system models and representations.

Research into the design of mixed-initiative planning and scheduling systems is concerned fundamentally with solving this general problem of interfacing a user with the automated system and placing a user into the problem-solving loop. One basic issue concerns mechanisms for specifying planning and scheduling problems to the automated system, i.e., for translating user specifications of domain constraints and objectives into internal system models. However, to effectively close the loop and actually involve the user in the planning/scheduling process, a second, somewhat inverse issue must be addressed: that of explaining system results in user-comprehensible terms. Human planners tend to be skeptical of automated systems in general, and an ability on the system's part to provide user-level rationalization of generated plans and schedules can promote user acceptance. Perhaps even more important to effective mixed-initiative planning and scheduling behavior is an ability to provide explanatory support in the event of system failure. As suggested above, the experienced human user often possesses deeper knowledge of strategic decision options that is outside of system models. She could manage unforeseen situations and retract specific constraints to recover from system failure, if properly informed of the specifics of the impasse that the automated system has encountered. Most current systems provide no guidance in such cases, and force the user to diagnose the problem at the level of the system's internal model.

In this paper, we consider this latter issue of explaining situations of solution failure in user-oriented terms. We focus specifically on the problem of explaining temporal constraint conflicts encountered by a constraint-based scheduling system. In contrast to previous work on explanation in Constraint Satisfaction Problem Solving (CSP) domains which operates at the level of individual decision variables and constraints, we propose use of a scheduling domain ontology to compute higher-level explanations. The reference system for our work is COMIREM, a web-based mixed-initiative problem solver [10]. We demonstrate how COMIREM's ontology can be used to isolate user-relevant constraints in a given conflict situation and provide guidance in exploring resolution options. Before describing our approach, we first review relevant aspects of the COMIREM ontology and problem solver and then briefly summarize prior work in explanation.

2 COMIREM: A Mixed-Initiative Planner/Scheduler

COMIREM is a web-based system devoted to the problem of interactive and dynamic allocation of resources to activities over specific time intervals. The system is based on a CSP paradigm and promotes a problem solving process that combines the actions of the automated solver and the human planner. COMIREM is composed of two main modules, named respectively *Automated Solver* and *Interaction Module*. The first is devoted to modeling domain entities through a CSP representation and provides the algorithm to solve the problem. It models the domain through the OZONE *scheduling domain ontology* which allows a user-interpretable description of an application domain to be mapped to application system functionalities [9]. Domain objects and features are represented in terms of entities very close to the human representation level of abstraction, and can be easily presented to the user through the module devoted to the user-system interaction. The Interaction Module directly interacts with the user, and allows her to take part in the process of finding a solution via advanced interactive facilities. It represents the communication channel between the user and the automated solver and a means to exploit various features of the automated system. Major aspects of the COMIREM architecture are summarized in the subsections below.

2.1 The Underlying OZONE Scheduling Ontology

The main primitives for constructing domain models in COMIREM derive from the OZONE Ontology [9]. Considered originally as a vehicle for high-level specification of scheduling problems, entities in the ontology can be broadly subdivided into *Activities, Resources and Constraints*:

- Activities. An activity represents a process that can be executed over a certain time interval. Execution of an activity requires resources. In COMIREM activities can be organized hierarchically into multi-level activity networks.

- Resources. A resource is an entity that supports or enables the execution of activities. Resources are generally in finite supply and their availability constrains *when* and *how* activities execute. An important objective of scheduling is to make efficient use of resources that support multiple competing activities. Two types of resources are modeled in COMIREM: single and multi-capacity resources.

- Constraints. Generally speaking, a constraint restricts the set of values that can be assigned to a variable. COMIREM provides the means to model three types of constraints: (a) *temporal constraints*, which constrain the start times and/or end times of one or more activities; (b) *resource constraints*: which require sequentialization of activities competing for the same resources; (c) *causal constraints*: which define what conditions must be met before an activity can be executed.

2.2 The Automated Solver

COMIREM utilizes an opportunistic constraint-posting scheduling procedure to allocate resources to activities over time, relying on a planning sub-procedure as necessary to determine appropriate resource reconfiguration actions. COMIREM takes as input an initial *plan sketch* that specifies, at some level of abstraction, the actions necessary to accomplish certain end goals for a given scenario. For example, to rescue people from an embassy in a foreign capital, an initial plan describing necessary actions such as securing the local airport, transporting rescuers to the airport, etc. is provided by the human planner, together with any associated causal dependences and temporal constraints. Starting from this initial plan, the scheduling procedure tries to feasibly allocate resources to input activities. In some cases, feasible assignment entails the generation of resource support plans (e.g., for "positioning" an aircraft to the location where it is needed), such planning subproblems are solved dynamically as specific resource assignments are considered. If successful, the procedure returns a detailed plan, where each activity is assigned the resources it requires and is designated to execute in a specified finite time interval. Due to its interactive nature, the system can exploit human-planner knowledge and decision making, and in fact promotes a mixed-initiative problem solving process. Through the Interaction Module it is possible to either generate a solution automatically or iteratively build a solution through a *step by step* mixed-initiative procedure that interleaves human choices with system calculation of consequences.

2.3   Mixed-Initiative Problem Solving in COMIREM

As just mentioned, COMIREM provides a user with two options: (a) automatically generate a solution to the problem; (b) iteratively build a solution. In the first case a user decides to completely entrust the system with the task of finding a solution. In the second case, the system provides constraint checking and option generation support for user decisions. When an initial plan is loaded, COMIREM performs a temporal feasibility check, and creates new activities as necessary to carry out entailed supporting actions. A visual representation of the problem and its main features is provided to the user through a graphical spreadsheet-style model. For each unassigned activity in the plan, COMIREM maintains the current set of feasible allocation options and presents them to the user through the Interaction Module. At any time and in any order, the user can manually specify resource assignments for particular activities. Whenever a user allocates a resource to a given activity, the impact of the user's choice is reflected in the plan and the system updates the set of possible options available for other pending decisions. At any point in the process, the automatic algorithm can be invoked to make all remaining assignments and produce a complete solution. Both activity and resource attributes can also be edited to change the constraints and requirements of the problem. The system provides a general ability to *undo* any user action (or sequence of actions) previously taken, providing a flexible framework for what-if analysis.

The interaction module in COMIREM can be seen as an intelligent blackboard that allows a user to reason incrementally on a solution, providing both (1) visualization functionalities to inspect problem and domain features and (2) interactive services to involve a user in the problem solving. The ambitious idea behind COMIREM is to capture different skills that a user and an automated system can apply to the resolution process. Typically an automated algorithm is better suited to conducting repetitive search steps that are not possible for a human user, while a user typically has more specific knowledge about the target domain that is difficult to formalize in general terms to be used by an algorithm. The development of principles for mixed-initiative interaction [2, 3] represents a key to the development of more powerful problem solving environments.

2.4   Explanation as a means to foster mixed-initiative problem solving

Among the numerous aspects involved in the development of mixed-initiative systems, one important requirement is the need to maintain continuous communication between the user and the automated problem solver. Current interactive systems are usually lacking with respect to providing such a continuity. System failures that may be encountered in finding a solution typify this sort of deficiency. Typically, when a planning/scheduling system fails during the problem solving, or when the solution is found to be inconsistent due to introduction of new world state information, the user is not properly supported and left alone to determine the reasons for the break (e.g., no solution exists, the particular algorithm did not find a solution, there was a bug in the solver etc.).

This leads to an interruption in the problem solving process that could be otherwise used as an event to determine a shift in the *initiative*. A conflicted situation might, for example, be resolved by a user who has a deeper knowledge of the domain and/or agrees to slightly change the problem in order to obtain a solution. Obviously in transferring the initiative to the user, a system should inform her about the reasons of the failure or problem encountered to ease and promote her participation. On this subject the concept of *explanation* is becoming of increasing interest in many different research communities. Our interest in this paper focuses on the use of explanation within COMIREM as a means to explain and inform a user about the reasons underlying system search failures and solution inconsistencies.

3   Explanation and CSPs

As already mentioned current work on explanation in CSP forces users to understand the system's underlying search model and reasoning in terms of variables and constraints that are usually not comprehensible for the final users. The CSP paradigm is a powerful means for representing and solving problems but it is far from users' models. In order to provide useful information a translation from the low level technicality to the high level human model is necessary. In classical constraint programming, an explanation is a set of constraints justifying propagation events generated by the solver (e.g., value removal from the domain of a certain variable, bound update, contradiction). In [6, 5] two kinds of explanation are introduced: (a) *contradiction explanation* and (b) *eliminating explanation*. The former is a subset of the current problem constraints, which if left alone, leads to a contradiction. It is composed of two parts, a subset of the original constraints, and a subset of the decision constraints introduced so far in the search. The latter, is an implication justifying the removal of a value from the domain of a variable. A very similar approach to this problem is the notion of *justification* introduced by Bessier [1]. A justification is an additional piece of information that is stored each time a value is deleted from a variable's domain. One general approach to computing explanations, then, is to make explicit the knowledge that the solver has while, for example, removing a value from a domain or dealing with an inconsistency. In this way, each time an event is generated (e.g., a value removal), the corresponding explanation is computed within the propagation code of the constraints and the *trace* of the solver reasoning is used as an explanation. Computation of explanations in this manner assumes that the basic CSP model is understandable, and neglects the issue of finding effective ways to present them to a naive user. In [11] the explanation problem is investigated and the need of designing effective ways to organize and present it to the user is highlighted. A crucial aspect in the presentation problem is one of finding effective ways to structure and present the information in order to enhance a user's ability to understand and possibly solve an occurred problem. In [7] a set of tools for providing user-friendly explanations in an explanation based constraint programming system is introduced. The basic hypothesis this work relies on is that all aspects of a constraint-based application can be represented in a hierarchical way. The implicit hierarchy that appears when encoding the problem is used to group constraints into "user-friendly boxes" which are used to add structured information while posting the constraints. In particular a textual representation of the set of constraints is introduced in the system which is used as a user-comprehensible explanation when a conflict arises.

4   Using the OZONE ontology to compute *user-oriented* explanations

In this section, we outline an approach to translating system-level explanations into a more user-comprehensible and user-actionable form via the use of an underlying domain ontology. Our previous work has argued the use of a scheduling domain ontology to facilitate user construction of an executable system model in a given application domain [9]. Here we consider its complementary use in driving the generation of user-oriented explanations. We focus specifically on the problem of explaining temporal constraint conflicts within COMIREM. Our idea is to use the COMIREM domain ontology knowledge (1) to compute the set of constraints that form the explanation, (2) to identify various constraint relaxation options that the user might consider to resolve the conflict, and (3) to provide content for generating user-understandable explanations of conflicts and possible resolving actions. Figure 1 illustrates the layers of a domain model in COMIREM. The first layer in the picture models the

Domain Layer (Ozone Ontology)

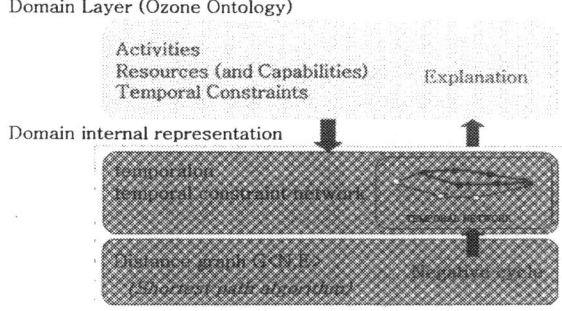

Figure 1: Domain Modeling in COMIREM

constraints of the target domain in terms of *activities*, *resources* and *constraints* using the scheduling ontology described in Section 2.1. This level of description provides an abstraction of the low level CSP representation used internally, that can be reasonably considered to be closer to the human model of the domain.

The second layer shows how this translation is implemented within COMIREM. The problem is represented internally as a Simple Temporal Problem (STP) constraint network [4] and the core scheduling procedure relies on an incremental STP constraint network solver. Planning/scheduling decisions generally correspond to the introduction of new constraints into the network (e.g., a sequencing constraint between two activities that require the same resource) or the adjustment of one or more existing constraints (e.g., refinement of an activity's duration, modification of an anchor). In either case, constraint propagation updates the bounds of affected nodes and checks for negative cycles in the resulting network. The lack of any such cycle ensures continued temporal feasibility of the plan. Otherwise a *conflict* has been detected, and either backtracking or some amount of constraint relaxation is necessary.

The intermediate level in Figure 1 represents a level of description in an OZONE domain model that captures various temporal constraints using a construct in the ontology called a *temporalon*. A temporalon [8] designates a temporal constraint between two time points. Two basic types of temporalons are definable. The first type is *temporalon-activity*, in which case the temporalon represents the temporal characteristics of an activity. Its two time points designate the activity's start and end, and the distance constraint (i.e., lower-bound, upper-bound pair) defines the activity's duration. The second basic type is *temporalon-link*, used to specify temporal relations between activities (e.g., Activity A must precede Activity B), or to designate absolute temporal restrictions (e.g., Activity A cannot start earlier than t1). Temporalons of this form either link the start/end points of distinct activities or link the start/end point of a single activity to an absolute time origin. Temporalons are specialized into a hierarchy of different types, each of which models and captures a particular aspect of the scheduling domain (e.g., *due-date* temporalon, *release-date* temporalon, *move-activity* temporalon, etc.). There is a one-to-one correspondence between the set of temporalons defined in the domain model and the temporal constraints contained in the underlying STP constraint network.

It is possible to notice some similarity between the user-friendly boxes introduced in [7] and temporalons. In [7], an assumption is made according to which each problem can be represented as a hierarchy of constraints. When this hierarchy of constraints is posted, some amount of information (user-friendly boxes) is coded into the system which can be reused to present explanation to the user. Within COMIREM the extension of the OZONE ontology based on temporalons, provides an analogous categorization and gives information at a higher level of abstraction about the constraints involved in a conflict. The temporalon layer is indeed domain oriented and its embedded knowledge can be integrated, interpreted and translated to support human intelligible explanations. The ontology used in COMIREM represents an attempt to capture different aspects of the domain and represent them through the use of domain entities close to a human model of the world. This effort previously made to model scheduling domains and problems (*user → system* translation) grants us useful structures that can be reused when the contrary translation is needed (*user ← system* translation).

4.1 A filtering classification to compute the explanation set

Within a COMIREM domain model, we can distinguish several categories of temporalons. Some temporalons represent input constraints that have been imposed by the user (e.g., Activity A must end by t2). Others represent inherent properties of the domain theory defined by the scheduling domain ontology (e.g., the fact that a "move activity" decomposes into a "load", "travel", "unload" sequence of finer level activities). Still others designate decisions that the automated solver has taken (e.g., use resource R first for activity A and then for activity B). Although all temporal constraints look identical at the level of the STP constraint network, the sets of constraints falling into each of the above categories have different implications from the standpoint of conflict explanation and resolution. For example, constraints relating to the structural characteristics of a hierarchical domain model, though likely to be identified as contributing constraints in a detected conflict, are not really relevant to understanding the conflict at the user-level. Alternatively, constraints directly attributable to user decisions are clearly relevant and may be retractable if they are found to be problematic. In general, one obvious pre-requisite to generating meaningful, actionable explanations is to first isolate the subset of those constraints returned by the STP cycle detector that are relevant to user decision-making. We call this subset the *explanation set*.

To make this notion more precise, we classify COMIREM temporalon subtypes into three main categories:

- *Problem constraints.* They derive directly from the user's specification of the problem and represent user requirements. Since these constraints originated from the user, they represent one set of constraints that she may be willing to compromise when faced with an *over-constrained* problem. Temporalons falling into this category include various user-specifiable activities (*move* and *paired-event*[1] temporalons), timing restrictions (*release-date*, *due-date*, *est* and *lft* temporalons), and various activity to activity synchronization constraints (*before*, *same-start* and *same-finish* temporalons).

- *Structural constraints.* These constraints either model physically motivated causal dependencies in the ontology's domain theory that cannot be relaxed, or express structural temporal relationships between activities residing at different levels in hierarchical activity networks (*activity-subactivity*, *demand-activity* temporalons, etc.).

- *Search constraints.* These are constraints introduced by the search algorithm in the course of solving the problem (*sequencing* temporalon), and of course can also be retracted in the event of a conflict.

Given this categorization, our approach to determining the explanation set for a given conflict is straightforward. Upon detection of a cycle, the STP network solver returns two pieces of information: the set of constraints (temporalons) involved in the cycle, and a magnitude m indicating the amount by which some temporal constraint (or combination of constraints) must be relaxed to resolve the inconsistency. The first filtering step simply removes all *structural temporalons* from the set of constraints returned by the STP cycle detector. The resulting subset is then further pruned by eliminating those temporalons that cannot be feasibly relaxed (e.g., would result in an activity with a negative duration). The remaining temporalons constitute the explanation set and are used to characterize the conflict to the user.

4.2 Conflict resolution options

A temporal constraint conflict detected in the temporal network can be resolved by modifying the bounds of one or more temporalons in the explanation set (using the magnitude m reported with the original conflict). Given the domain level typing of temporalons, the low level action of modifying temporalon bounds can be mapped directly to higher-level, user-oriented actions (i.e., *conflict resolution options*). For each temporalon contained in the explanation set, information captured in the domain ontology is used to compute a type-specific set of possible resolution options. The union of all computed options is then presented to the user.

5 Examples of conflict explanation and resolution options

To illustrate the basic conflict explanation procedure just described consider the following two examples.

Example 1 Figure 2(a) shows an example of a temporal conflict discovered during feasibility checking of an input plan in COMIREM. The computed duration Dur(MH-60), of a *move* activity from location B to location A using resource (helicopter) MH-60 is greater than the difference between the latest finish time and the earliest start time constraints on the activity.

---

[1] a paired-event is an activity that takes place at one location.

The solver detects the inconsistency and returns the set of involved temporalons along with the conflict magnitude m.

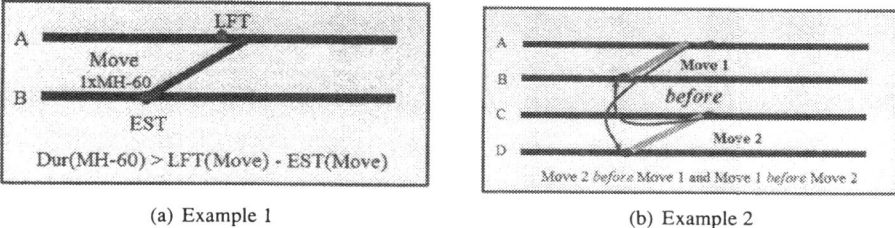

| (a) Example 1 | (b) Example 2 |

Figure 2: Two examples of possible temporal constraints conflicts

In this example, there are three conflicting temporalons: a *move* temporalon, a *release-date* temporalon and a *due-date* temporalon. Since all belong to the *problem constraints* category (see Section 4.1) and each can be feasibly relaxed, no filtering is possible and this conflict set becomes the explanation set. Relevant resolutions are computed for each temporalon and the results are shown in Table 1.

explanation set	explanation	resolution options
	Temporal inconsistency is due to:	choose an option:
move	duration of activity move(A,B)	1 override computed duration
		2 use a faster resource
release-date	release-date constraint	3 deploy earlier
due-date	due-date constraint	4 delay engagement

Table 1: Explanation and resolution options for the conflict of Example 1

Example 2 Figure 2(b) shows a conflict due to an attempt to assert conflicting sequencing constraints between two move activities $move_1$, from location B to location A and $move_2$ from location D to location C (i.e., both $move_1$ before $move_2$ and $move_2$ before $move_1$). Given the hierarchical structure of move activities, the cycle detector actually returns a cycle with sixteen temporalons, in particular 8 structural temporalons, 2 move temporalons, 4 paired-event [2] and 2 *before* temporalons. The higher complexity of this example (16 temporalons against 3) highlights the general difficulty in providing a user with a comprehensible explanation. Using the classification, the eight structural temporalons are first eliminated from the explanation set. Subsequently, both the four paired-event and the two move temporalons are eliminated since none can be feasibly relaxed. Table 2 shows the final explanation set and the generated resolution options.

6 Conclusions

One potential source of difficulty in transitioning automated planning and scheduling theories and tools into practice is the gap between the user and system's models. Bridging this gap re-

---

[2] paired-event temporalons derive from the decomposition of a move activity into a "load", "travel" and "unload" sequence of activities.

explanation set	explanation	resolution options
	Temporal inconsistency is due to:	choose an option:
before	move1(A,B) before move2(C,D)	1 relax *before* constraint
before	move2(C,D) before move1(A,B)	2 relax *before* constraint

Table 2: Explanation and resolution options for the conflict of Example 2

quires a system to translate information from internal algorithmic representations into higher level descriptions that are more comprehensible to the user. In this paper we considered the problem of closing the loop with the user in situations where the automated solver reaches an impasse, so that initiative can be redirected back to the user and cooperative problem solving can continue. We focused specifically on the problem of explaining temporal constraint conflicts, and using the COMIREM planner/scheduler as a reference model, proposed the use of a scheduling domain ontology as a means of generating user-oriented explanations. We showed a couple of explanation generation examples, which give preliminary evidence of the potential of our approach.

Acknowledgments

Stephen F. Smith, David Hildum and Christian Ohler were funded in part by the Department of Defense Advanced Research Projects Agency (DARPA) under contract F30602-00-2-0503 and the CMU Robotics Institute. Gabriella Cortellessa's work is partially supported by ASI (Italian Space Agency) under projects ARISCOM and SACSO. This work has been developed during her visit at the CMU Robotics Institute as a visiting student scholar.

References

[1] C. Bessiere. Arc consistency in dynamic constraint satisfaction problems. In *Proceedings AAAI'91*, 1991.

[2] Mark Burstein and Drew McDermott. Issues in the development of human-computer mixed-initiative planning. In B. Gorayska and J.L. Mey, editors, *Cognitive Technology*, pages 285–303. Elsevier, 1996.

[3] R. Cohen, C. Allaby, C. Cumbaa, M. Fitzgerald, K. Ho, B. Hui, C. Latulipe, F. Lu, N. Moussa, D. Pooley, A. Qian, and S. Siddiqi. What is initiative? In S. Haller, S. McRoy, and A. Kobsa, editors, *Computational Models of Mixed-Initiative Interaction*, pages 171–212. Kluwer Academic Publishers, 1999.

[4] R. Dechter, I. Meiri, and J. Pearl. Temporal constraint networks. *Artificial Intelligence*, 49:61–95, 1991.

[5] N. Jussien and V. Barichard. The PaLM system: explanation-based constraint programming. In *Proceedings of TRICS: Techniques foR Implementing Constraint programming Systems, a post-conference workshop of CP 2000*, pages 118–133, Singapore, September 2000.

[6] Narendra Jussien. e-constraints: explanation-based constraint programming. In *CP01 Workshop on User-Interaction in Constraint Satisfaction*, Paphos, Cyprus, 1 December 2001.

[7] Narendra Jussien and Samir Ouis. User-friendly explanations for constraint programming. In *ICLP'01 11th Workshop on Logic Programming Environments*, Paphos, Cyprus, 1 December 2001.

[8] S. Smith and H. Hildum. Interacting with freon: A quick overview. Technical report, Carnegie Mellon University.

[9] S. F. Smith and M. A. Becker. An ontology for constructing scheduling systems. In *Working Notes of 1997 AAAI Symposium on Ontological Engineering*, Palo Alto, CA, March 1997. AAAI Press.

[10] S.F. Smith, D.W. Hildum, and D.A. Crimm. Interactive Resource Management in the Comirem Planner. In *IJCAI-03 Workshop on Mixed-Initiative Intelligent Systems*, Acapulco Mexico, August 2003.

[11] Richard Wallace and Eugene Freuder. Explanation for Whom? In *CP01 Workshop on User-Interaction in Constraint Satisfaction*, Paphos, Cyprus, 1 December 2001.

Planning, Scheduling and Constraint Satisfaction: From Theory to Practice
L. Castillo et al. (Eds.)
IOS Press, 2005

Project Planning Under Temporal Uncertainty

Susanne Biundo   Roland Holzer
Bernd Schattenberg
Dept. of Artificial Intelligence, University of Ulm, 89069 Ulm, Germany
phone: +49 731 50 24121   fax: +49 731 50 24199
mail: firstName.lastName@informatik.uni-ulm.de

Abstract. This paper presents an approach towards probabilistic planning with continuous time. It adopts stochastic concepts for continuous probabilities and integrates them into an HTN-based planning framework. Based on uncertain time durations associated with primitive tasks the time consumption probabilities of non-linear plans can be accumulated and thus an overall probability for a successful execution of complex plans can be computed. Furthermore, heuristics for the decomposition of abstract tasks can be derived that guide the search towards plans with a minimized average value/variance of their overall time consumption. An example from software project planning is used to demonstrate our approach.

1 Introduction and Motivation

The process of software development has to deal with a variety of unpredictable events, which make it particularly hard to calculate costs, to provide adequate buffer times, and finally to meet project deadlines. Keeping to the project's time schedule is obviously critical for every software company, and consequently there is a growing market for supporting tools helping to keep such projects manageable. This work is motivated by the observation that present-day tools mostly offer limited management support by basically highlighting already off-schedule project threads. AI planning techniques offer a notably more intelligent support in the project definition phase, especially if they are able to deal with uncertain information about actual implementation times and the like.

In this paper, we introduce an approach to handle uncertain time consumption of actions in planning. We adopt the concepts for continuous probabilities and their computations from stochastics and integrate them into a standard HTN-based planning framework. The resulting probabilistic planning approach allows for an adequate representation of (a continuous model of) uncertain time consumption. The duration probabilities of single actions and action sequences can be efficiently computed during planning. This enables the construction of plans that are guaranteed to meet certain probability thresholds w.r.t. given time limits. Furthermore, the approach can be generalized to handle parallel threads of execution and to accumulate alternative task decompositions. Not only does this enable a qualified decision if various alternative solutions are at hand, it even suggests a useful pruning of the search space. Furthermore, we show how heuristics for HTN-planning can be generated that lead to the synthesis of plans with a minimized average duration and/or variance of time consumption.

The rest of the paper is organized as follows. Section 2 introduces the foundations of HTN planning and the basic concepts of our probabilistic approach. In Section 3 the techniques are generalized to partially ordered plans, while Section 4 shows how the uncertain duration of primitive operations can be propagated along the task hierarchy into abstract tasks. An example taken from software project planning illustrates our approach in Section 5 and its implementation is sketched in Section 6. We conclude with a review of related work and some final remarks.

2 Basic Definitions

Our HTN-based planning formalism relies on the usual STRIPS representations of states and operators for the primitive action level. A *state* is a finite set of ground atoms. An *operator* instance $o = (\text{prec}(o), \text{add}(o), \text{del}(o))$ consists of three such sets: the *preconditions* and the *positive* and *negative effects*, respectively. It appears to be a ground instance of a respective operator schema. Such an operator instance o is *applicable* in a state s iff $\text{prec}(o) \subseteq s$. The result of applying operator $o = (\text{prec}(o), \text{add}(o), \text{del}(o))$ in state s is a state $\text{result}(s, o) = (s \cup \text{add}(o)) \setminus \text{del}(o)$. Operators are also called *primitive tasks*.

A *plan* $p = \langle o_0 \ldots o_n \rangle$ is a sequence of operator instances such that for every state s_i, in which o_i is applicable, we have that o_{i+1} is applicable in $\text{result}(s_i, o_i)$, where $s_{i+1} = \text{result}(s_i, o_i)$ for $0 \leq i \leq n$. A plan p is then *applicable* in s_0, and the resulting state $\text{result}(\text{result}(\ldots \text{result}(s_0, o_0), o_1) \ldots, o_n)$ of p is denoted by $\text{result}(s_0, p)$.

Abstract actions are represented by *complex tasks* t. For each complex task t, there exists at least one *method* $m = (t, d)$, relating t and a *task network* d which implements t. Task networks are structures $d = (T, \prec, V)$, where T is the set of complex and/or primitive tasks into which t is decomposed, $\prec$ is a partial order on T, and V is a set of codesignation and non-codesignation constraints on the variables occurring in $T \cup \{t\}$. Plans are generated by *expanding* abstract tasks, i.e. by subsequently applying methods in the following way: given a task network $(T, \prec, V)$, an abstract task $t \in T$, and a method $m = (t, (T_t, \prec_t, V_t))$. Let furthermore $\prec_\delta$ be the subset of $\prec$ in which t occurs. The network resulting from applying m is $d' = (T', \prec', V')$ with

$$
\begin{aligned}
T' &= (T \setminus t) \cup T_t \\
\prec' &= (\prec \setminus \prec_\delta) \cup \prec_t \cup \{(t_a, t_t) \mid (t_a, t) \in \prec, t_t \in T_t\} \cup \{(t_t, t_a) \mid (t, t_a) \in \prec, t_t \in T_t\} \\
V' &= V \cup V_t
\end{aligned}
$$

A *planning problem* is a quadruple $(d, \text{Init}, \mathcal{T}, \mathcal{M})$, where d is a task network, Init a set of ground atoms, the *initial state*, $\mathcal{T}$ a set of complex and primitive task schemas, and $\mathcal{M}$ a set of methods for the complex tasks in $\mathcal{T}$. Given a task network $d' = (T', \prec', V')$ which results from d by subsequently expanding all abstract tasks in d. Then d' is a *solution* to such a planning problem iff T' only contains primitive tasks from $\mathcal{T}$ and all operator sequences which can be built from the ground instances represented by T' and V' and which are in consistency with $\prec'$ represent a plan p which is applicable in Init.

In order to represent uncertain durations of operators, we make use of continuous random variables which are used in stochastics to model continuous events. A *random variable* $\mathcal{X} : \Omega \rightarrow \mathbb{R}$ is a measurable function that maps the event space Ω onto the real numbers $\mathbb{R}$.

The *distribution* of $\mathcal{X}$ is described by a *probability density* $D : \mathbb{R} \to \mathbb{R}$, denoted by $\mathcal{X}_D$ or $\mathcal{X} \sim D$. The *mean value* $\mu = E(\mathcal{X}_D)$ of a random variable with density D is defined as $\int_{-\infty}^{+\infty} x D(x) dx$, and the *variance* $\mathrm{Var}(\mathcal{X}_D)$ of a random variable is given as $E((\mathcal{X}_D)^2) - E(\mathcal{X}_D)^2$, also denoted by σ^2.

For this presentation we focus on random variables with the normal-distribution density, denoted by $\mathcal{X}_{\mathcal{N}(\mu,\sigma^2)}$. We will see below, that this choice does not imply any loss of generality. The probability that the value of a such random variable is lower than a given value a is computed as follows:

$$Pr[\mathcal{X}_{\mathcal{N}(\mu,\sigma^2)} < a] := \int\limits_{-\infty}^{a} \mathcal{N}(\mu,\sigma^2) dx = \int\limits_{-\infty}^{a} \frac{1}{\sqrt{2\sigma^2\pi}} e^{-\frac{(x-\mu)^2}{\sigma^2}} dx$$

Please note, that there is no antiderivative for the normal distribution. We therefore use a standard approximation to compute the probabilities (the error introduced by this approximation is however less than 10^{-8}).

Our operator description is extended by an annotation $rv(o)$, which is the random variable that describes the uncertain duration of the operator o. The mean value of such a random variable represents the average amount of time consumed by the operator, while the variance describes the uncertainty of its duration. The mean value of the density of a random variable $rv(o)$ is negative or zero. A mean value of zero means that the operator takes no time for execution. Variance is zero for absolutely certain operator durations. In addition, the description of a planning problem is extended by a random variable $\mathcal{I}$, that represents a limit to the maximum duration of the plan. $\mathcal{I}$ has a positive mean value and may have a variance of zero. Furthermore, a threshold is added to the problem description. A plan that has been generated in the HTN fashion described above is now considered valid only if the probability of exceeding the given duration limit is less than the user-defined threshold.

3 Computing the Uncertain Duration of Plans

The random variable describing the duration of a *totally ordered* plan is the sum of all durations, i.e. random variables of the single operators. The density of a sum of random variables is computed by the *convolution* of the single densities. Given two random variables $\mathcal{X}_{D_1}^1$ and $\mathcal{X}_{D_2}^2$ where D_1 and D_2 are the respective density functions, the density of their sum is defined by:

$$D_{\mathcal{X}_{D_1}^1 + \mathcal{X}_{D_2}^2}(t) := \int\limits_{-\infty}^{+\infty} D_1(\tau) D_2(t-\tau) d\tau = \int\limits_{-\infty}^{+\infty} D_1(t-\tau) D_2(\tau) d\tau$$

Computing the convolution of densities is analytically hard in the general case and for some cases even impossible (depending on the kind of the random variables densities). Furthermore, simulation techniques like Monte Carlo Simulation are not applicable in the case of continuous random variables, because the simulation converges to the value of the real integral only for finite intervals. To compute the probability for a plan to exceed a given duration, we need to compute the integral value over intervals like $(-\infty, \dots, 0]$. Stochastics literature shows, that when dealing with continuous random variables, most stochastic processes can be approximated using the normal-distribution. This property can be utilized effectively because the distribution of the sum of two normal distributed random variables is again normal-distributed. Furthermore, the convolution of normal-distributed random variables can be very efficiently computed. However, there exists no formula for the antiderivative of the normal-density, but at least there exists a good approximation for it.

Given n normal-distributed random variables $\mathcal{X}^i$, the density of the sum of these variables can be computed by:

$$\mathcal{X}^i \sim \mathcal{N}(\mu_i, \sigma_i^2) : \sum_i \mathcal{X}^i \sim \mathcal{N}\left(\sum_i \mu_i, \sum_i \sigma_i^2\right)$$

The overall duration of a plan $p =< o_1, \ldots, o_n >$ is represented by a new single random variable $\mathcal{Y}$. Given operator durations $rv(o_i) = \mathcal{X}_{\mathcal{N}(\mu_i, \sigma_i^2)}$, the density of $\mathcal{Y}$ is calculated by convoluting the densities $\mathcal{N}(\mu_i, \sigma_i^2)$ of all operators. Using the formula above, we get the following density for $\mathcal{Y}$:

$$\mathcal{Y} \sim \mathcal{N}\left(\sum_{i=0}^n \mu_i, \sum_{i=0}^n \sigma_i^2\right)$$

In order to compute the density of the duration of a *partially ordered* plan or a task network, it is necessary to find a sequence of operators or tasks that leads from a "start" task to an "end" task and has a maximum duration. We call such a sequence the *critical path*. Calculating $\mathcal{Y}^i$ for every path p_i in a partially ordered task network or plan can be done efficiently. The complex part is to determine which path is the critical one, as there exists no comparison metric on random variables. The critical path is consequently defined over the probabilities for the linear sub-sequences to over-run the given maximum duration $\mathcal{I}$.

Our approach to solve this problem extends previous work on resource consumption for linear plans [1]: We extract every possible path p_i in the partially ordered task network and compute the random variable $\mathcal{Y}^i$ for the total time consumption of the respective sequence. The density of $\mathcal{Y}^i$ is calculated analogous to the duration of a totally ordered plan. After that, we add the initial time-bound $\mathcal{I}$ (i.e. the maximum duration allowed for the plan) to each $\mathcal{Y}^i$, resulting in a new random variable $\mathcal{Z}^i$ which characterizes the time left after executing the actions of p_i. The critical path is now the path p_i with maximum probability of failure $Pr[\mathcal{I} + \mathcal{Y}^i < 0] = Pr[\mathcal{Z}^i < 0]$.

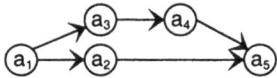

Figure 1: A partially ordered plan.

A short example illustrates the computation of the critical path. Given the operators $a_1, \ldots, a_5$ with $rv(a_1) = \mathcal{X}_{\mathcal{N}(-4,0.5)}$, $rv(a_2) = \mathcal{X}_{\mathcal{N}(-3,1)}$, $rv(a_3) = \mathcal{X}_{\mathcal{N}(-1,0.8)}$, $rv(a_4) = \mathcal{X}_{\mathcal{N}(-1.5,0.8)}$, and $rv(a_5) = \mathcal{X}_{\mathcal{N}(-2,0)}$ ordered like shown in Figure 1. The duration random variable $\mathcal{Y}^1$ for the first path a_1, a_3, a_4, a_5 has the density $\mathcal{N}(-8.5, 2.1)$ while that of $\mathcal{Y}^2$ for the second path a_1, a_2, a_5 has the density $\mathcal{N}(-9, 1.5)$. Let $\mathcal{I}_{\mathcal{N}(12,0)}$ be the random variable that describes the allowed maximum duration of the plan. We compute the probabilities for a failure, represented by random variables $\mathcal{Z}^1$ and $\mathcal{Z}^2$, as follows:

$$Pr[\mathcal{I}_{\mathcal{N}(12,0)} + \mathcal{Y}^1_{(-8.5,2.1)} < 0] = Pr[\mathcal{Z}^1_{\mathcal{N}(3.5,2.1)} < 0] \approx 0.00786$$
$$Pr[\mathcal{I}_{\mathcal{N}(12,0)} + \mathcal{Y}^2_{(-9,1.5)} < 0] = Pr[\mathcal{Z}^2_{\mathcal{N}(3,1.5)} < 0] \approx 0.00715$$

The resulting probabilities show, that the path a_1, a_3, a_4, a_5 is the critical one, because it is more likely to exceed the total duration time.

4 Propagation

As described above, duration random variables are annotated to primitive tasks only. This means, an HTN planner has to arrive at a primitive task network before it is able to reason about durations at all. However, it would perform much better if it were able to reason about the duration of abstract tasks and their possible refinements as well. One possibility to enable this would be to integrate the required information into the domain model, i.e. the domain modeler declares the abstract "duration" by hand. This alternative may be very time-consuming and may often lead to flawed models. We propose to propagate the abstract duration automatically, instead. Our approach guarantees that the propagated values are always under-estimations and can therefore be used to compute heuristic values for abstract plans. We will describe how the propagation works, and will show how this information is used to prune the search space during the planning process.

Note that, we can compute the duration of a given task network if all tasks in the network are assigned a random variable describing their duration. To compute an underestimation for an abstract task, we need to know the durations $\mathcal{Y}^j_{\mathcal{N}(\mu_j,\sigma_j^2)}$ of all task networks j the abstract task can be decomposed into. Given these durations, the underestimation for the abstract task is defined by the min function:

$$\min \left(\mathcal{Y}^j_{\mathcal{N}(\mu_j,\sigma_j^2)} \right) := \mathcal{Y}'_{\mathcal{N}\left(-\min_j(|\mu_j|), \min_j(\sigma_j^2) \right)}$$

It can easily be shown that the random variable $\mathcal{Y}'$ which describes the duration of the abstract task is always an underestimation of the real duration. This is because the density of $\mathcal{Y}'$ has the minimal mean value and variance of all possible decompositions. This means, the real duration will be equal or greater than the duration described by $\mathcal{Y}'$.

The propagation algorithm terminates if all tasks in the domain model are non-recursive, because the propagation can be done bottom-up starting with the task networks containing only primitive tasks. In the case of recursive tasks definitions, we cannot reason about all possible decompositions of the abstract recursive task. Nevertheless, to get an underestimation for recursive tasks we compute the minimum of the termination cases for the recursion. The result of this computation is a legal underestimation, because the termination case has to appear at least once in the recursion.

```
propagation:                a.1 process_task-nets:         b.1 process_tasks:
1 process_primitive_tasks   a.2 ∀ task-nets tn do          b.2 ∀ tasks t do
2 mark_recursion_cycles     a.3   if not processed(tn)     b.3   if not processed(t)
3 while not finished() do   a.4     if (∀t∈tn: processed(t))  b.4     if (∀methods m(t,tn_j):
4   process_task-nets       a.5       underestimation(tn) =           processed(tn_j))
5   process_tasks                       sum_critical_path(tn)  b.5       underestimation(t) =
6 done                      a.6 done                                     min(underestimation(tn_j))
                                                            b.6 done
```

Figure 2: The three core procedures of the propagation algorithm.

Figure 2 shows the propagation algorithm. In line 1 the primitive tasks get their underestimations assigned, which is the random variable of the corresponding operator. This procedure also sets `processed` true for every primitive task. The recursion cycles are marked in line 2, with a standard depth-first search. The main loop (lines 3 to 6) of the algorithm terminates if `finished` becomes true. This is the case if all tasks and task networks are processed (i.e.,

if all of them have been assigned an underestimation). The `process_task-nets` procedure called in line 4 is one of the main procedures of the algorithm and is shown in Figure 2.
It iterates over all task networks (a.2–a.6) and searches for not yet processed task networks
(a.3). If such a task network is found, the procedure tries to compute an underestimation for
it. To do so, all tasks in the network have to have assigned a proper random variable for their
duration (a.4). If all these conditions are met, the underestimation for the task network is
processed by the critical-path algorithm described in the section above.

The second core procedure is `process_task` (cf. Figure 2). The main-loop (b.2–b.6)
of this procedure is similar to that in `process_task-nets`. It iterates over all tasks in the
domain model which are not already processed (b.3). To compute the underestimation for the
current task, all task networks into which the task can be decomposed have to be processed
(b.4). The underestimation is then computed by the min function described above.

As it is not easy to see that the algorithm always terminates, we will give a sketch of
a proof. Suppose we are given a legal domain model, i.e., among other properties, a domain model which includes at least one task network which contains only primitive tasks.
That means, there exists at least one abstract task which can be decomposed into a task
network containing only primitive ones (recursive methods have been "eliminated" during
pre-processing). After processing the primitive tasks, all these primitive networks have been
assigned an underestimation. Therefore, in every iteration of the main loop there exists at
least one abstract task for which the duration estimation can be propagated. The complexity
of this procedures is discussed in [1].

5 Project Planning for Software Development

Our example domain is taken from the daily work of a fictitious small software company
which develops end-user tailored business software. In this domain we find much procedu-
ral knowledge capturing well proven "best practice". However, these routines offer certain
degrees of freedom which are hard to overview even for relatively simple applications.

Figure 3 shows what the planning domain for such projects can look like if we follow a
(somewhat simplified) waterfall-based development approach: Each project is basically divided into 4 consecutive phases in which the requirements for the application are specified
and refined, a software design is chosen and implemented, the resulting system is thoroughly
tested, and finally installed on the customer's hardware.

As one example for the variation in the procedure, we can identify 4 different ways to per-

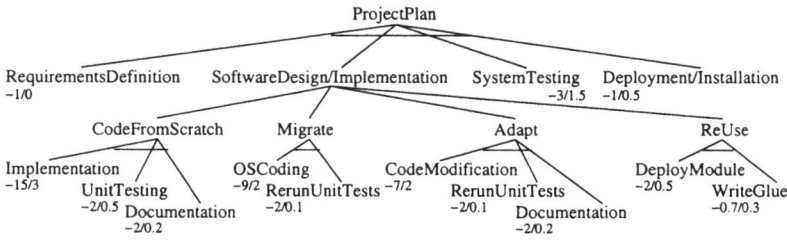

Figure 3: The decomposition hierarchy for the software project domain (numbers denote mean value and variance for the duration of primitive tasks).

form the design and implementation task. The company can develop a completely new piece of software "from scratch", it can re-use an existing component unchanged, functionally extended or adapted, or it can re-implement software written for another operating system (migrate). All these alternatives imply different sub-tasks for documenting newly written code, testing, etc. For the presentation in this paper we omit many of the possible details, so the presented section of the decomposition hierarchy only shows the primitive tasks' duration annotations and no further preconditions or effects (e.g., only components can be installed which have been implemented for the respective operating system, components have to match requirement specifications, interfacing relations, etc.). Concerning the precision of the distribution parameters, it has to be noted, that in general there exist relatively good estimations about how much time an action needs on average and typical fluctuations of it. Alternatively, the parameters can be reliably determined from small samples of the companies project history by standard statistical methods, e.g. the maximum-likelihood estimate.

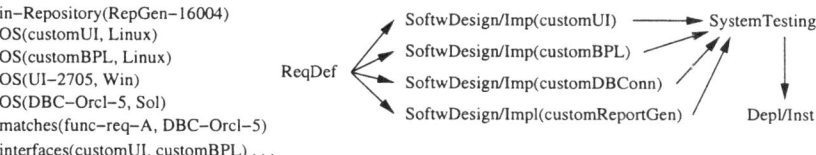

Figure 4: The initial state and the initial task network in the software project domain.

Planning problems in this domain specify which software components are ordered by the customer: in our example it is a Linux application consisting of a user interface, a component implementing the respective business process logic, a database connection interface, and a report generator. The initial state specifies, among other things, the components present in the developers' repository, the operating system the component is specified for, for which functional requirements a component is suitable, and how the components interface each other (cf. Figure 4). Furthermore, the developers are given a total project deadline in 36 days plus a heavy contractual penalty fee if this deadline is missed by more than 4 more days. Given this situation, the project team is willing to accept an 85% probability of success for the first deadline, but they want to be more than 99% sure to meet the penalty deadline. We will start our analysis focusing on the first deadline.

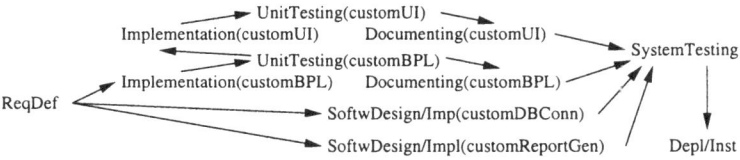

Figure 5: The first expansions in the initial task network.

After the first expansions, the resulting task network depicted in Figure 5 is under analysis. As no requirement matching modules for the user interface and business logic modules are in the repository, the system develops this (partial) plan for implementing both from scratch. The *interfaces* relation between the components enforces the business logic module to be implemented and tested before the implementation of the user interface can be done. Consequently, the critical path contains the two implementation tasks, resulting in a duration distribution for the network of $\mathcal{N}(-5, 9.2)$. This means, that the probability of meeting the first deadline is only $Pr[\mathcal{X}_{\mathcal{N}(-5,9.2)} \geq 0] = 4.96\%$

At this stage the plan is already unacceptable for the team. Therefore, the search continues with another expansion possibility, namely adapting an existing user interface instead. Figure 6 shows the task network after some more expansion steps: a suitable database interface exists for a related operating system, and an existing report generator could be re-used in the application.

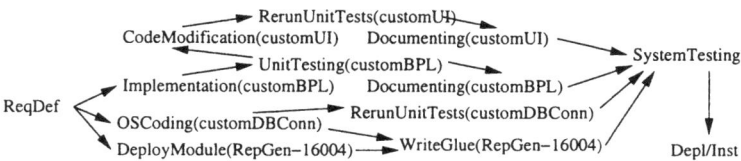

Figure 6: The final expansions in the initial task network.

The critical path includes the implementation and the adaptation with a distribution of $\mathcal{N}(7, 7.8)$, so we can assume that the team finishes its task within the given time of 36 days with a probability of $Pr[\mathcal{X}_{\mathcal{N}(7,7.8)} \geq 0] = 85.86\%$ Repeating the computation for the extended deadline of 40 days, the project leader can also be 99.39% sure that with the plan found, the company will not be sued for the delay. We see, that in contrast to an interval algebra based solution, the company's risk becomes quantifiable.

6 Implementation

The mechanisms for handling uncertain durations of operations are integrated in a multi-agent planning framework, originally developed for hybrid planning [2]. The basic architecture is depicted in Figure 7. Briefly, *detector* agents encapsulate checking routines which announce *flaws* in the shared blackboard data-structure, i.e. the current task network. Flaws consist in the presence of abstract tasks and unsatisfied preconditions of operators, among others. *Modifier* agents receive flaws and calculate solution proposals (e.g. task expansions, adding ordering constraints, etc.) which in turn are sent to the *strategy* agent. The strategy organizes the search by choosing such a task network modification at each step and executes it. After that the detectors are invoked again. Backtracking is initiated if no modification is issued for

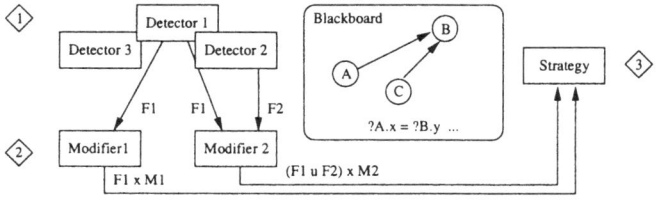

Figure 7: The components of the planning system architecture and their life-cycle.

at least one flaw. A deeper presentation of these mechanisms is beyond the scope of this paper, but it has to be noted that the representation of modification proposals allows the strategy to identify areas of interest in the plan (to guide its search), and that for our purposes it does not have to be adapted to make use of information delivered by additional agents. The framework has also been used to integrate scheduling capabilities in a similar way [11].

The integration of temporal uncertainty is done by utilizing the independence of the single agents. We just add a *duration-detector* which reasons about the uncertain time needed to execute the plan like it is described above. It roughly works as follows: After its invocation, the agent calculates the duration $\mathcal{Y}$ of the critical path for the (incomplete) plan on the blackboard. The presented propagation procedure allows for this on every level of abstraction. Note, that $\mathcal{Y}$ has a negative mean value, as it stands for usage of time. In the next step the agent adds the maximum allowable duration for the plan from the problem description to $\mathcal{Y}$ and determines the resulting random variable $\mathcal{Z}$. $\mathcal{Z}$ represents the time difference between the time limit and the expected duration of the plan. The probability of failure of the plan (w.r.t. the duration) is consequently $Pr[\mathcal{Z} < 0]$: the probability for exceeding the time limit. If this probability is higher than the given threshold, the duration-agent generates a *duration-exceeded-flaw*. As there is no modifier in the agent community to propose a modification step to fix this kind of flaw, the planner has to initiate backtracking.

By propagating duration under-estimations up to the abstract task level, the detector is able to compute a heuristic value for the duration on every level of abstraction during plan generation. To prune the search space, an abstract plan that already exceeds the maximum duration can be rejected at any stage, as the duration propagation always under-estimates.

7 Related Work

Related approaches in the literature mainly use intervals to represent temporal uncertainty.

β-robust scheduling for single machines is presented in [6], where the total flow time of all scheduled jobs is minimized. In this context, information is gathered about the execution time of single tasks and the duration of the abstract action is estimated by a maximum likelihood, the result of which is a random variable. A fast heuristic function for scheduling performance is compared with correct but slow computations, and it is shown how to select the schedule which promises the best performance.

A lot of work is done in the field of handling *discrete* probabilities in planning, of which we address that about epsilon-safe planning here [8]. It deals with the feature of uncertain sensing actions and introduces an approach to generate an ε-safe plan, which means to generate a plan that has only a probability of ε to fail in execution.

O-Plan, e.g., performs an optimistic and a pessimistic estimation of each resource profile [7]. If the optimistic profile falls below zero, i.e. if all consumption steps are performed as late as possible allocating the minimal quantity possible and all production steps are performed as early as possible producing as much as possible, and there is still a point in time in the plan where the capacity is exceeded, then this plan cannot be repaired and search has to backtrack. Furthermore, O-Plan can introduce constraints to evade potentially conflicting plans.

Simple Temporal Networks (STN) are constraint networks, in which nodes are time points and edges represent constraints like upper and lower bounds. [9] introduces the Temporal Constraint Satisfaction Problem (TCSP) in which a preference value is added to the temporal constraints. As solving the TCSP is NP-hard, a restriction on convex intervals is presented, which can be solved in polynomial time. Another extension to STN is presented in [10], which focuses on the execution of STN w.r.t. events of uncertain timing. It describes how the STN has to be adapted if uncertain timing occurs during execution, and how the existing procedures for this problem can be improved in this way.

Alternatively, duration uncertainty can be modeled qualitatively by using fuzzy temporal nets. Approaches like [4] use them to obtain approximate solutions.

The presented idea on heuristic propagation of operator durations is loosely based on [5], in which intervals on abstract tasks are used as a heuristic function for resource consumption on the action layer. But uncertain resources consumption in operators is not discussed.

8 Conclusion

We have described an approach to handle uncertainty w.r.t. time consumption of operations in HTN planning. Durations are represented by continuous normal-distributed random variables. By adopting appropriate stochastic concepts the duration probabilities of critical execution paths can be accumulated. With that, overall probabilities for the successful execution of non-linear plans/task networks can be computed. We have shown how it can be embedded into an multi-agent based planning framework, where it allows for the derivation and use of heuristics to guide the decomposition-based planning process towards solutions that meet a certain probability threshold.

References

[1] Susanne Biundo, Roland Holzer, and Bernd Schattenberg. Dealing with continuous resources in AI planning. In *Proc. of the 4th Intern. Workshop on Planning and Scheduling for Space*, 2004.

[2] Susanne Biundo and Bernd Schattenberg. From abstract crisis to concrete relief – A preliminary report on combining state abstraction and HTN planning. In A. Cesta and D. Borrajo, editors, *Proc. of the 6th European Conf. on Planning (ECP-01)*, LNCS, pages 157–168. Springer Verlag, 2001.

[3] J. Bresina, R. Dearden, N. Meuleau, S. Ramakrishnan, D. Smith, and R. Washington. Planning under continuous time and resource uncertainty: A challenge for AI. In A. Darwiche and N. Friedman, editors, *Proc. of the 18th Conf. in Uncertainty in AI*, pages 77–84. Morgan Kaufmann, 2002.

[4] L. Castillo and J. Fdez.-Olivares and A. Gonzalez. Integration of fuzzy scheduling into a planning framework. In L. Castillo, D. Borrajo, M.A. Salido and A. Oddi editors, *Planning and Scheduling*, IOS Press, 2004.

[5] Bradley J. Clement, Anthony C. Barrett, Gregg R. Rabideau, and Edmund H. Durfee. Using abstraction in planning and scheduling. In A. Cesta and D. Borrajo, editors, *Proc. of the 6th European Conf. on Planning (ECP-01)*, LNCS, pages 145–156. Springer Verlag, 2001.

[6] Richard Daniels and Janice Carrillo. β-robust scheduling for single-machine systems with uncertain processing times. *IIE Transactions*, 29(11):977–985, 1997.

[7] Brian Drabble and Austin Tate. The use of optimistic and pessimistic resource profiles to inform search in an activity based planner. In K. Hammond, editor, *Proc. of the 2nd Intern. Conf. on AI Planning Systems (AIPS-94)*, pages 243–248. AAAI Press, 1994.

[8] Robert P. Goldman and Mark S. Boddy. Epsilon-safe planning. In R. López de Mántaras and D. Poole, editors, *Proc. of the 10th Annual Conf. on Uncertainty in AI*, pages 253–261. Morgan Kaufmann, 1994.

[9] Lina Khatib, Paul H. Morris, Robert A. Morris, and Francesca Rossi. Temporal constraint reasoning with preferences. In B. Nebel, editor, *Proc. of the 17th Intern. Joint Conf. on AI (IJCAI-01)*, pages 322–327, Morgan Kaufmann, 2001.

[10] Paul Morris and Nicola Muscettola. Execution of temporal plans with uncertainty. In *Proc. of the 17th National Conf. on AI (AAAI-2000)*. AAAI Press, July 2000.

[11] Bernd Schattenberg and Susanne Biundo. On the identification and use of hierarchical resources in planning and scheduling. In M. Ghallab, J. Hertzberg, and P. Traverso, editors, *Proc. of the 6th Intern. Conf. on AI Planning and Scheduling (AIPS'02)*, pages 263–272. AAAI Press, 2002.

Author Index